P9-CDT-196

Dale Emerson served as the chief financial officer for Reliant Electric Company, a distributor of electricity serving portions of Montana and North Dakota. Reliant was in the final stages of planning a takeover of Dakota Gasworks, Inc., a natural gas distributor that operated solely within North Dakota. Emerson went on a weekend fishing trip with his uncle, Ernest Wallace. Emerson mentioned to Wallace that he had been putting in a lot of extra hours at the office planning a takeover of Dakota Gasworks. On returning from the fishing trip, Wallace met with a broker from Chambers Investments and purchased $20,000 of Reliant stock. Three weeks later, Reliant made a tender offer to Dakota Gasworks stockholders and purchased 57 percent of Dakota Gasworks stock. Over the next two weeks, the price of Reliant stock rose 72 percent before leveling out. Wallace then sold his Reliant stock for a gross profit of $14,400. Using the information presented in the chapter, answer the following questions.

1 Would registration with the SEC be required for Dakota Gasworks securities? Why or why not?

2 Did Emerson violate Section 10(b) of the Securities Exchange Act of 1934 and SEC Rule 10b-5? Why or why not?

3 What theory or theories might a court use to hold Wallace liable for insider trading?

4 Under the Sarbanes-Oxley Act of 2002, who would be required to certify the accuracy of financial statements filed with the SEC?

THE INTERNET: Exercises, Enrichment, and Support

ON THE WEB

These margin features give specific Uniform Resource Locators (URLs), or Internet addresses, concerning topics discussed in the text. You will find over one hundred such references throughout this text. Two examples are shown here.

ON THE WEB

An excellent Web site for information on employee benefits—including the full text of relevant statutes, such as the FMLA and COBRA, as well as case law and current articles—is BenefitsLink. Go to **www.benefitslink.com/index.shtml**.

ON THE WEB

The U.S. Department of Justice offers an impressive collection of statistics on crime, including cyber crime, at the following Web site:

www.ojp.usdoj.gov/bjs.

ONLINE ACTIVITIES

Included at the end of every chapter are at least two Internet exercises that students can perform to learn more about topics covered in the chapter. These exercises, as well as interactive quiz questions, are available on the *Business Law Today: The Essentials,* Eighth Edition, Web site at:

academic.cengage.com/blaw/blt

Cengage Advantage Books — *The Essentials*

Text & Summarized Cases • E-Commerce • Legal • Ethical • International Environment

BUSINESS LAW TODAY

MILLER / JENTZ

Eighth Edition

For this edition of *Business Law Today: The Essentials,* we have redesigned and streamlined the text's Web site so that users can easily locate the resources they seek.

Business Law Today: The Essentials

8ᵀᴴ Edition

TEXT & SUMMARIZED CASES

E-Commerce, Legal, Ethical,
and International Environment

Roger LeRoy Miller
Institute for University Studies
Arlington, Texas

Gaylord A. Jentz
Herbert D. Kelleher
Emeritus Professor in Business Law
MSIS Department
University of Texas at Austin

SOUTH-WESTERN
CENGAGE Learning

Australia • Brazil • Japan • Korea • Mexico • Singapore • Spain • United Kingdom • United States

SOUTH-WESTERN
CENGAGE Learning

Business Law Today: The Essentials

8TH Edition

TEXT & SUMMARIZED CASES
E-Commerce, Legal, Ethical, and International Environment
Roger LeRoy Miller   Gaylord A. Jentz

COPYRIGHT © 2008
South-Western, a part of Cengage Learning.

Printed in the United States of America
2   3   4   5   09   08

ISBN-13: 978–0–324–65454–7
ISBN-10: 0–324–65454–5

Library of Congress Control Number: 2007935133

For more information, contact:

South-Western Cengage Learning
5191 Natorp Boulevard
Mason, Ohio, 45040
USA

Or you can visit our Internet site at **academic.cengage.com/blaw**.

Vice President and Editorial Director
Jack Calhoun

Publisher, Business Law, and Accounting
Rob Dewey

Acquisition Editor
Steve Silverstein

Senior Developmental Editor
Jan Lamar

Executive Marketing Manager
Lisa L. Lysne

Marketing Manager
Jenny Garamy

Production Manager
Bill Stryker

Technology Project Manager
Rob Ellington

Manufacturing Buyer
Kevin Kluck

Compositor
Parkwood Composition
New Richmond, WI

Printer
Quebecor World Versailles

Senior Art Director
Michelle Kunkler

Internal Designer
Bill Stryker

Cover Designer
Diane Gliebe/Design Matters

Web site Coordinator
Brian Courter

Cover Images
© Getty Images, Inc.

INTERNATIONAL LOCATIONS

ASIA (including India)
Cengage Learning
www.cengageasia.com
tel: (65) 6410 1200

AUSTRALIA/NEW ZEALAND
Cengage Learning
www.cengage.com.au
tel: (61) 3 9685 4111

LATIN AMERICA
Cengage Learning
www.cengage.com.mx
tel: +52 (55) 1500 6000

Represented in Canada by Nelson Education, Ltd.
www.nelson.com
tel: (416) 752 9100 / (800) 668 0671

UK/EUROPE/MIDDLE EAST/AFRICA
Cengage Learning
www.cengage.co.uk
tel: (44) 207 067 2500

SPAIN (includes Portugal)
Cengage Learning
http://www.paraninfo.es

Contents in Brief

APPENDICES

Contents*

*Consult the inside front and back covers of this book for easy reference to the many special features in this textbook.

Preface to the Instructor

We have always felt that business law and the legal environment should be an exciting, contemporary, and interesting course. We believe that *Business Law Today: The Essentials*, Eighth Edition, imparts this excitement to your students. We have spent a great deal of effort in giving this book a visual appeal that will encourage students to learn the law. We have also worked hard to make sure that *Business Law Today: The Essentials* continues its established tradition of being the most up-to-date text on the market. The law presented in the Eighth Edition of *Business Law Today: The Essentials* includes new statutes, regulations, and cases, as well as the most recent developments in cyberlaw.

You will find that coverage of traditional business law has not been sacrificed in the process of creating this text. Additionally, *Business Law Today: The Essentials* explicitly addresses the American Assembly of Collegiate Schools of Business's (AACSB's) broad array of curriculum requirements. For example, many of the features and special pedagogical devices in this text focus on the global, political, ethical, social, environmental, technological, and cultural contexts of business law. In addition, critical-thinking skills are reinforced throughout.

WHAT'S NEW TO THE EIGHTH EDITION

Instructors have come to rely on the coverage, accuracy, and applicability of *Business Law Today: The Essentials*. For this edition, we have added a number of features to make the text more practical for today's business environment and to promote critical-thinking skills.

Practical Elements in Every Chapter

For the Eighth Edition of *Business Law Today: The Essentials*, we have added a **special new feature entitled** *Preventing Legal Disputes* in each chapter. These brief features offer practical guidance on steps that businesspersons can take in their daily transactions to avoid legal disputes and litigation. These features are integrated throughout the text as appropriate to the topics being discussed.

In addition, every chapter in the Eighth Edition concludes with an *Application* **feature** that focuses on practical considerations related to the chapter's contents and concludes with a checklist of tips for the businessperson. Many of these features are new or have been substantially revised for this edition. For example, some of the new *Application* features include:

■ How Can You Create an Ethical Workplace? (Chapter 2).

■ How Can You Protect against Identity Theft? (Chapter 6).

■ Establishing an Electronic Communications Policy (Chapter 10).

We have also revised the Internet exercises that conclude each chapter to focus on the practical aspects of doing business in today's global legal environment.

Critical Thinking and Legal Reasoning

Today's business leaders are often required to think "outside the box" when making business decisions. For this reason, **we have added a number of critical-thinking elements for the Eighth Edition** that are designed to challenge students' understanding of the materials beyond simple retention. Your students' critical-thinking and legal-reasoning skills will be increased as they work through the numerous pedagogical devices within the book. Nearly every feature and every case presented in the text conclude with some type of critical-thinking question. These questions include *For Critical Analysis, What If the Facts Were Different? Why Is This Case Important?* and *Why Is This Case Important to Businesspersons?*

In addition, we have also added an entirely new section to the chapter-ending *Questions and Case Problems* that focuses on critical thinking and writing. Questions in that section include *Critical Legal Thinking, Critical Thinking and Writing Assignment for Business,* and *Video Questions,* each of which will be described shortly.

Reviewing Features Added to Every Chapter

For the Eighth Edition of *Business Law Today: The Essentials,* we have added a special new feature at the end of every chapter that helps solidify students' understanding of the chapter materials. Each of these *Reviewing . . .* features presents a hypothetical scenario and then asks a series of questions that require students to identify the issues and apply the legal concepts discussed in the chapter. An instructor can use these features as the basis for a lively in-class discussion or can encourage students to use them for self-study and assessment prior to completing homework assignments. **Suggested answers to the** *Reviewing* **features' questions are available in the** *Instructor's Manual* **and the** *Answers Manual* **that accompany this text.**

New Hypothetical Questions with Sample Answers in Appendix F

In response to those instructors who would like students to have sample answers available for some of the *Questions and Case Problems,* for this edition we have added a special question in each chapter entitled **Hypothetical Question with Sample Answer.** In addition to each chapter providing one **Case Problem with Sample Answer** that is based on an actual case and answered on the text's Web site, students can now also access a sample answer to one hypothetical question per chapter by going to Appendix F at the end of the text. The answers to these questions are also posted on the text's Web site (located at **academic.cengage.com/blaw/blt**). Students can compare their own answers to the answers provided to determine whether they have applied the law correctly and to learn what needs to be included when answering the end-of-chapter *Questions and Case Problems.*

New Streamlined Organization for the Chapter-Ending *Questions and Case Problems*

For the Eighth Edition of *Business Law Today: The Essentials,* we have completely reorganized and streamlined the *Questions and Case Problems* that conclude each chapter. To facilitate assessment, the problems are now divided by subheadings into the following three categories:

1 Hypothetical Scenarios—We begin with a section of *Hypothetical Scenarios,* which present simple situations and ask students to apply the legal concepts from the chapter.

Included in this group of questions is the new *Hypothetical Question with Sample Answer,* discussed previously (for which a sample answer is available in Appendix F of the text and on the Web site).

2 **Case Problems**—Next are the *Case Problems,* which present the facts of recent cases and ask students to analyze how the law applies. These problems include a *Case Problem with Sample Answer* (that is provided on the text's Web site) and *A Question of Ethics,* the majority of which are new to this edition and based on 2007 cases.

3 **Critical Thinking and Writing Assignments**—The third subsection consists of the *Critical Thinking and Writing Assignments,* which are designed to enhance critical-thinking skills and include several types of questions that are new to this edition.

- Every chapter includes a **Critical Legal Thinking** question that requires students to think critically about some aspect of the law discussed in the chapter.

- Selected chapters include a **Critical Thinking and Writing Assignment for Business** question that focuses on critical thinking in a business-oriented context.

- Many chapters also include a special **Video Question** under this subheading that directs students to the text's Web site (at **academic.cengage.com/blaw/blt**) to access a video relevant to a topic covered in the chapter (a passcode is required—see the discussion of the Business Law Digital Video Library later in this preface). The students view the video clip, some of which are from Hollywood movies, and then answer a series of questions on how the law applies to the situation depicted in the video.

New Appendix on the Sarbanes-Oxley Act of 2002

In a number of places in this text, we refer to the Sarbanes-Oxley Act of 2002 and the corporate scandals that led to the passage of that legislation. For example, Chapter 2 mentions how the requirements of the Sarbanes-Oxley Act were intended to deter unethical corporate conduct and make certain corporate acts illegal. In Chapter 21, we discuss this act in the context of securities law and corporate governance and present an exhibit (Exhibit 21–4) containing some of the key provisions of the act relating to corporate accountability in securities transactions. In Chapter 25, we discuss whether this act can be applied extraterritorially.

Because the Sarbanes-Oxley Act is a topic of significant concern in today's business climate, for the Eighth Edition, we have added **excerpts and explanatory comments on the Sarbanes-Oxley Act of 2002 as Appendix D.** Students and instructors alike will find it useful to have the provisions of the act immediately available for reference and explained in plain language.

New Bankruptcy Reform Act of 2005 Incorporated

Chapter 16 has been significantly revamped due to the passage of the 2005 bankruptcy reform legislation. Bankruptcy reform has been a topic of major debate for many years. Now that the reform act has been enacted, we have overhauled the content of this chapter to reflect fully the changes. We also include a *Landmark in the Law* feature discussing the 2005 act.

Impact of This Case on Today's Law

Many students are unclear about how some of the older cases presented in this text affect today's courts. We have therefore added a special section for this edition entitled **Impact of This Case on Today's Law.** These sections appear at the end of all *Landmark and Classic Cases* to clarify the relevance of the particular case to modern law.

BUSINESS LAW TODAY: THE ESSENTIALS ON THE WEB

For this edition of *Business Law Today: The Essentials*, we have redesigned and stream-lined the text's Web site so that users can easily locate the resources they seek. When you visit our Web site at **academic.cengage.com/blaw/blt**, you will find a broad array of teaching/learning resources, including the following:

■ *Relevant Web Sites* for all of the *Landmark in the Law* features and *Landmark and Classic Cases* that are presented in this text.

■ *Sample Answers* to the *Case Problem with Sample Answer*, which appears at the end of every chapter, are posted on the student companion Web site. This problem-answer set is designed to help your students learn how to answer case problems by acquainting them with model answers to selected problems. In addition, we post the answers to the *Hypothetical Questions with Sample Answers* on the Web site as well as in the text (Appendix F).

■ *Videos* referenced in the *Video Questions* that appear at the ends of selected chapters of *Business Law Today: The Essentials*, Eighth Edition (available only with a passcode).

■ *Practical Internet Exercises* for every chapter in the text (at least two per chapter). The Internet exercises have been refocused to provide more practical information to business law students on topics covered in the chapters and to acquaint students with the legal resources that are available online.

■ *Interactive Quizzes* for every chapter in this text that include a number of questions related to each chapter's contents.

■ *Key Terms* for every chapter in the text.

■ *Flashcards* that provide students with an optional study tool to review the key terms in every chapter.

■ *Appendix A: How to Brief Cases and Analyze Case Problems* is featured in the book and is also posted on the Web site.

■ *PowerPoint slides* for this edition.

■ *Legal Reference Materials* that include a "Statutes" page that offers links to the full text of selected statutes referenced in the text, a Spanish glossary, the text of the appendices that were removed for the Eighth Edition, and links to other important legal resources available for free on the Web.

■ *Online Legal Research Guide* that offers complete yet brief guidance to using the Internet and evaluating information obtained from the Internet. As an online resource, it now includes hyperlinks to the Web sites discussed for click-through convenience.

■ *Court Case Updates* that present summaries of new cases from various West legal publications, all specifically keyed to chapters in this text.

Business Law Digital Video Library

For this edition of *Business Law Today: The Essentials*, we have included special *Video Questions* at the end of selected chapters. Each of these questions directs students to the text's Web site (at **academic.cengage.com/blaw/blt**) to view a video relevant to a topic covered in the chapter. This instruction is followed by a series of questions based on the video. The questions are repeated on the Web site, when the student accesses the video. An access code for the videos can be packaged with each new copy of this textbook for no additional charge. If the Business Law Digital Video Library access did not come packaged with your textbook, it can be purchased online at **digitalvideolibrary.westbuslaw.com**.

ity, (3) conduct or participate in the affairs of an enterprise through racketeering activity, or (4) conspire to do any of the preceding activities.

RICO incorporates by reference twenty-six separate types of federal crimes and nine types of state felonies[10] and declares that if a person commits two of these offenses, he or she is guilty of "racketeering activity." Under the criminal provisions of RICO, any individual found guilty is subject to a fine of up to $25,000 per violation, imprisonment for up to twenty years, or both. Additionally, the statute provides that those who violate RICO may be required to forfeit (give up) any assets, in the form of property or cash, that were acquired as a result of the illegal activity or that were "involved in" or an "instrumentality of" the activity.

The broad language of RICO has allowed it to be applied in cases that have little or nothing to do with organized crime. In fact, today the statute is more often used to attack white-collar crimes than organized crime. In addition, RICO creates civil as well as criminal liability. The government can seek civil penalties, including the divestiture of a defendant's interest in a business (called forfeiture) or the dissolution of the business. Moreover, in some cases, the statute allows private individuals to sue violators and potentially recover three times their actual losses (treble damages), plus attorneys' fees, for business injuries caused by a violation of the statute. This is perhaps the most controversial aspect of RICO and one that continues to cause debate in the nation's federal courts.

ETHICAL ISSUE 6.1

Should courts allow private parties to file RICO actions against their employers based on a pattern of hiring illegal immigrants? The civil sanctions authorized by RICO have given plaintiffs a tremendous financial incentive to pursue businesses and employers for RICO violations. In one recent case, for example, a group of employees sued their employer, Mohawk Industries, Inc. The employees claimed that Mohawk had engaged in a pattern of hiring illegal immigrants willing to work for lower wages in an effort to drive down the wages of legal employees. Mohawk, the second-largest carpet manufacturer in the United States with more than 30,000 employees, allegedly conspired with recruiting agencies to hire undocumented workers and even provided illegal immigrants with transportation from the border. The plaintiffs claimed that this pattern of illegal hiring expanded Mohawk's hourly workforce and resulted in lower wages for the plaintiffs (and other legal employees). Mohawk filed a motion to dismiss for lack of evidence of racketeering activity, which the federal court denied, and the case was appealed.

The United States Supreme Court initially granted a writ of *certiorari* in this case but later dismissed the writ as "improvidently granted" and remanded the case to the U.S. Court of Appeals for the Eleventh Circuit. In September 2006, the federal appellate court ruled that the plaintiffs had presented sufficient evidence of racketeering activity to go forward with the RICO suit.[11] Although the merits of the case have not yet been resolved, the potential treble (triple) damages award against Mohawk could be substantial. In addition, the case is likely to open the door to other actions against employers that have a history of employing illegal immigrants and thereby causing injury to the economic interests of other employees.

The *Concept Summary* on the following page provides definitions and examples of the crime categories just discussed.

---

10. See 18 U.S.C. Section 1961(1)(A).
11. *Williams v. Mohawk Industries, Inc.,* 465 F.3d 1277 (11th Cir. 2006); *cert.* granted ___ U.S. ___, 126 S.Ct. 830, 163 L.Ed.2d 705 (2005); and *cert.* dismissed at ___ U.S. ___, 126 S.Ct. 2016, 164 L.Ed.2d 776 (2006). The holding in this case conflicts with a decision in another federal circuit; see *Baker v. IBP, Inc.,* 357 F.3d 685 (7th Cir. 2004).

CONCEPT SUMMARY Types of Crimes

CRIME CATEGORY	DEFINITIONS AND EXAMPLES
Violent Crime	1. *Definition*—Crimes that cause others to suffer harm or death. 2. *Examples*—Murder, assault and battery, sexual assault (rape), and robbery.
Property Crime	1. *Definition*—Crimes in which the goal of the offender is some form of economic gain or the damaging of property; the most common form of crime. 2. *Examples*—Burglary, larceny, obtaining goods by false pretenses, receiving stolen goods, arson, and forgery.
Public Order Crime	1. *Definition*—Crimes contrary to public values and morals. 2. *Examples*—Public drunkenness, prostitution, gambling, and illegal drug use.
White-Collar Crime	1. *Definition*—An illegal act or series of acts committed by an individual or business entity using some nonviolent means to obtain a personal or business advantage; usually committed in the course of a legitimate occupation. 2. *Examples*—Embezzlement, mail and wire fraud, bribery, bankruptcy fraud, the theft of trade secrets, and insider trading.
Organized Crime	1. *Definition*—A form of crime conducted by groups operating illegitimately to satisfy the public's demand for illegal goods and services (such as gambling or illegal narcotics). 2. *Money laundering*—The establishment of legitimate enterprises through which "dirty" money (obtained through criminal activities, such as organized crime) can be "laundered" (made to appear to be legitimate income). 3. *The Racketeer Influenced and Corrupt Organizations Act (RICO) of 1970*—RICO makes it a federal crime to (a) use income obtained from racketeering activity to purchase any interest in an enterprise, (b) acquire or maintain an interest in an enterprise through racketeering activity, (c) conduct or participate in the affairs of an enterprise through racketeering activity, or (d) conspire to do any of the preceding activities. RICO provides for both civil and criminal liability.

Classification of Crimes

FELONY
A crime—such as arson, murder, rape, or robbery—that carries the most severe sanctions, ranging from one year in a state or federal prison to the death penalty.

MISDEMEANOR
A lesser crime than a felony, punishable by a fine or incarceration in jail for up to one year.

PETTY OFFENSE
In criminal law, the least serious kind of criminal offense, such as a traffic or building-code violation.

Depending on their degree of seriousness, crimes typically are classified as felonies or misdemeanors. **Felonies** are serious crimes punishable by death or by imprisonment for more than a year. **Misdemeanors** are less serious crimes, punishable by a fine or by confinement for up to a year. In most jurisdictions, **petty offenses** are considered to be a subset of misdemeanors. Petty offenses are minor violations, such as jaywalking or violations of building codes. Even for petty offenses, however, a guilty party can be put in jail for a few days, fined, or both, depending on state or local law.

Whether a crime is a felony or a misdemeanor can determine in which court the case is tried and, in some states, whether the defendant has a right to a jury trial. Many states also define different degrees of felony offenses (first, second, and third degree murder, for example) and vary the punishment according to the degree. Some states also have different classes (degrees) of misdemeanors.

DEFENSES TO CRIMINAL LIABILITY

In certain circumstances, the law may allow a person to be excused from criminal liability because she or he lacks the required mental state. Criminal defendants may also be relieved of criminal liability if they can show that their criminal actions were justified, given the circumstances. Among the most important defenses to criminal liability are infancy, intoxication, insanity, mistake, consent, duress, justifiable use of force, entrapment, and the statute of limitations. Also, in some cases, defendants are given immunity and thus relieved, at least in part, of criminal liability for crimes they committed. We look at each of these defenses here.

Note that procedural violations, such as obtaining evidence without a valid search warrant, may operate as defenses also. As you will read later in this chapter, evidence obtained in violation of a defendant's constitutional rights normally may not be admitted in court. If the evidence is suppressed, then there may be no basis for prosecuting the defendant.

Infancy

The term *infant*, as used in the law, refers to any person who has not yet reached the age of majority (see Chapter 8). In all states, certain courts handle cases involving children who are alleged to have violated the law. In some states, juvenile courts handle children's cases exclusively. In other states, however, courts that handle children's cases may also have jurisdiction over additional matters. In most states, a child may be treated as an adult and tried in a regular court if she or he is above a certain age (usually fourteen) and is charged with a felony, such as rape or murder.

Intoxication

The law recognizes two types of intoxication, whether from drugs or from alcohol: *involuntary* and *voluntary*. Involuntary intoxication occurs when a person either is physically forced to ingest or inject an intoxicating substance or is unaware that a substance contains drugs or alcohol. Involuntary intoxication is a defense to a crime if its effect was to make a person incapable of obeying the law or of understanding that the act committed was wrong. Voluntary intoxication is rarely a defense, but it may be effective in cases in which the defendant was so *extremely* intoxicated as to negate the state of mind that a crime requires.

Insanity

Just as a child is often judged to be incapable of the state of mind required to commit a crime, so also may someone suffering from a mental illness. Thus, insanity may be a defense to a criminal charge. The courts have had difficulty deciding what the test for legal insanity should be, however, and psychiatrists as well as lawyers are critical of the tests used. Almost all federal courts and some states use the relatively liberal standard set forth in the Model Penal Code:

> A person is not responsible for criminal conduct if at the time of such conduct as a result of mental disease or defect he [or she] lacks substantial capacity either to appreciate the wrongfulness of his [or her] conduct or to conform his [or her] conduct to the requirements of the law.

Some states use the *M'Naghten* test,[12] under which a criminal defendant is not responsible if, at the time of the offense, he or she did not know the nature and quality of the act or did not know that the act was wrong. Other states use the irresistible-impulse test. A person operating under an irresistible impulse may know an act is wrong but cannot refrain from doing it. Under any of these tests, proving insanity is extremely difficult. For this reason, the insanity defense is rarely used and usually is not successful.

---

12. A rule derived from *M'Naghten's Case*, 8 Eng.Rep. 718 (1843).

ON THE WEB

You can gain insights into criminal law and criminal procedures, including a number of the defenses that can be raised to avoid criminal liability, by looking at some of the famous criminal law cases included on Court TV's Web site. Go to

www.courttv.com/index.html.

These two brothers were only thirteen and fourteen years old when they killed their father with a baseball bat and then set their Florida house on fire. In court, they did not deny their wrongdoing. They were sentenced to terms of seven to eight years for third degree murder and arson. Under what circumstances should they not be held responsible for their reprehensible actions? (The Smoking Gun)

Mistake

COMPARE "Ignorance" is a lack of information. "Mistake" is a confusion of information.

Everyone has heard the saying "Ignorance of the law is no excuse." Ordinarily, ignorance of the law or a mistaken idea about what the law requires is not a valid defense. In some states, however, that rule has been modified. Criminal defendants who claim that they honestly did not know that they were breaking a law may have a valid defense if (1) the law was not published or reasonably made known to the public or (2) the defendant relied on an official statement of the law that was erroneous.

A *mistake of fact*, as opposed to a *mistake of law*, operates as a defense if it negates the mental state necessary to commit a crime. **■EXAMPLE 6.6** If Oliver Wheaton mistakenly walks off with Julie Tyson's briefcase because he thinks it is his, there is no theft. Theft requires knowledge that the property belongs to another. ■

Consent

CONSENT
Voluntary agreement to a proposition or an act of another; a concurrence of wills.

What if a victim consents to a crime or even encourages the person intending a criminal act to commit it? Ordinarily, **consent** does not operate as a bar to criminal liability. In some rare circumstances, however, the law may allow consent to be used as a defense. In each case, the question is whether the law forbids an act that was committed against the victim's will or forbids the act without regard to the victim's wish. The law forbids murder, prostitution, and drug use regardless of whether the victim consents to it. Also, if the act causes harm to a third person who has not consented, there is no escape from criminal liability. Consent or forgiveness given after a crime has been committed is not really a defense, though it can affect the likelihood of prosecution or the severity of the sentence. Consent operates most successfully as a defense in crimes against property.

■EXAMPLE 6.7 Barry gives Phong permission to stay in Barry's lakeside cabin and hunt for deer on the adjoining land. After observing Phong carrying a gun into the cabin at night, a neighbor calls the police, and an officer subsequently arrests Phong. If charged with burglary (or aggravated burglary, because he had a weapon), Phong can assert the defense of consent. He had obtained Barry's consent to enter the premises. ■

Duress

DURESS
Unlawful pressure brought to bear on a person, causing the person to perform an act that she or he would not otherwise perform.

Duress exists when the *wrongful threat* of one person induces another person to perform an act that she or he would not otherwise perform. In such a situation, duress is said to negate the mental state necessary to commit a crime. For duress to qualify as a defense, the following requirements must be met:

1 The threat must be of serious bodily harm or death.
2 The harm threatened must be greater than the harm caused by the crime.
3 The threat must be immediate and inescapable.
4 The defendant must have been involved in the situation through no fault of his or her own.

Justifiable Use of Force

SELF-DEFENSE
The legally recognized privilege to protect oneself or one's property against injury by another. The privilege of self-defense usually applies only to acts that are reasonably necessary to protect oneself, one's property, or another person.

Probably the best-known defense to criminal liability is **self-defense.** Other situations, however, also justify the use of force: the defense of one's dwelling, the defense of other property, and the prevention of a crime. In all of these situations, it is important to distinguish between deadly and nondeadly force. *Deadly force* is likely to result in death or serious bodily harm. *Nondeadly force* is force that reasonably appears necessary to prevent the imminent use of criminal force.

Generally speaking, people can use the amount of nondeadly force that seems necessary to protect themselves, their dwellings, or other property or to prevent the commission of a crime. Deadly force can be used in self-defense (1) if the defender *reasonably believes* that imminent death or grievous bodily harm will otherwise result, (2) if the attacker is using unlawful force (an example of lawful force is that exerted by a police officer), and (3) if the defender has not initiated or provoked the attack. Deadly force normally can be used to defend a dwelling only if the unlawful entry is violent and the person believes deadly force is necessary to prevent imminent death or great bodily harm or—in some jurisdictions—if the person believes deadly force is necessary to prevent the commission of a felony (such as arson) in the dwelling.

Entrapment

Entrapment is a defense designed to prevent police officers or other government agents from enticing persons to commit crimes in order to later prosecute them for criminal acts. In the typical entrapment case, an undercover agent *suggests* that a crime be committed and somehow pressures or induces an individual to commit it. The agent then arrests the individual for the crime.

For entrapment to be considered a defense, both the suggestion and the inducement must take place. The defense is intended not to prevent law enforcement agents from setting a trap for an unwary criminal but rather to prevent them from pushing the individual into it. The crucial issue is whether the person who committed a crime was predisposed to commit the illegal act or did so because the agent induced it.

ENTRAPMENT
In criminal law, a defense in which the defendant claims that he or she was induced by a public official—usually an undercover agent or police officer—to commit a crime that he or she would otherwise not have committed.

Statute of Limitations

With some exceptions, such as for the crime of murder, statutes of limitations apply to crimes just as they do to civil wrongs. In other words, the state must initiate criminal prosecution within a certain number of years. If a criminal action is brought after the statutory time period has expired, the accused person can raise the statute of limitations as a defense.

Immunity

At times, the state may wish to obtain information from a person accused of a crime. Accused persons are understandably reluctant to give information if it will be used to prosecute them, and they cannot be forced to do so. The privilege against *self-incrimination* is granted by the Fifth Amendment to the U.S. Constitution, which reads, in part, "nor shall [any person] be compelled in any criminal case to be a witness against himself." In cases in which the state wishes to obtain information from a person accused of a crime, the state can grant *immunity* from prosecution or agree to prosecute for a less serious offense in exchange for the information. Once immunity is given, the person can no longer refuse to testify on Fifth Amendment grounds because he or she now has an absolute privilege against self-incrimination.

Often, a grant of immunity from prosecution for a serious crime is part of the **plea bargaining** between the defendant and the prosecuting attorney. The defendant may be convicted of a lesser offense, while the state uses the defendant's testimony to prosecute accomplices for serious crimes carrying heavy penalties.

PLEA BARGAINING
The process by which a criminal defendant and the prosecutor in a criminal case work out a mutually satisfactory disposition of the case, subject to court approval; usually involves the defendant's pleading guilty to a lesser offense in return for a lighter sentence.

CONSTITUTIONAL SAFEGUARDS AND CRIMINAL PROCEDURES

Criminal law brings the power of the state, with all its resources, to bear against the individual. Criminal procedures are designed to protect the constitutional rights of individuals and to prevent the arbitrary use of power on the part of the government.

The U.S. Constitution provides specific safeguards for those accused of crimes. Most of these safeguards protect individuals against state government actions, as well as federal government actions, by virtue of the due process clause of the Fourteenth Amendment. These protections are set forth in the Fourth, Fifth, Sixth, and Eighth Amendments.

Fourth Amendment Protections

SEARCH WARRANT
An order granted by a public authority, such as a judge, that authorizes law enforcement personnel to search a particular premise or property.

PROBABLE CAUSE
Reasonable grounds for believing that a person should be arrested or searched.

The Fourth Amendment protects the "right of the people to be secure in their persons, houses, papers, and effects." Before searching or seizing private property, law enforcement officers must obtain a **search warrant**—an order from a judge or other public official authorizing the search or seizure. To obtain a search warrant, law enforcement officers must convince a judge that they have reasonable grounds, or **probable cause,** to believe a search will reveal a specific illegality. Probable cause requires the officers to have trustworthy evidence that would convince a reasonable person that the proposed search or seizure is more likely justified than not. Furthermore, the Fourth Amendment prohibits general warrants. It requires a particular description of what is to be searched or seized. General searches through a person's belongings are not permissible. The search cannot extend beyond what is described in the warrant. Although search warrants require specificity, if a search warrant is issued for a person's residence, items that are in that residence may be searched even if they do not belong to that individual.

■EXAMPLE 6.8 Paycom Billing Services, Inc., facilitates payments from Internet users to its client Web sites and stores vast amounts of credit-card information in the process. Three partners at Paycom received a letter from an employee, Christopher Adjani, threatening to sell Paycom's confidential client information if the company did not pay him $3 million. Pursuant to an investigation, the Federal Bureau of Investigation (FBI) obtained a search warrant to search Adjani's person, automobile, and residence, including computer equipment. When the FBI agents served the warrant, they discovered evidence of the criminal scheme in the e-mail communications on a computer in the residence. The computer belonged to Adjani's live-in girlfriend. Adjani filed a motion to suppress this evidence, claiming that because he did not own the computer, it was beyond the scope of the warrant. Although the federal trial court granted the defendant's motion and suppressed the incriminating e-mails, the U.S. Court of Appeals for the Ninth Circuit reversed the decision in 2006. According to the appellate court, despite the novel Fourth Amendment issues raised in the case, the search of the computer was proper given the alleged involvement of computers in the crime.[13] ■

13. *United States v. Adjani*, 452 F.3d 1140 (9th Cir. 2006). The parties have filed a petition to have the United States Supreme Court review the case.

Passengers and their carry-on items are searched at an airport security checkpoint. Do such searches violate passengers' Fourth Amendment right? (Ralf Roletschek/Wikimedia Commons)

Constitutional protection against unreasonable searches and seizures also extends to businesses and professionals. As government regulation of business increased, government inspectors conducted frequent and unannounced inspections to ensure compliance with the regulations. Such inspections could be extremely disruptive. In 1978, the United States Supreme Court held that government inspectors do not have the right to enter business premises without a warrant, although the standard of probable cause is not the same as that required in nonbusiness contexts.[14] The existence of a general and neutral plan of enforcement will justify the issuance of a warrant.

Lawyers and accountants frequently possess the business records of their clients, and inspecting these documents while they are out of the hands of their true owners also requires a warrant. No warrant is required, however, for seizures of spoiled or contaminated food. Nor are warrants required for searches of businesses in such highly regulated industries as liquor, guns, and strip mining. General manufacturing is not considered to be one of these highly regulated industries, however.

The administrative search standard used for highly regulated industries is sometimes applied in other contexts as well. In the following case, the court considered whether the standard applies to airports and thus permits a suspicionless checkpoint search to screen airline passengers.

ON THE WEB

You can learn about some of the constitutional questions raised by various criminal laws and procedures by going to the Web site of the American Civil Liberties Union at

www.aclu.org.

---

14. *Marshall v. Barlow's, Inc.*, 436 U.S. 307, 98 S.Ct. 1816, 56 L.Ed.2d 305 (1978).

CASE 6.2   **United States v. Hartwell**

United States Court of Appeals, Third Circuit, 436 F.3d 174 (2006).

FACTS Christian Hartwell arrived at the Philadelphia International Airport on May 17, 2003, to catch a flight to Phoenix, Arizona. He reached the security checkpoint, placed his hand luggage on a conveyor belt to be X-rayed, and approached the metal detector. Hartwell's luggage was scanned without incident, but when he walked through the checkpoint, he set off the magnetometer. He was told to remove all items from his pockets and try again. Hartwell removed several items from his pocket but still set off the alarm. Carlos Padua, a federal Transportation Security Administration (TSA) agent, took Hartwell aside and scanned him with a handheld magnetometer. The wand revealed a solid object in Hartwell's pants pocket. Padua asked what it was, but Hartwell did not respond. Escorted to a private screening room, Hartwell refused several requests to empty his pocket. By Hartwell's account, Padua then reached into the pocket and removed two packages of crack cocaine. Hartwell was arrested and convicted on charges related to the possession of the drugs. He appealed to the U.S. Court of Appeals for the Third Circuit, arguing that the search violated the Fourth Amendment.

ISSUE Does a checkpoint search conducted in an airport to screen airline passengers violate the Fourth Amendment?

DECISION No. The U.S. Court of Appeals for the Third Circuit held that Hartwell's search was permissible under the Fourth Amendment, "even though it was initiated without individualized suspicion and was conducted without a warrant. It is permissible * * * because the State has an overwhelming interest in preserving air travel safety, and the procedure is tailored to advance that interest while proving to be only minimally invasive."

REASON Referring to the administrative search doctrine, the court balanced "the gravity of the public concerns" that have given rise to airport searches, the extent to which the searches advance the public interest, and the impact of the searches on "individual liberty." The court identified the public concern as "preventing terrorist attacks on airplanes," which "is of paramount importance." With respect to advancing the public interest, "absent a search, there is no effective means of detecting which airline passengers are reasonably likely to hijack an airplane." The court added that airport checkpoints and searches have been effective. As for any interference with liberty, the procedures in this case were "minimally intrusive. They were well tailored to protect personal privacy, escalating in invasiveness only after a lower level of screening disclosed a reason to conduct a more probing search." Besides, every airline passenger is subject to a supervised search "not far from the

CASE 6.2–Continues next page

1 Did Amstel's bid meet the requirements of an offer? Explain.

2 Was there an acceptance of the offer? Why or why not?

3 Suppose that the court determines that the parties did not reach an agreement. Further suppose that Amstel, in anticipation of building Durbin's studio, had purchased materials and refused other jobs so that he would have time in his schedule for Durbin's project. Under what theory discussed in the chapter might Amstel attempt to recover these costs?

4 Now suppose that Durbin had gone forward with his plan to build the studio and immediately accepted Amstel's bid without discussing the type or quality of materials. After Amstel began construction, Durbin asked Amstel to substitute a superior brand of acoustic tiles for the tiles that Amstel had intended to use at the time that he bid on the project. Amstel installed the tiles, then asked Durbin to pay the difference in price, but Durbin refused. Can Amstel sue to obtain the price differential from Durbin in this situation? Why or why not?

APPLICATION   Controlling the Terms of the Offer*

T he courts normally attempt to "save" contracts whenever feasible, but sometimes it is impossible to do so. Two common reasons that contracts fail are that (1) the terms of the offer were too unclear or indefinite to constitute a binding contract on the offer's acceptance, and (2) the acceptance was not timely. If you are an offeror, you can control both of these factors: you can determine what the terms of the future contract will be, as well as the time and mode of acceptance.

Include Clear and Definite Terms

If a contract's terms are too unclear or indefinite, the contract will fail. Unless a court can ascertain exactly what the rights and duties of the parties are under a particular contract, the court cannot enforce those rights and duties. Therefore, as an offeror, make sure that the terms of your offer are sufficiently definite to constitute a binding contract if the offer is accepted. A statement such as "Quantity to be determined later" may allow the offeree, after acceptance, to claim that a contract was never formed because the quantity term was not specified or is ambiguous. (Note, however, that sales and lease contracts governed by the Uniform Commercial Code may be formed even though terms are missing or ambiguous.)

Another reason an offeror should make sure that the offer's terms are clear and definite is that if a contract results, any ambiguous provision may be interpreted against the party that drafted the contract.

Specify the Time and Mode of Acceptance

Problems concerning contract formation also arise when it is unclear whether an acceptance is effective or at what time it became effective. To avoid such problems, you should take some precautions when phrasing the offer. Whether your offer is made via the Internet, fax, express delivery, or mail, you can specify that the offer must be accepted (or even that you must receive the acceptance) by a certain time, and if it is not, the offer will terminate. Similarly, you can specify the mode of acceptance. In online offers, you can indicate that to accept the offer, the user must click on a certain box on the screen. If you make an offer and want the acceptance to be faxed to you, make sure that you clearly indicate that the acceptance must be faxed to you at a given fax number by a specific time, or it will not be effective.

CHECKLIST FOR THE OFFEROR

1 Make sure that the terms of the offer are sufficiently clear and definite to allow both the parties and a court to determine the specific rights and obligations of the parties. Otherwise, the contract may fail for its ambiguity.

2 Specify in the offer the date on which the offer will terminate and the authorized mode of acceptance. For example, you can indicate that an acceptance, to be effective, must be faxed to you at a specific fax number by a specific time or date. You can even specify that the acceptance will not be effective until you receive it.

---

* This *Application* is not meant to substitute for the services of an attorney who is licensed to practice law in your state.

KEY TERMS

acceptance 219
accord and satisfaction 226
agreement 211
bilateral contract 205
consideration 222
contract 203
counteroffer 217
covenant not to sue 228
estopped 228
executed contract 208
executory contract 208
express contract 207
forbearance 222

formal contract 207
implied-in-fact contract 207
informal contract 207
liquidated debt 226
mailbox rule 221
mirror image rule 218
offer 211
offeree 205
offeror 205
option contract 216
past consideration 225
promise 202
promisee 203

promisor 203
promissory estoppel 228
quasi contract 210
release 226
rescission 225
revocation 216
unenforceable contract 209
unilateral contract 205
valid contract 209
void contract 210
voidable contract 209

CHAPTER SUMMARY Contracts: Nature, Classification, Agreement, and Consideration

**An Overview
of Contract Law**
(See pages 202–204.)

1. *Sources of contract law*—The common law governs all contracts except when it has been modified or replaced by statutory law, such as the Uniform Commercial Code (UCC), or by administrative agency regulations. The UCC governs contracts for the sale or lease of goods (see Chapter 11).

2. *The function of contracts*—Contract law establishes what kinds of promises will be legally binding and supplies procedures for enforcing legally binding promises, or agreements.

3. *The definition of a contract*—A contract is an agreement that can be enforced in court. It is formed by two or more competent parties who agree to perform or to refrain from performing some act in the present or in the future.

4. *Requirements of a valid contract*—Agreement, consideration, contractual capacity, and legality.

5. *Defenses to the enforcement of a contract*—Genuineness of assent and form.

Types of Contracts
(See pages 204–211.)

1. *Bilateral*—A promise for a promise.

2. *Unilateral*—A promise for an act (acceptance is the completed—or substantial—performance of the contract by the offeree).

3. *Formal*—Requires a special form for contract formation.

4. *Informal*—Requires no special form for contract formation.

5. *Express*—Formed by words (oral, written, or a combination).

6. *Implied in fact*—Formed at least in part by the conduct of the parties.

7. *Executed*—A fully performed contract.

8. *Executory*—A contract not yet fully performed.

9. *Valid*—A contract that has the necessary contractual elements of offer and acceptance, consideration, parties with legal capacity, and having been made for a legal purpose.

10. *Voidable*—A contract in which a party has the option of avoiding or enforcing the contractual obligation.

11. *Unenforceable*—A valid contract that cannot be enforced because of a legal defense.

12. *Void*—No contract exists, or there is a contract without legal obligations.

13. *Quasi contract*—A quasi contract, or a contract implied in law, is a contract that is imposed by law to prevent unjust enrichment.

CHAPTER SUMMARY	**Contracts: Nature, Classification, Agreement, and Consideration–Continued**
Requirements of the Offer (See pages 211–215.)	1. *Intention*—There must be a serious, objective intention by the offeror to become bound by the offer. Nonoffer situations include (a) expressions of opinion; (b) statements of future intent; (c) preliminary negotiations; (d) generally, advertisements, catalogues, price lists, and circulars; (e) solicitations for bids made by an auctioneer; and (f) traditionally, agreements to agree in the future. 2. *Definiteness*—The terms of the offer must be sufficiently definite to be ascertainable by the parties or by a court. 3. *Communication*—The offer must be communicated to the offeree.

Termination of the Offer (See pages 216–219.)	1. *By action of the parties—*
	  a. Revocation—Unless the offer is irrevocable, it can be revoked at any time before acceptance without liability. Revocation is not effective until received by the offeree or the offeree's agent. Some offers, such as a merchant's firm offer and option contracts, are irrevocable.
	  b. Rejection—Accomplished by words or actions that demonstrate a clear intent not to accept the offer; not effective until received by the offeror or the offeror's agent.
	  c. Counteroffer—A rejection of the original offer and the making of a new offer.
	
	2. *By operation of law—*
	  a. Lapse of time—The offer terminates (1) at the end of the time period specified in the offer or (2) if no time period is stated in the offer, at the end of a reasonable time period.
	  b. Destruction of the specific subject matter of the offer—Automatically terminates the offer.
	  c. Death or incompetence—Terminates the offer unless the offer is irrevocable.
	  d. Illegality—Supervening illegality terminates the offer.

Acceptance (See pages 219–222.)	1. Can be made only by the offeree or the offeree's agent.
	
	2. Must be unequivocal. Under the common law (mirror image rule), if new terms or conditions are added to the acceptance, it will be considered a counteroffer.
	
	3. Acceptance of a unilateral offer is effective on full performance of the requested act. Generally, no communication is necessary.
	
	4. Acceptance of a bilateral offer can be communicated by the offeree by any authorized mode of communication and is effective on dispatch. Unless the mode of communication is expressly specified by the offeror, the following methods are impliedly authorized:
	  a. The same mode used by the offeror or a faster mode.
	  b. Mail, when the two parties are at a distance.
	  c. In sales contracts, by any reasonable medium.

Elements of Consideration (See pages 222–223.)	Consideration is broken down into two parts: (1) something of *legally sufficient value* must be given in exchange for the promise, and (2) there must be a *bargained-for exchange*.
Legal Sufficiency and Adequacy of Consideration (See page 223.)	Legal sufficiency of consideration relates to the first element of consideration—something of legal value must be given in exchange for a promise. Adequacy of consideration relates to "how much" consideration is given and whether a fair bargain was reached. Courts will inquire into the adequacy of consideration (whether the consideration is legally sufficient) only when fraud, undue influence, duress, or unconscionability may be involved.

(Continued)

CHAPTER SUMMARY	Contracts: Nature, Classification, Agreement, and Consideration–Continued
Contracts That Lack Consideration (See pages 223–226.)	Consideration is lacking in the following situations: 1. *Preexisting duty*—Consideration is not legally sufficient if one is either by law or by contract under a *preexisting duty* to perform the action being offered as consideration for a new contract. 2. *Past consideration*—Actions or events that have already taken place do not constitute legally sufficient consideration. 3. *Illusory promises*—When the nature or extent of performance is too uncertain, the promise is rendered illusory (without consideration and unenforceable).
Settlement of Claims (See pages 226–228.)	1. *Accord and satisfaction*—An *accord* is an agreement in which a debtor offers to pay a lesser amount than the creditor purports to be owed. *Satisfaction* may take place when the accord is executed. 2. *Release*—An agreement in which, for consideration, a party forfeits the right to seek further recovery beyond the terms specified in the release. 3. *Covenant not to sue*—An agreement not to sue on a present, valid claim.
Promissory Estoppel (See page 228.)	The equitable doctrine of promissory estoppel applies when a promisor reasonably expects a promise to induce definite and substantial action or forbearance by the promisee, and the promisee does act in reliance on the promise. Such a promise is binding if injustice can be avoided only by enforcement of the promise. Also known as the doctrine of *detrimental reliance*.

FOR REVIEW

Answers for the even-numbered questions in this **For Review** *section can be found in Appendix E at the end of this text.*

1 What is a contract? What are the four basic elements necessary to the formation of a valid contract?

2 What are the various types of contracts?

3 What are the requirements of an offer?

4 How can an offer be accepted?

5 What are the elements of consideration?

■

QUESTIONS AND CASE PROBLEMS

HYPOTHETICAL SCENARIOS

7.1 Express versus Implied Contracts. Suppose that a local businessperson, McDougal, is a good friend of Krunch, the owner of a local candy store. Every day on his lunch hour McDougal goes into Krunch's candy store and spends about five minutes looking at the candy. After examining Krunch's candy and talking with Krunch, McDougal usually buys one or two candy bars. One afternoon, McDougal goes into Krunch's candy shop, looks at the candy, and picks up a $1 candy bar. Seeing that Krunch is very busy, he catches Krunch's eye, waves the candy bar at Krunch without saying a word, and walks out. Is there a contract? If so, classify it within the categories presented in this chapter.

7.2 Hypothetical Question with Sample Answer. Chernek, the sole owner of a small business, has a large piece of used farm equipment for sale. He offers to sell the equipment to Bollow for $10,000. Discuss the legal effects of the following events on the offer:

1 Chernek dies prior to Bollow's acceptance, and at the time she accepts, Bollow is unaware of Chernek's death.

2 The night before Bollow accepts, a fire destroys the equipment.

3 Bollow pays $100 for a thirty-day option to purchase the equipment. During this period, Chernek dies, and Bollow accepts the offer, knowing of Chernek's death.

4 Bollow pays $100 for a thirty-day option to purchase the equipment. During this period, Bollow dies, and Bollow's estate accepts Chernek's offer within the stipulated time period.

 **For a sample answer to Question 7.2, go to Appendix F at the end of this text.**

7.3 **Contract Classification.** High-Flying Advertising, Inc., contracted with Big Burger Restaurants to fly an advertisement above the Connecticut beaches. The advertisement offered $5,000 to any person who could swim from the Connecticut beaches to Long Island across the Long Island Sound in less than a day. McElfresh saw the streamer and accepted the challenge. He started his marathon swim that same day at 10 A.M. After he had been swimming for four hours and was about halfway across the sound, McElfresh saw another plane pulling a streamer that read, "Big Burger revokes." Is there a contract between McElfresh and Big Burger? If there is a contract, what type(s) of contract is (are) formed?

CASE PROBLEMS

7.4 **Implied Contract.** Thomas Rinks and Joseph Shields developed Psycho Chihuahua, a caricature of a Chihuahua dog with a "do-not-back-down" attitude. They promoted and marketed the character through their company, Wrench, L.L.C. Ed Alfaro and Rudy Pollak, representatives of Taco Bell Corp., learned of Psycho Chihuahua and met with Rinks and Shields to talk about using the character as a Taco Bell "icon." Wrench sent artwork, merchandise, and marketing ideas to Alfaro, who promoted the character within Taco Bell. Alfaro asked Wrench to propose terms for Taco Bell's use of Psycho Chihuahua. Taco Bell did not accept Wrench's terms, but Alfaro continued to promote the character within the company. Meanwhile, Taco Bell hired a new advertising agency, which proposed an advertising campaign involving a Chihuahua. When Alfaro learned of this proposal, he sent the Psycho Chihuahua materials to the agency. Taco Bell made a Chihuahua the focus of its marketing but paid nothing to Wrench. Wrench filed a suit against Taco Bell in a federal district court, claiming in part that it had an implied contract with Taco Bell, which the latter breached. Do these facts satisfy the requirements for an implied contract? Why or why not? [*Wrench, L.L.C. v. Taco Bell Corp.*, 256 F.3d 446 (6th Cir. 2001), *cert.* denied, 534 U.S. 1114, 122 S.Ct. 921, 151 L.Ed.2d 885 (2002)]

7.5 **Case Problem with Sample Answer.** As a child, Martha Carr once visited her mother's 108-acre tract of unimproved land in Richland County, South Carolina. In 1968, Betty and Raymond Campbell leased the land. Carr, a resident of New York, was diagnosed as having schizophrenia and depression in 1986, was hospitalized five or six times, and takes prescription drugs for the illnesses. In 1996, Carr inherited the Richland property and, two years later, contacted the Campbells about selling the land. Carr asked Betty about the value of the land, and Betty said that the county tax assessor had determined that the land's *agricultural value* was $54,000.

The Campbells knew at the time that the county had assessed the total property value at $103,700 for tax purposes. On August 6, Carr signed a contract to sell the land to the Campbells for $54,000. Believing the price to be unfair, however, Carr did not deliver the deed. The Campbells filed a suit in a South Carolina state court against Carr, seeking specific performance of the contract. At trial, an expert real estate appraiser testified that the *real market value* of the property was $162,000 at the time of the contract. Under what circumstances will a court examine the adequacy of consideration? Are those circumstances present in this case? Should the court enforce the contract between Carr and the Campbells? Explain. [*Campbell v. Carr*, 361 S.C. 258, 603 S.E.2d 625 (2004)]

After you have answered Problem 7.5, compare your answer with the sample answer given on the Web site that accompanies this text. Go to academic.cengage.com/blaw/blt**, select "Chapter 7," and click on "Case Problem with Sample Answer."**

7.6 **Offer.** In August 2000, in California, Terry Reigelsperger sought treatment for pain in his lower back from chiropractor James Siller. Reigelsperger felt better after the treatment and did not intend to return for more, although he did not mention this to Siller. Before leaving the office, Reigelsperger signed an "informed consent" form that read, in part, "I intend this consent form to cover the entire course of treatment for my present condition and for any future condition(s) for which I seek treatment." He also signed an agreement that required the parties to submit to arbitration "any dispute as to medical malpractice. . . . This agreement is intended to bind the patient and the health care provider . . . who now or in the future treat[s] the patient." Two years later, Reigelsperger sought treatment from Siller for a different condition relating to his cervical spine and shoulder. Claiming malpractice with respect to the second treatment,

Reigelsperger filed a suit in a California state court against Siller. Siller asked the court to order the submission of the dispute to arbitration. Does Reigelsperger's lack of intent to return to Siller after his first treatment affect the enforceability of the arbitration agreement and consent form? Why or why not? [*Reigelsperger v. Siller*, 40 Cal.4th 574, 53 Cal.Rptr.3d 887, 150 P.3d 764 (2007)]

7.7 Contract Enforceability. California's Subdivision Map Act (SMA) prohibits the sale of real property until a map of its subdivision is filed with, and approved by, the appropriate state agency. In November 2004, Black Hills Investments, Inc., entered into two contracts with Albertson's, Inc., to buy two parcels of property in a shopping center development. Each contract required that "all governmental approvals relating to any lot split [or] subdivision" be obtained before the sale but permitted Albertson's to waive this condition. Black Hills made a $133,000 deposit on the purchase. A few weeks later, before the sales were complete, Albertson's filed with a local state agency a map that subdivided the shopping center into four parcels, including the two that Black Hills had agreed to buy. In January 2005, Black Hills objected to concessions that Albertson's had made to a buyer of one of the other parcels, told Albertson's that it was terminating its deal, and asked for a return of its deposit. Albertson's refused. Black Hills filed a suit in a California state court against Albertson's, arguing that the contracts were void. Are these contracts valid, voidable, unenforceable, or void? Explain. [*Black Hills Investments, Inc. v. Albertson's, Inc.*, 146 Cal.App.4th 883, 53 Cal.Rptr.3d 263 (4 Dist. 2007)]

7.8 **A Question of Ethics.** *John Sasson and Emily Springer met in January 2002. John worked for the U.S. Army as an engineer. Emily was an attorney with a law firm. When, six months later, John bought a townhouse in Randolph, New Jersey, he asked Emily to live with him. She agreed, but retained the ownership of her home in Monmouth Beach. John paid the mortgage and the other expenses on the townhouse. He urged Emily to quit her job and work from "our house." In May 2003, Emily took John's advice and started her own law practice. In December, John made her the beneficiary of his $150,000 individual retirement account (IRA) and said that he would give her his 2002 BMW M3 car before the end of the next year. He proposed to her in September 2004, giving her a diamond engagement ring and promising to "take care of her" for the rest of her life. Less than a month later, John was critically injured by an accidental blow to his head during a basketball game and died. On behalf of John's estate, which was valued at $1.1 million, his brother Steven filed a complaint in a New Jersey state court to have Emily evicted from the townhouse. Given these facts, consider the following questions. [In re Estate of Sasson, 387 N.J.Super. 459, 904 A.2d 769 (App.Div. 2006)]*

1 Based on John's promise to "take care of her" for the rest of her life, Emily claimed that she was entitled to the townhouse, the BMW, and an additional portion of John's estate. Under what circumstances would such a promise constitute a valid, enforceable contract? Does John's promise meet these requirements? Why or why not?

2 Whether John's promise is legally binding, is there an ethical basis on which it should be enforced? Is there an ethical basis for *not* enforcing it? Are there any circumstances under which a promise of support should be—or should *not* be—enforced? Discuss.

CRITICAL THINKING AND WRITING ASSIGNMENTS

7.9 Critical Legal Thinking. Review the list of basic requirements for contract formation given at the beginning of this chapter. In view of those requirements, analyze the relationship entered into when a student enrolls in a college or university. Has a contract been formed? If so, is it a bilateral contract or a unilateral contract? Discuss.

7.10 Critical Legal Thinking. Under what circumstances should courts examine the adequacy of consideration?

7.11 **Video Question.** Go to this text's Web site at **academic. cengage.com/blaw/blt** and select "Chapter 7." Click on "Video Questions" and view the video titled *Bowfinger*. Then answer the following questions.

1 In the video, Renfro (Robert Downey, Jr.) says to Bowfinger (Steve Martin), "You bring me this script and Kit Ramsey and you've got yourself a 'go' picture." Assume for the purposes of this question that their agreement is a contract. Is the contract bilateral or unilateral? Is it express or implied? Is it formal or informal? Is it executed or executory? Explain your answers.

2 Recall from the video that the contract between Bowfinger and the producer was oral. Suppose that a statute requires contracts of this type to be in writing. In that situation, would the contract be void, voidable, or unenforceable? Explain.

ONLINE ACTIVITIES

PRACTICAL INTERNET EXERCISES

Go to this text's Web site at **academic.cengage.com/blaw/blt**, select "Chapter 7," and click on "Practical Internet Exercises." There you will find the following Internet research exercises that you can perform to learn more about the topics covered in this chapter.

PRACTICAL INTERNET EXERCISE 7–1   LEGAL PERSPECTIVE—Contract Terms

PRACTICAL INTERNET EXERCISE 7–2   MANAGEMENT PERSPECTIVE—Implied Employment Contracts

PRACTICAL INTERNET EXERCISE 7–3   ETHICAL PERSPECTIVE—Offers and Advertisements

BEFORE THE TEST

Go to this text's Web site at **academic.cengage.com/blaw/blt**, select "Chapter 7," and click on "Interactive Quizzes." You will find a number of interactive questions relating to this chapter.

CHAPTER 8
Contracts: Capacity, Legality, Assent, and Form

CHAPTER OUTLINE

- CONTRACTUAL CAPACITY
- LEGALITY
- GENUINENESS OF ASSENT
- THE STATUTE OF FRAUDS– REQUIREMENT OF A WRITING
- THE STATUTE OF FRAUDS– SUFFICIENCY OF THE WRITING

LEARNING OBJECTIVES

AFTER READING THIS CHAPTER, YOU SHOULD BE ABLE TO ANSWER THE FOLLOWING QUESTIONS:

1 What are some exceptions to the rule that a minor can disaffirm (avoid) any contract?

2 Does an intoxicated person have the capacity to enter into an enforceable contract?

3 In what types of situations might genuineness of assent to a contract's terms be lacking?

4 What elements must exist for fraudulent misrepresentation to occur?

5 What contracts must be in writing to be enforceable?

Courts generally want contracts to be enforceable, and much of the law is devoted to aiding the enforceability of contracts. Nonetheless, as indicated in the chapter-opening quotation, "liberty of contract" is not absolute. In other words, not all people can make legally binding contracts at all times. Contracts entered into by persons lacking the capacity to do so may be voidable. Similarly, contracts calling for the performance of an illegal act are illegal and thus void—they are not contracts at all.

In this chapter, we first examine contractual capacity and some aspects of illegal bargains. We then look at genuineness of assent. An otherwise valid contract may be unenforceable if the parties have not genuinely assented to its terms. As mentioned in Chapter 7, lack of genuine assent is a *defense* to the enforcement of a contract. A contract that is otherwise valid may also be unenforceable if it is not in the proper form. For example, if a contract is required by law to be in writing and there is no written evidence of the contract, it may not be enforceable. In the concluding section of this chapter, we examine the kinds of contracts that require a writing under what is called the *Statute of Frauds*.

CONTRACTUAL CAPACITY

CONTRACTUAL CAPACITY
The threshold mental capacity required by law for a party who enters into a contract to be bound by that contract.

Contractual capacity is the legal ability to enter into a contractual relationship. Courts generally presume the existence of contractual capacity, but in some situations, capacity is lacking or may be questionable. A person who has been determined by a court to be mentally incompetent, for example, cannot form a legally binding contract with another party. In other situations, a party may have the capacity to enter into a valid contract but may also have the right to avoid liability under it. For example, minors—or *infants*, as they are commonly referred to in the law—usually are not legally bound by contracts. In this section, we look at the effect of youth, intoxication, and mental incompetence on contractual capacity.

Minors

Today, in virtually all states, the *age of majority* (when a person is no longer a minor) for contractual purposes is eighteen years—the so-called coming of age. (The age of majority may still be twenty-one for other purposes, however, such as the purchase and consumption of alcohol.) In addition, some states provide for the termination of minority on marriage. Minority status may also be terminated by a minor's **emancipation,** which occurs when a child's parent or legal guardian relinquishes the legal right to exercise control over the child. Normally, minors who leave home to support themselves are considered emancipated. Several jurisdictions permit minors to petition a court for emancipation themselves. For business purposes, a minor may petition a court to be treated as an adult.

The general rule is that a minor can enter into any contract an adult can, provided that the contract is not one prohibited by law for minors (for example, the sale of alcoholic beverages or tobacco). A contract entered into by a minor, however, is voidable at the option of that minor, subject to certain exceptions (to be discussed shortly). To exercise the option to avoid a contract, a minor need only manifest an intention not to be bound by it. The minor "avoids" the contract by disaffirming it.

Disaffirmance   The legal avoidance, or setting aside, of a contractual obligation is referred to as **disaffirmance.** To disaffirm, a minor must express, through words or conduct, his or her intent not to be bound to the contract. The minor must disaffirm the entire contract, not merely a portion of it. For instance, a minor cannot decide to keep part of the goods purchased under a contract and return the remaining goods. When a minor disaffirms a contract, the minor can recover any property that she or he transferred to the adult as consideration for the contract, even if it is then in the possession of a third party.[1]

A contract can ordinarily be disaffirmed at any time during minority[2] or for a reasonable time after the minor comes of age. What constitutes a "reasonable" time may vary. Two months would probably be considered reasonable, but except in unusual circumstances, a court may not find it reasonable to wait a year or more after coming of age to disaffirm. If an individual fails to disaffirm an executed contract within a reasonable time after reaching the age of majority, a court will likely hold that the contract has been ratified (*ratification* will be discussed shortly).

Note that an adult who enters into a contract with a minor cannot avoid his or her contractual duties on the ground that the minor can do so. Unless the minor exercises the option to disaffirm the contract, the adult party normally is bound by it.

A Minor's Obligations on Disaffirmance   Although all states' laws permit minors to disaffirm contracts (with certain exceptions), including executed contracts, state laws differ on the extent of a minor's obligations on disaffirmance.

ON THE WEB

The Legal Information Institute at Cornell Law School provides a table with links to state statutes governing the emancipation of minors. Go to

www.law.cornell.edu/topics/ Table_Emancipation.htm.

EMANCIPATION
In regard to minors, the act of being freed from parental control; occurs when a child's parent or legal guardian relinquishes the legal right to exercise control over the child. Normally, a minor who leaves home to support himself or herself is considered emancipated.

DISAFFIRMANCE
The legal avoidance, or setting aside, of a contractual obligation.

This minor is discussing the purchase of a used car with a salesperson. When a minor disaffirms a contract, such as a contract to buy a car, most states require the minor to return whatever he or she purchased, if it is within his or her control. Why do some states require more?
(Michael Newman/PhotoEdit)

---

1. The Uniform Commercial Code, in Section 2–403(1), allows an exception if the third party is a "good faith purchaser for value."
2. In some states, however, a minor who enters into a contract for the sale of land cannot disaffirm the contract until she or he reaches the age of majority.

Majority Rule.   Courts in a majority of states hold that the minor need only return the goods (or other consideration) subject to the contract, provided the goods are in the minor's possession or control. ▪**EXAMPLE 8.1** Jim Garrison, a seventeen-year-old, purchases a computer from Radio Shack. While transporting the computer to his home, Garrison, through no fault of his own, is involved in a car accident. As a result of the accident, the plastic casing of the computer is broken. The next day, he returns the computer to Radio Shack and disaffirms the contract. Under the majority view, this return fulfills Garrison's duty even though the computer is now damaged. Garrison is entitled to receive a refund of the purchase price (if paid in cash) or to be relieved of any further obligations under an agreement to purchase the computer on credit. ▪

Minority Rule.   A growing number of states, either by statute or by court decision, place an additional duty on the minor—the duty to restore the adult party to the position she or he held before the contract was made. The trend among today's courts is to hold a minor responsible for damage, ordinary wear and tear, and depreciation of goods that the minor used prior to disaffirmance.

Exceptions to the Minor's Right to Disaffirm   State courts and legislatures have carved out several exceptions to the minor's right to disaffirm. Some contracts cannot be avoided simply as a matter of law, on the ground of public policy. For example, marriage contracts and contracts to enlist in the armed services fall into this category. Other contracts may not be disaffirmed for different reasons, including those discussed here.

Misrepresentation of Age.   Suppose that a minor tells a seller she is twenty-one years old when she is really seventeen. Ordinarily, the minor can disaffirm the contract even though she has misrepresented her age. Moreover, in some jurisdictions the minor is not liable for the tort of fraudulent misrepresentation, the rationale being that such a tort judgment might indirectly force the minor to perform the contract.

In many jurisdictions, however, a minor who has misrepresented his or her age can be bound by a contract under certain circumstances. First, several states have enacted statutes for precisely this purpose. In these states, misrepresentation of age is enough to prohibit disaffirmance. Other statutes prohibit disaffirmance by a minor who has engaged in business as an adult. Second, some courts refuse to allow minors to disaffirm executed (fully performed) contracts unless they can return the consideration received. The combination of the minors' misrepresentations and their unjust enrichment has persuaded these courts to *estop* (prevent) the minors from asserting contractual incapacity.

Contracts for Necessaries, Insurance, and Loans.   A minor who enters into a contract for necessaries may disaffirm the contract but remains liable for the reasonable value of the goods used. **Necessaries** are basic needs, such as food, clothing, shelter, and medical services, at a level of value required to maintain the minor's standard of living or financial and social status. Thus, what will be considered a necessary for one person may be a luxury for another. Additionally, what is considered a necessary depends on whether the minor is under the care or control of his or her parents, who are required by law to provide necessaries for the minor. If a minor's parents provide the minor with shelter, for example, then a contract to lease shelter (such as an apartment) normally will not be regarded as a contract for necessaries.

Generally, then, to qualify as a contract for necessaries, (1) the item contracted for must be necessary to the minor's existence, (2) the value of the necessary item may be up to a level required to maintain the minor's standard of living or financial and social status, and (3) the minor must not be under the care of a parent or guardian who is required

NECESSARIES
Necessities required for life, such as food, shelter, clothing, and medical attention; may include whatever is believed to be necessary to maintain a person's standard of living or financial and social status.

BE AWARE   A minor's station in life (including financial and social status and lifestyle) is important in determining whether an item is a necessary or a luxury. For example, clothing is a necessary, but if a minor from a low-income family contracts for the purchase of a $2,000 leather coat, a court may deem the coat a luxury. In this situation, the contract would not be for "necessaries."

to supply this item. Unless these three criteria are met, the minor can normally disaffirm the contract *without* being liable for the reasonable value of the goods used.

Traditionally, insurance has not been viewed as a necessary, so minors can ordinarily disaffirm their insurance contracts and recover all premiums paid. Nevertheless, some jurisdictions prohibit disaffirming insurance contracts—for example, when minors contract for life insurance on their own lives. Financial loans are seldom considered to be necessaries, even if the minor spends the borrowed funds on necessaries. If, however, a lender makes a loan to a minor for the express purpose of enabling the minor to purchase necessaries, and the lender personally makes sure the funds are so spent, the minor normally is obligated to repay the loan.

Ratification   In contract law, **ratification** is the act of accepting and giving legal force to an obligation that previously was not enforceable. A minor who has reached the age of majority can ratify a contract expressly or impliedly. *Express* ratification occurs when the individual, on reaching the age of majority, states orally or in writing that she or he intends to be bound by the contract. *Implied* ratification takes place when the minor, on reaching the age of majority, indicates an intent to abide by the contract.

■EXAMPLE 8.2 Lin enters a contract to sell her laptop to Arturo, a minor. If Arturo does not disaffirm the contract and, on reaching the age of majority, writes a letter to Lin stating that he still agrees to buy the laptop, he has expressly ratified the contract. If, instead, Arturo takes possession of the laptop as a minor and continues to use it well after reaching the age of majority, he has impliedly ratified the contract. ■

If a minor fails to disaffirm a contract within a reasonable time after reaching the age of majority, then a court must determine whether the conduct constitutes implied ratification or disaffirmance. Generally, courts presume that a contract that is *executed* (fully performed by both sides) was ratified. A contract that is still *executory* (not yet performed by both parties) is normally considered to be disaffirmed. The *Concept Summary* on this page summarizes the rules relating to contracts by minors.

RATIFICATION
The act of accepting and giving legal force to an obligation that previously was not enforceable.

Intoxicated Persons

Contractual capacity also becomes an issue when a party to a contract was intoxicated at the time the contract was made. Intoxication is a condition in which a person's normal capacity to act or think is inhibited by alcohol or some other drug. If the person was

CONCEPT SUMMARY **Contracts by Minors**

General Rule	Contracts entered into by minors are voidable at the option of the minor.
Rules of Disaffirmance	A minor may disaffirm a contract at any time while still a minor and within a reasonable time after reaching the age of majority. Most states only require that the minor return the goods that were subject to the contract, regardless of any damage, wear and tear, or depreciation of those goods. Some states require that the minor pay for any damage to, or depreciation of, the goods being returned.
Exceptions to Basic Rules of Disaffirmance	1. *Fraud or misrepresentation*—In many jurisdictions, a minor who misrepresents her or his age is denied the right of disaffirmance. 2. *Necessaries*—Minors may disaffirm contracts for necessaries but remain liable for the reasonable value of the goods or services. 3. *Ratification*—After reaching the age of majority, a person can ratify a contract that he or she formed as a minor, thereby becoming fully liable on the contract.

sufficiently intoxicated to lack mental capacity, the contract may be voidable even if the intoxication was purely voluntary. For the contract to be voidable, however, the person must prove that the intoxication impaired her or his reason and judgment so severely that she or he did not comprehend the legal consequences of entering into the contract. In addition, to avoid the contract in the majority of states, the person claiming intoxication must be able to return all consideration received.

If, despite intoxication, the person understood the legal consequences of the agreement, the contract is enforceable. The fact that the terms of the contract are foolish or obviously favor the other party does not make the contract voidable (unless the other party fraudulently induced the person to become intoxicated). As a practical matter, courts rarely permit contracts to be avoided on the ground of intoxication, because it is difficult to determine whether a party was sufficiently intoxicated to avoid legal duties. Rather than inquire into the intoxicated person's mental state, many courts instead focus on objective indications of capacity to determine whether the contract is voidable owing to intoxication.[3]

Mentally Incompetent Persons

Contracts made by mentally incompetent persons can be void, voidable, or valid. If a court has previously determined that a person is mentally incompetent and has appointed a guardian to represent the person, any contract made by that mentally incompetent person is *void*—no contract exists. Only the guardian can enter into a binding contract on behalf of the mentally incompetent person.

If a court has not previously judged a person to be mentally incompetent but in fact the person was incompetent at the time, the contract may be *voidable*. A contract is voidable if the person did not know he or she was entering into the contract or lacked the mental capacity to comprehend its nature, purpose, and consequences. In such situations, the contract is voidable at the option of the mentally incompetent person but not the other party. The contract may then be disaffirmed or ratified (if the person regains mental competence). Like intoxicated persons, mentally incompetent persons must return any consideration and pay for the reasonable value of any necessaries they receive.

A contract entered into by a mentally incompetent person (whom a court has not previously declared incompetent) may also be *valid* if the person had capacity *at the time the contract was formed*. For instance, a person may be able to understand the nature and effect of entering into a certain contract yet simultaneously lack capacity to engage in other activities. In such cases, the contract ordinarily will be valid because the person is not legally mentally incompetent for contractual purposes.[4] Similarly, an otherwise mentally incompetent person may have a *lucid interval*—a temporary restoration of sufficient intelligence, judgment, and will to enter into contracts—during which she or he will be considered to have full legal capacity.

LEGALITY

To this point, we have discussed three of the requirements for a valid contract to exist—agreement, consideration, and contractual capacity. Now we examine the fourth—legality. For a contract to be valid and enforceable, it must be formed for a legal purpose. A contract

---

3. See, for example, the court's decision in *Lucy v. Zehmer*, presented as Case 7.2 in Chapter 7.

4. Modern courts no longer require a person to be completely irrational to disaffirm contracts on the basis of mental incompetence. A contract may be voidable if, by reason of a mental illness or defect, an individual was unable to act reasonably with respect to the transaction and the other party had reason to know of the condition.

to do something that is prohibited by federal or state statutory law is illegal and, as such, void from the outset and thus unenforceable. Additionally, a contract to commit a tortious act or to commit an action that is contrary to public policy is illegal and unenforceable.

Contracts Contrary to Statute

Statutes often set forth rules specifying which terms and clauses may be included in contracts and which are prohibited. We examine here several ways in which contracts may be contrary to a statute and thus illegal.

Contracts to Commit a Crime   Any contract to commit a crime is a contract in violation of a statute. Thus, a contract to sell an illegal drug (the sale of which is prohibited by statute) is not enforceable. If the object or performance of the contract is rendered illegal by statute *after* the contract has been entered into, the contract is considered to be discharged by law. (See the discussion of *impossibility of performance* in Chapter 9.)

Usury   Virtually every state has a statute that sets the maximum rate of interest that can be charged for different types of transactions, including ordinary loans. A lender who makes a loan at an interest rate above the lawful maximum commits **usury.** The maximum rate of interest varies from state to state, as do the consequences for lenders who make usurious loans. Some states allow the lender to recover only the principal of a loan along with interest up to the legal maximum. In effect, the lender is denied recovery of the excess interest. In other states, the lender can recover the principal amount of the loan but no interest.

USURY
Charging an illegal rate of interest.

Although usury statutes place a ceiling on allowable rates of interest, exceptions are made to facilitate business transactions. For example, many states exempt corporate loans from the usury laws. In addition, almost all states have special statutes allowing much higher interest rates on small loans to help those borrowers who need funds and could not otherwise obtain loans.

Gambling   All states have statutes that regulate gambling—defined as any scheme that involves the distribution of property by chance among persons who have paid valuable consideration for the opportunity (chance) to receive the property.[5] Gambling is the creation of risk for the purpose of assuming it. Traditionally, the states have deemed gambling contracts illegal and thus void.

In several states, however, including Louisiana, Michigan, Nevada, and New Jersey, casino gambling is legal. In other states, certain forms of gambling are legal. California, for example, has not defined draw poker as a crime, although criminal statutes prohibit numerous other types of gambling games. A number of states allow gambling on horse races, and the majority of states have legalized state-operated lotteries, as well as lotteries (such as bingo) conducted for charitable purposes. Many states also allow gambling on Indian reservations.

Sometimes, it is difficult to distinguish a gambling contract from the risk sharing inherent in almost all contracts.   **■EXAMPLE 8.3**   In one case, five co-workers each received a free lottery ticket from a customer and agreed to split the winnings if one of the tickets turned out to be the winning one. At first glance, this may seem entirely legal. The court, however, noted that the oral contract in this case "was an exchange of promises to share winnings from the parties' individually owned lottery tickets upon the happening of the uncertain event" that one of the tickets

Payday loans are popular with individuals who do not have regular banking relationships. A client writes a check for some relatively small amount to be cashed at "pay day," usually in two weeks. About 10 million U.S. residents apply for these loans in any given year. The implicit interest rates are extremely high, sometimes more than 100 percent on an annualized basis. Why would anyone agree to pay so much for such a short-term loan?
(Seth Anderson/Creative Commons)

5. See *Wishing Well Club v. Akron,* 112 N.E.2d 41 (Ohio Com.Pl. 1951).

would win. Consequently, concluded the court, the agreement at issue was "founded on a gambling consideration" and therefore was void.[6] ◾

Online Gambling   A significant issue today is how gambling laws can be applied in the Internet context. Because state laws pertaining to gambling differ, online gambling raises a number of unique issues. For example, in those states that do not allow casino gambling or offtrack betting, what can a state government do if residents of the state place bets online? Also, where does the actual act of gambling occur? For example, suppose that a resident of New York places bets via the Internet at a gambling site located in Antigua. Is the actual act of "gambling" taking place in New York or in Antigua? According to a New York court in one case, "if the person engaged in gambling is located in New York, then New York is the location where the gambling occurred."[7] Courts of other states may take a different view, however.

Another issue that is being debated is whether entering contracts that involve gambling on sports teams that do not really exist—fantasy sports—is a form of gambling. For a discussion of this issue, see this chapter's *Adapting the Law to the Online Environment* feature.

Sabbath (Sunday) Laws   Statutes referred to as Sabbath (Sunday) laws prohibit the formation or performance of certain contracts on a Sunday. These laws, which date back to colonial times, are often called **blue laws,** as mentioned in Chapter 1. Blue laws get their name from the blue paper on which New Haven, Connecticut, printed its town ordinance in 1781 that prohibited work and required businesses to close on Sunday. According to a few state and local laws, all contracts entered into on a Sunday are illegal. Laws in other states or municipalities prohibit only the sale of certain types of merchandise, such as alcoholic beverages, on a Sunday.

In most states with such statutes, contracts that were entered into on a Sunday can be ratified during a weekday. Also, if a contract that was entered into on a Sunday has been fully performed (executed), normally it cannot be rescinded (canceled). Exceptions to Sunday laws permit contracts for necessities (such as food) and works of charity. Many states do not enforce Sunday laws, and some state courts have held these laws to be unconstitutional because they interfere with the freedom of religion.

Licensing Statutes   All states require that members of certain professions obtain licenses allowing them to practice. Physicians, lawyers, real estate brokers, architects, electricians, and stockbrokers are but a few of the people who must be licensed. Some licenses are obtained only after extensive schooling and examinations, which indicate to the public that a special skill has been acquired. Others require only that the particular person be of good moral character and pay a fee.

The Purpose of Licensing Statutes.   Generally, business licenses provide a means of regulating and taxing certain businesses and protecting the public against actions that could threaten the general welfare. For example, in nearly all states, a stockbroker must be licensed and must file a bond with the state to protect the public from fraudulent transactions in stocks. Similarly, a plumber must be licensed and bonded to protect the public against incompetent plumbers and to protect the public health. Only persons or businesses possessing the qualifications and complying with the conditions required by statute are entitled to licenses. For instance, the owner of a bar can be required to sell food as a condition of obtaining a license to serve liquor.

BLUE LAWS
State or local laws that prohibit the performance of certain types of commercial activities on a Sunday.

ON THE WEB

If you are interested in reading the earliest legislation regulating activities on the Sabbath in colonial America (and about some of the punishments meted out for failing to obey these regulations), go to

www.natreformassn.org/statesman/99/colfound.html.

---

6. *Dickerson v. Deno*, 770 So.2d 63 (Ala. 2000).
7. *United States v. Cohen*, 260 F.3d. 68 (2d Cir. 2001).

ADAPTING THE LAW TO THE ONLINE ENVIRONMENT | Are Online Fantasy Sports Just Another Form of Real-Life Gambling?

According to the Fantasy Sports Trade Association, between 16 million and 20 million U.S. adults play some form of fantasy sports. A fantasy sport is a game in which the participants, or "owners," build a team composed of real-life players from different real-life teams. For example, an owner might include a quarterback from the New England Patriots and a running back from the San Diego Chargers. The fantasy team then competes against other fantasy sports teams with different owners. Each week during the season for the particular sport, the statistical performances of the real-life players are translated into points, and the points of all the players on an owner's fantasy team are totaled. Although fantasy baseball, basketball, golf, hockey, and other sports—even professional wrestling—are available, most participants play fantasy football.

Enter the Internet

Although the origin of fantasy sports supposedly can be traced back to 1962, when an owner of the Oakland Raiders football team and four other football fans created the Greater Oakland Professional Pigskin Prognosticators League, or GOPPPL, fantasy sports did not become big business until access to the Internet became widespread in the 1990s. Today, the number of players is increasing at a rate of 7 to 10 percent per year, and the game contributes as much as $4 billion annually to the U.S. economy. Fantasy sports sites have proliferated on the Internet, as have fantasy sports news sites, such as RotoWire.com and Fantasyfootballnews.com.

One of the appeals of online fantasy sports is that the participants can gamble on the outcome. In a fantasy football league, for example, each participant-owner adds a given amount to the pot and then "drafts" his or her fantasy team from the actual National Football League (NFL) players. Each week, as described earlier, the owner receives points based on his or her players' statistical performances. At the end of the season, the weekly points are totaled, and the owner with the most points wins the pot.

Exemption from Online Gambling Prohibitions

As online gambling has expanded, Congress has stepped in to attempt to regulate it. In October 2006, Congress passed and President George W. Bush signed into law a bill that, in essence, outlaws Internet gambling by making it illegal for credit-card companies and banking institutions to engage in transactions with Internet gambling companies.[a] Note that the act does not prohibit individuals from placing bets online, but rather focuses on restricting their ability to obtain financing for online gambling. Although the legislation seems comprehensive, it specifically exempts Internet wagers on horse racing, state lotteries, and fantasy sports. In other words, Congress explicitly determined that fantasy sports do *not* constitute a prohibited Internet gambling activity.

But Aren't Participants in Fantasy Sports Leagues Really Gambling?

In a lawsuit filed in New Jersey, Charles Humphrey claimed that media companies, including Viacom, CBS, ESPN, and *The Sporting News* had engaged in illegal gambling by hosting pay-to-play fantasy leagues. Humphrey argued that fantasy sports leagues are games of chance and not games of skill, and claimed that he was entitled to recover as gambling losses all of the entry fees paid by participants. The U.S. District Court rejected the argument, ruling that Humphrey's complaint failed to state a claim because it did not identify any individual who paid an entry fee to play in one of the fantasy sports.

Although the court dismissed the case on procedural grounds, the opinion stated that fantasy sports leagues are not bets or wagers because the entry fees are paid unconditionally. The court also found that the federal statute on Internet gambling (previously mentioned) confirms its conclusion that "fantasy sports leagues such as those operated by Defendants do not constitute gambling as a matter of law."[b]

FOR CRITICAL ANALYSIS *What arguments can be used to support the idea that playing fantasy sports requires skill?*

a. Security and Accountability for Every Port Act, Public Law No. 109-347, Sections 5361–5367, 120 Stat. 1884 (2006). (A version of the Unlawful Internet Gambling Enforcement Act of 2006 was incorporated into this statute.) See 31 U.S.C. Section 5361 *et seq.*

b. *Humphrey v. Viacom, Inc.*, 2007 WL 1797648 (D.N.J. 2007).

Contracts with Unlicensed Practitioners. A contract with an unlicensed practitioner may still be enforceable, depending on the nature of the licensing statute. Some states expressly provide that the lack of a license in certain occupations bars the enforcement of work-related contracts. If the statute does not expressly state this, one must look to the underlying purpose of the licensing requirements for a particular occupation. If the purpose is to protect the public from unauthorized practitioners, a contract involving an unlicensed individual is illegal and unenforceable. If, however, the underlying purpose of the statute is to raise government revenues, a contract with an unlicensed practitioner is enforceable—although the unlicensed person is usually fined.

Contracts Contrary to Public Policy

Although contracts involve private parties, some are not enforceable because of the negative impact they would have on society. These contracts are said to be *contrary to public policy*. Examples include a contract to commit an immoral act, such as selling a child, and a contract that prohibits marriage. **EXAMPLE 8.4** Everett offers a young man $10,000 if he refrains from marrying Everett's daughter. If the young man accepts, no contract is formed (the contract is void) because it is contrary to public policy. Thus, if the man marries Everett's daughter, Everett cannot sue him for breach of contract. ■ Business contracts that may be contrary to public policy include contracts in restraint of trade and unconscionable contracts or clauses.

Contracts in Restraint of Trade   Contracts in restraint of trade (anticompetitive agreements) usually adversely affect the public policy that favors competition in the economy. Typically, such contracts also violate one or more federal or state statutes.[8] An exception is recognized when the restraint is reasonable and is part of, or supplemental to, a contract for the sale of a business or an **employment contract** (a contract stating the terms and conditions of employment). Many such exceptions involve a type of restraint called a **covenant not to compete,** or a restrictive covenant.

Covenants Not to Compete and the Sale of an Ongoing Business.   Covenants (promises) not to compete are often contained as ancillary (secondary, or subordinate) clauses in contracts concerning the sale of an ongoing business. A covenant not to compete is created when a seller agrees not to open a new store in a certain geographic area surrounding the old store. Such agreements enable the seller to sell, and the purchaser to buy, the goodwill and reputation of an ongoing business. If, for example, a well-known merchant sells his or her store and opens a competing business a block away, many of the merchant's customers will likely do business at the new store. This renders less valuable the good name and reputation sold to the other merchant for a price. If a covenant not to compete is not ancillary to a sales agreement, however, it will be void because it unreasonably restrains trade and is contrary to public policy.

Covenants Not to Compete in Employment Contracts.   Agreements not to compete can also be included in employment contracts. People in middle-level and upper-level management positions commonly agree not to work for competitors or not to start a competing business for a specified period of time after terminating employment. Such agreements are generally legal so long as the specified period of time is not excessive in duration and the geographic restriction is reasonable. Basically, the restriction on competition must be reasonable—that is, not any greater than necessary to protect a legitimate business interest. Although a court might find that a time restriction of one year is reasonable, a time restriction of two, three, or five years may not be considered reasonable.

Determining what constitutes "reasonable" time and geographic restrictions in the online environment is a more difficult issue that is being addressed by the courts. The Internet environment has no physical borders, so geographic restrictions are no longer relevant. Also, a reasonable time period may be shorter in the online environment than in conventional employment contracts because the restrictions would apply worldwide.

EMPLOYMENT CONTRACT
A contract between an employer and an employee in which the terms and conditions of employment are stated.

COVENANT NOT TO COMPETE
A contractual promise of one party to refrain from conducting business similar to that of another party for a certain period of time and within a specified geographic area. Courts commonly enforce such covenants if they are reasonable in terms of time and geographic area and are part of, or supplemental to, a contract for the sale of a business or an employment contract.

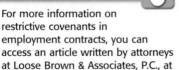

ON THE WEB

For more information on restrictive covenants in employment contracts, you can access an article written by attorneys at Loose Brown & Associates, P.C., at **www.loosebrown.com/Articles/bl2.htm.**

---

8. Federal statutes prohibiting anticompetitive agreements include the Sherman Antitrust Act, the Clayton Act, and the Federal Trade Commission Act. See Chapter 22.

Enforcement Problems.   The laws governing the enforceability of covenants not to compete vary significantly from state to state. In some states, such as Texas, such a covenant will not be enforced unless the employee has received some benefit in return for signing the noncompete agreement. This is true even if the covenant is reasonable as to time and area. If the employee receives no benefit, the covenant will be deemed void. California prohibits the enforcement of covenants not to compete altogether.

Occasionally, depending on the jurisdiction, courts will *reform* covenants not to compete. If a covenant is found to be unreasonable in time or geographic area, the court may convert the terms into reasonable ones and then enforce the reformed covenant. This presents a problem, however, in that the judge has implicitly become a party to the contract. Consequently, courts usually resort to contract **reformation** only when necessary to prevent undue burdens or hardships.

REFORMATION
A court-ordered correction of a written contract so that it reflects the true intentions of the parties.

Unconscionable Contracts or Clauses   Ordinarily, a court does not look at the fairness or equity of a contract; for example, a court normally will not inquire into the adequacy of consideration. Persons are assumed to be reasonably intelligent, and the court does not come to their aid just because they have made unwise or foolish bargains. In certain circumstances, however, bargains are so oppressive that the courts relieve innocent parties of part or all of their duties. Such a bargain is called an **unconscionable contract** (or **unconscionable clause**). Both the Uniform Commercial Code (UCC) and the Uniform Consumer Credit Code (UCCC) embody the unconscionability concept—the former with regard to the sale of goods and the latter with regard to consumer loans and the waiver of rights.[9] A contract can be unconscionable on either procedural or substantive grounds, as discussed in the following subsections and illustrated graphically in Exhibit 8–1.

**UNCONSCIONABLE CONTRACT
(OR UNCONSCIONABLE CLAUSE)**
A contract or clause that is void on the basis of public policy because one party, as a result of disproportionate bargaining power, is forced to accept terms that are unfairly burdensome and that unfairly benefit the dominating party.

---

9. See, for example, UCC 2–302 and 2–719, and UCCC 5–108 and 1–107.

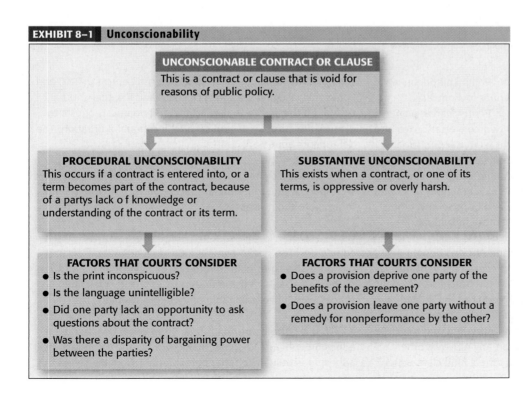

EXHIBIT 8–1   Unconscionability

UNCONSCIONABLE CONTRACT OR CLAUSE
This is a contract or clause that is void for reasons of public policy.

PROCEDURAL UNCONSCIONABILITY
This occurs if a contract is entered into, or a term becomes part of the contract, because of a partys lack of knowledge or understanding of the contract or its term.

SUBSTANTIVE UNCONSCIONABILITY
This exists when a contract, or one of its terms, is oppressive or overly harsh.

FACTORS THAT COURTS CONSIDER
● Is the print inconspicuous?
● Is the language unintelligible?
● Did one party lack an opportunity to ask questions about the contract?
● Was there a disparity of bargaining power between the parties?

FACTORS THAT COURTS CONSIDER
● Does a provision deprive one party of the benefits of the agreement?
● Does a provision leave one party without a remedy for nonperformance by the other?

Procedural Unconscionability. Procedural unconscionability has to do with how a term becomes part of a contract and relates to factors bearing on a party's lack of knowledge or understanding of the contract terms because of inconspicuous print, unintelligible language ("legalese"), lack of opportunity to read the contract, lack of opportunity to ask questions about the contract's meaning, and other factors. Procedural unconscionability sometimes relates to purported lack of voluntariness because of a disparity in bargaining power between the two parties. Contracts entered into because of one party's vastly superior bargaining power may be deemed unconscionable. Such contracts are often referred to as **adhesion contracts.** An adhesion contract is written exclusively by one party (the dominant party, usually the seller or creditor) and presented to the other (the adhering party, usually the buyer or borrower) on a take-it-or-leave-it basis.[10] In other words, the adhering party has no opportunity to negotiate the terms of the contract.

Standard-form contracts often contain fine-print provisions that shift a risk naturally borne by one party to the other. A variety of businesses use such contracts. Life insurance policies, residential leases, loan agreements, and employment agency contracts are often standard-form contracts. To avoid enforcement of the contract or of a particular clause, the aggrieved party must show that the parties had substantially unequal bargaining positions and that enforcement would be manifestly unfair or oppressive. If the required showing is made, the contract or particular term is deemed unconscionable and is not enforced.

In the following case, the question was whether a standard-form contract clause that mandated individual arbitration of any dispute and precluded class action[11] was unconscionable.

ADHESION CONTRACT
A "standard-form" contract, such as that between a large retailer and a consumer, in which the stronger party dictates the terms.

---

10. See, for example, *Henningsen v. Bloomfield Motors, Inc.*, 32 N.J. 358, 161 A.2d 69 (1960).

11. A *class action* is a means by which one or more individuals of a large group of persons interested in a dispute can sue as a class without every member of the group needing to appear in court.

CASE 8.1 Thibodeau v. Comcast Corp.

Superior Court of Pennsylvania, Philadelphia County, 2006 PA Super. 346, 912 A.2d 874 (2006).

FACTS Philip Thibodeau was a subscriber to Comcast Corporation's cable-television service in Pennsylvania. As part of his subscription, Thibodeau rented two converter boxes and two remote controls, which he thought were needed to receive the broadcasts. At the time, Comcast did not tell its customers that nonpremium programming could be viewed without the boxes and that the remotes were wholly unnecessary. In 2002, Comcast mailed Thibodeau and others a "customer agreement" that mandated the individual arbitration of all disputes and precluded class action. Meanwhile, also in Pennsylvania, Lorena Afroilan bought a Panasonic Corporation cell phone and contracted with the AT&T Wireless network for service. With the purchase, Afroilan was given a "Welcome Guide," which required the individual arbitration of all disputes and precluded class action. When Afroilan tried to switch providers, she discovered that her phone had a lock preventing its use on any network other than AT&T's. Thibodeau, Afroilan, and others filed class-action suits in a Pennsylvania state court against Comcast, AT&T, and Panasonic, alleging violations of state law. The trial court combined the suits and denied the defendants' requests to dismiss the complaints and compel individual arbitration. The defendants appealed.

ISSUE Should the court enforce the arbitration clauses that were part of the adhesion contracts and compel the plaintiffs to arbitrate their disputes?

DECISION No. The state appellate court affirmed the lower court's decision not to compel individual arbitration of these disputes. The court held that the preclusion of all class action in the defendants' "customer agreement" and "Welcome Guide" was "unconscionable and unenforceable."

REASON The court noted that "[n]ot every contract of adhesion contains unconscionable provisions. A contract of adhesion is only unconscionable if it unreasonably favors the

CASE 8.1–Continued

drafter." In this case, the customer contracts of both Comcast and AT&T attempted to require all customers to arbitrate all claims as individuals and to prevent them from filing class actions. According to the court, class-action suits are particularly important for consumers because they provide a means for those with limited financial resources and time to join together and assert their lawful rights. The individual members of a class often suffer only minimal damages, and no consumer would expend the time, fees, and costs of litigation for this small potential recovery. For example, defendant Thibodeau alleged that he was overcharged $9.60

per month. The court reasoned that to enforce the provisions requiring arbitration and prohibiting class actions would effectively immunize Comcast and AT&T from liability for any minor consumer claims. Because it is clearly contrary to public policy to immunize large corporations from liability, the court held that the provisions of the adhesion contracts were unconscionable and unenforceable.

WHAT IF THE FACTS WERE DIFFERENT?
If the "customer agreement" and "Welcome Guide" had precluded only class litigation and mandated class arbitration, would the court have considered the provisions unconscionable? Why or why not?

Substantive Unconscionability. Substantive unconscionability characterizes those contracts, or portions of contracts, that are oppressive or overly harsh. Courts generally focus on provisions that deprive one party of the benefits of the agreement or leave that party without remedy for nonperformance by the other. For example, suppose that a person with little income and only a fourth-grade education agrees to purchase a refrigerator for $3,000 and signs a two-year installment contract. The same type of refrigerator usually sells for $900 on the market. Despite the general rule that the courts will not inquire into the adequacy of the consideration, some courts have held that this type of contract is unconscionable because the contract terms are so oppressive as to "shock the conscience" of the court.[12]

Exculpatory Clauses Often closely related to the concept of unconscionability are **exculpatory clauses,** which release a party from liability in the event of monetary or physical injury, *no matter who is at fault.* Indeed, courts frequently refuse to enforce such clauses because they deem them to be unconscionable. Exculpatory clauses found in rental agreements for commercial property are normally held to be contrary to public policy. Such clauses are almost universally held to be illegal and unenforceable when they are included in residential property leases. Depending on the situation, exculpatory clauses in the employment context may be deemed unconscionable.

EXCULPATORY CLAUSE
A clause that releases a contractual party from liability in the event of monetary or physical injury, no matter who is at fault.

EXAMPLE 8.5 Suppose, for example, that Madison Manufacturing Company requires all of its employees to sign an employment contract with a clause stating that employees bear the risks incident to the position. Specifically, the contract states that the employer (Madison) is not responsible for any injury or damage that an employee may suffer as a result of accidents, carelessness, or misconduct of that employee or any other Madison worker. In this situation, because the exculpatory clause attempts to remove the employer's potential liability for any injuries to its employees, a court would usually find that the clause is contrary to public policy and unenforceable.[13] ■

Exculpatory clauses may be enforced, however, when the parties seeking their enforcement are not involved in businesses considered important to the public interest. Businesses such as health clubs, amusement parks, horse-rental concessions, golf-cart

REMEMBER Nearly everyone is liable for her or his own torts, and this responsibility cannot be contracted away.

---

12. See, for example, *Jones v. Star Credit Corp.*, 59 Misc.2d 189, 298 N.Y.S.2d 264 (1969). This case will be presented in Chapter 11 as Case 11.2.

13. For a case with similar facts, see *Little Rock & Fort Smith Railway Co. v. Eubanks*, 48 Ark. 460, 3 S.W. 808 (1887). In such a case, the exculpatory clause may also be illegal because it violates a state workers' compensation law.

concessions, and skydiving organizations frequently use exculpatory clauses to limit their liability for patrons' injuries. Because these services are not essential, the firms offering them are sometimes considered to have no relative advantage in bargaining strength, and anyone contracting for their services is considered to do so voluntarily.

ETHICAL ISSUE 8.1

Should exculpatory clauses allow the signer an opportunity to bargain? Before you may engage in a variety of activities, such as joining a gym or taking a lap around a miniature car racecourse, you may be asked to sign an agreement containing a clause releasing the owner of the operation from liability for any injury that you may suffer. Such exculpatory clauses are common. Nevertheless, courts frequently refuse to enforce them.

The Wisconsin Supreme Court, for example, has invalidated every exculpatory clause brought before it in the last twenty-five years. A recent case involved the death of a woman who drowned in a private swimming and fitness facility after signing a general waiver release statement.[14] The Wisconsin Supreme Court ruled that the exculpatory agreement was invalid because, among other things, the signer did not have "any opportunity to bargain." Indeed, waiver-of-liability agreements are almost always presented on a take-it-or-leave-it basis. Thus, if all courts were to make "an opportunity to bargain" a requirement for a valid agreement, virtually all exculpatory clauses would be deemed invalid. That would mean that under no circumstances could the creator of the waiver-of-liability agreement avoid liability—even if the signer of the agreement was 100 percent at fault and negligent. The result would be higher liability insurance rates for all businesses dealing with the public. Such higher insurance rates would be ultimately passed on to consumers in the form of higher prices for those who engage in downhill skiing, go to gyms, and do bungee jumping. Is this a fair outcome?

The Effect of Illegality

In general, an illegal contract is void: the contract is deemed never to have existed, and the courts will not aid either party. In most illegal contracts, both parties are considered to be equally at fault—*in pari delicto*. If the contract is executory (not yet fulfilled), neither party can enforce it. If it has been executed, there can be neither contractual nor quasi-contractual recovery.

That one wrongdoer in an illegal contract is unjustly enriched at the expense of the other is of no concern to the law—except under certain circumstances (to be discussed shortly). The major justification for this hands-off attitude is that it is improper to place the machinery of justice at the disposal of a plaintiff who has broken the law by entering into an illegal bargain. Another justification is the hoped-for deterrent effect of this general rule. A plaintiff who suffers a loss because of an illegal bargain will presumably be deterred from entering into similar illegal bargains in the future.

There are exceptions to the general rule that neither party to an illegal bargain can sue for breach and neither party can recover for performance rendered. We look at these exceptions here.

Justifiable Ignorance of the Facts   When one of the parties to a contract is relatively innocent (has no reason to know that the contract is illegal), that party can often recover any benefits conferred in a partially executed contract. In this situation, the courts will not enforce the contract but will allow the parties to return to their original positions.

---

14. *Atkins v. Swimwest Family Fitness Center,* 2005 WI 4, 277 Wis.2d 303, 691 N.W.2d 334 (2005).

A court may sometimes permit an innocent party who has fully performed under a contract to enforce the contract against the guilty party. **■EXAMPLE 8.6** A trucking company contracts with Gillespie to carry crated goods to a specific destination for a normal fee of $5,000. The trucker delivers the crates and later finds out that they contained illegal goods. Although the shipment, use, and sale of the goods are illegal under the law, the trucker, being an innocent party, can normally still legally collect the $5,000 from Gillespie. ■

Members of Protected Classes   When a statute protects a certain class of people, a member of that class can enforce an illegal contract even though the other party cannot. **■EXAMPLE 8.7** Statutes prohibit certain employees (such as flight attendants) from working more than a specified number of hours per month. These employees thus constitute a class protected by statute. An employee who is required to work more than the maximum can recover for those extra hours of service. ■

Other examples of statutes designed to protect a particular class of people are **blue sky laws**—state laws that regulate the offering and sale of securities for the protection of the public (see Chapter 21)—and state statutes regulating the sale of insurance. If an insurance company violates a statute when selling insurance, the purchaser can nevertheless enforce the policy and recover from the insurer.

BLUE SKY LAWS
State laws that regulate the offering and sale of securities for the protection of the public.

Withdrawal from an Illegal Agreement   If the illegal part of a bargain has not yet been performed, the party rendering performance can withdraw from the contract and recover the performance or its value. **■EXAMPLE 8.8** Suppose that Marta and Amil decide to wager (illegally) on the outcome of a boxing match. Each deposits money with a stakeholder, who agrees to pay the winner of the bet. At this point, each party has performed part of the agreement, but the illegal part of the agreement will not occur until the money is paid to the winner. Before such payment occurs, either party is entitled to withdraw from the agreement by giving notice to the stakeholder of his or her withdrawal. ■

Severable, or Divisible, Contracts   A contract that is *severable*, or divisible, consists of distinct parts that can be performed separately, with separate consideration provided for each part. With an *indivisible* contract, in contrast, the parties intended that complete performance by each party would be essential, even if the contract contains a number of seemingly separate provisions.

If a contract is divisible into legal and illegal portions, a court may enforce the legal portion but not the illegal one, so long as the illegal portion does not affect the essence of the bargain. This approach is consistent with the basic policy of enforcing the legal intentions of the contracting parties whenever possible. **■EXAMPLE 8.9** Suppose that Cole signs an employment contract that includes an overly broad and thus illegal covenant not to compete. In that situation, the court might allow the employment contract to be enforceable but reform the unreasonably broad covenant by converting its terms into reasonable ones. Alternatively, the court could declare the covenant illegal (and thus void) and enforce the remaining employment terms. ■

GENUINENESS OF ASSENT

Genuineness of assent may be lacking because of mistake, fraudulent misrepresentation, undue influence, or duress. Generally, a party who demonstrates that he or she did not genuinely assent (agree) to the terms of a contract can choose either to carry out the contract or to rescind (cancel) it and thus avoid the entire transaction.

Mistakes

We all make mistakes, so it is not surprising that mistakes are made when contracts are created. In certain circumstances, contract law allows a contract to be avoided on the basis of mistake. It is important to distinguish between *mistakes of fact* and *mistakes of value or quality*. Only a mistake of fact may allow a contract to be avoided.

■EXAMPLE 8.10 Suppose that Paco buys a violin from Beverly for $250. Although the violin is very old, neither party believes that it is extremely valuable. Later, however, an antiques dealer informs the parties that the violin is rare and worth thousands of dollars. Here, both parties were mistaken, but the mistake is a mistake of *value* rather than a mistake of *fact* that warrants contract rescission. Therefore, Beverly cannot rescind the contract. ■

Mistakes of fact occur in two forms—*unilateral* and *bilateral (mutual)*. A unilateral mistake is made by only one of the contracting parties; a mutual mistake is made by both. We look next at these two types of mistakes and illustrate them graphically in Exhibit 8–2.

Unilateral Mistakes A unilateral mistake occurs when only one party is mistaken as to a *material fact*—that is, a fact important to the subject matter of the contract. Generally, a unilateral mistake does not give the mistaken party any right to relief from the contract. In other words, the contract normally is enforceable against the mistaken party.

■EXAMPLE 8.11 Elena intends to sell her motor home for $17,500. When she learns that Chin is interested in buying a used motor home, she faxes a letter offering to sell the vehicle to him. When typing the fax, however, she mistakenly keys in the price of $15,700. Chin immediately sends Elena a fax accepting her offer. Even though Elena intended to sell her motor home for $17,500, she has made a unilateral mistake and is bound by contract to sell the vehicle to Chin for $15,700. ■

> **BE CAREFUL** What a party to a contract knows or should know can determine whether the contract is enforceable.

There are at least two exceptions to this rule.[15] First, if the *other* party to the contract knows or should have known that a mistake of fact was made, the contract may not be enforceable. **■EXAMPLE 8.12** In the above example, if Chin knew that Elena intended to sell her motor home for $17,500, then Elena's unilateral mistake (stating $15,700 in her offer) may render the resulting contract unenforceable. ■ The second exception arises when a unilateral mistake of fact was due to a mathematical mistake in addition, subtraction, division, or multiplication and was made inadvertently and without gross (extreme)

---

15. The *Restatement (Second) of Contracts*, Section 153, liberalizes the general rule to take into account the modern trend of allowing avoidance in some circumstances even though only one party has been mistaken.

EXHIBIT 8–2 Mistakes of Fact

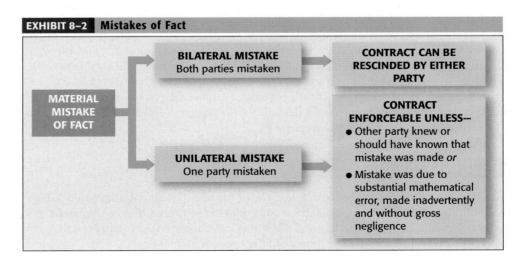

MATERIAL MISTAKE OF FACT

BILATERAL MISTAKE Both parties mistaken → **CONTRACT CAN BE RESCINDED BY EITHER PARTY**

UNILATERAL MISTAKE One party mistaken → **CONTRACT ENFORCEABLE UNLESS—**
- Other party knew or should have known that mistake was made *or*
- Mistake was due to substantial mathematical error, made inadvertently and without gross negligence

negligence. If a contractor's bid was significantly low because he or she made a mistake in addition when totaling the estimated costs, any contract resulting from the bid normally may be rescinded. Of course, in both situations, the mistake must still involve some *material fact*.

Bilateral (Mutual) Mistakes   When both parties are mistaken about the same material fact, the contract can be rescinded by either party.[16] Note that, as with unilateral mistakes, the mistake must be about a *material fact* (one that is important and central to the contract). **■EXAMPLE 8.13** Keeley buys a landscape painting from Umberto's art gallery. Both Umberto and Keeley believe that the painting is by the artist Vincent van Gogh. Later, Keeley discovers that the painting is a very clever fake. Because neither Umberto nor Keeley was aware of this fact when they made their deal, Keeley can rescind the contract and recover the purchase price of the painting. ■

A word or term in a contract may be subject to more than one reasonable interpretation. In that situation, if the parties to the contract attach materially different meanings to the term, their mutual misunderstanding may allow the contract to be rescinded. **■EXAMPLE 8.14** In a classic case, *Raffles v. Wichelhaus*,[17] Wichelhaus purchased a shipment of cotton from Raffles to arrive on a ship called the *Peerless* from Bombay, India. Wichelhaus meant a ship called *Peerless* sailing from Bombay in October; Raffles meant a different ship called *Peerless* sailing from Bombay in December. When the goods arrived on the December *Peerless* and Raffles tried to deliver them, Wichelhaus refused to accept them. The British court held for Wichelhaus, concluding that no mutual assent existed because the parties had attached materially different meanings to an essential term of the contract (which ship *Peerless* was to transport the goods). ■

In the following case, an injured worker sought to set aside a settlement agreement entered into with his employer, arguing that the agreement was based on a mutual mistake of fact—a physician's mistaken diagnosis of the worker's injury.

---

16. *Restatement (Second) of Contracts*, Section 152.
17. 159 Eng.Rep. 375 (1864).

| CASE 8.2 | **Roberts v. Century Contractors, Inc.** |

Court of Appeals of North Carolina, 162 N.C.App. 688, 592 S.E.2d 215 (2004).
www.aoc.state.nc.us/www/public/html/opinions.htm[a]

FACTS Bobby Roberts was an employee of Century Contractors, Inc., in July 1993, when a pipe struck him in a work-related accident, causing trauma to his neck and back. Dr. James Markworth of Southeastern Orthopaedic Clinic diagnosed Roberts's injuries. After surgery and treatment, Markworth concluded that Roberts was at maximum medical improvement (MMI) and stopped treating him. Roberts agreed with Century to accept $125,000 and payment of related medical expenses, and to waive any right to make further claims in regard to his injury. In June 1998, still experiencing pain, Roberts saw Dr. Allen Friedman, who determined that Roberts was not at MMI. Markworth then admitted that his diagnosis was a mistake. Roberts filed a claim for workers' compensation (see Chapter 18), seeking compensation and medical benefits for his injury. He alleged that his agreement with Century should be set aside due to a mutual mistake of fact. The North Carolina state administrative agency authorized to rule on workers' compensation claims awarded Roberts what he sought. Century appealed to a state intermediate appellate court.

a. Under the "Court of Appeals Opinions" heading, click on the year "2004." In your browser's "Find" box, type in the case title to access the full text of the court's opinion. The North Carolina Administrative Office of the Courts maintains this Web site.

CASE 8.2–Continues next page

CASE 8.2–Continued

ISSUE Should the agreement between Roberts and Century be set aside on the basis of a mutual mistake of fact?

DECISION Yes. The state intermediate appellate court affirmed the award of compensation and medical benefits to Roberts.

REASON The court explained that compromise settlement agreements, including settlement agreements in workers' compensation cases, are governed by general principles of contract law. The court stated that it is a well-settled principle of contract law that a valid contract exists only where there has been a meeting of the minds as to all essential terms of the agreement. "Therefore," said the court, "where a mistake is common to both parties and concerns a material past or presently existing fact, such that there is no meeting of the minds, a contract may be avoided." The mistake "must be as to a fact which enters into and forms the basis of the contract * * * and must be such that it animates and controls the conduct of the parties." Also, "relief from a contract due to mistake of fact will be had only where *both* parties to an agreement are mistaken." The court pointed out that Markworth's MMI diagnosis was "material to the settlement of this claim" and that both parties relied on this information in entering into settlement negotiations. Later, however, "Dr. Friedman testified, and the [state agency found] as fact, that plaintiff was not at maximum medical improvement." Thus, the court concluded that there was a mutual mistake with regard to the plaintiff's medical condition at the time of the signing of the settlement agreement.

FOR CRITICAL ANALYSIS–Social Consideration
Why did the court consider Markworth's misdiagnosis a bilateral mistake rather than a unilateral mistake?

Fraudulent Misrepresentation

Although fraud is a tort, the presence of fraud also affects the genuineness of the innocent party's consent to a contract. When an innocent party consents to a contract with fraudulent terms, the contract usually can be avoided because she or he has not *voluntarily* consented to the terms.[18] Normally, the innocent party can either rescind (cancel) the contract and be restored to her or his original position or enforce the contract and seek damages for injuries resulting from the fraud.

Typically, fraud involves three elements:

1 A misrepresentation of a material fact must occur.

2 There must be an intent to deceive.

3 The innocent party must justifiably rely on the misrepresentation.

Additionally, to collect damages, a party must have been injured as a result of the misrepresentation.

Fraudulent misrepresentation can also occur in the online environment. Because curbing Internet fraud is a major challenge in today's world, we explore the topic further in Chapter 13, in the context of consumer law.

Misrepresentation Must Occur The first element of proving fraud is to show that misrepresentation of a material fact has occurred. This misrepresentation can take the form of words or actions. For example, an art gallery owner's statement, "This painting is a Picasso" is a misrepresentation of fact if the painting was done by another artist.

A statement of opinion is generally not subject to a claim of fraud. For example, claims such as "This computer will never break down" and "This car will last for years and years" are statements of opinion, not fact, and contracting parties should recognize them as such and not rely on them. A fact is objective and verifiable; an opinion is usually subject to

A woman browses through some online personal ads. Individuals who post their profiles on an Internet dating site may tend to exaggerate their attractive traits and may even make statements about themselves that they know to be false. But what happens when an Internet service provider makes fraudulent misrepresentations about its users? (Photo by Bill Stryker)

---

18. *Restatement (Second) of Contracts*, Sections 163 and 164.

debate. Therefore, a seller is allowed to "huff and puff his [or her] wares" without being liable for fraud. In certain cases, however, particularly when a naïve purchaser relies on an expert's opinion, the innocent party may be entitled to *rescission* (cancellation) or *reformation* (an equitable remedy granted by a court in which the terms of a contract are altered to reflect the true intentions of the parties).

Intent to Deceive   The second element of fraud is knowledge on the part of the misrepresenting party that facts have been misrepresented. This element, usually called *scienter*,[19] or "guilty knowledge," generally signifies that there was an intent to deceive. *Scienter* clearly exists if a party knows that a fact is not as stated. *Scienter* also exists if a party makes a statement that he or she believes not to be true or makes a statement recklessly, without regard to whether it is true or false. Finally, this element is met if a party says or implies that a statement is made on some basis, such as personal knowledge or personal investigation, when it is not.

■EXAMPLE 8.15 A convicted felon, Robert Sarvis, applied for a position as an adjunct professor two weeks after his release from prison. On his résumé, he lied about his past work history by representing that he had been the president of a corporation for fourteen years and had taught business law at another college. At his interview, Sarvis stated that he was "well equipped to teach" business law and ethics and that he had "a great interest and knowledge of business law." After he was hired and began working, Sarvis's probation officer alerted the school to his criminal history. The school immediately fired Sarvis, and he brought a lawsuit against the school for breaching his employment contract. The school claimed that it was not liable for the breach because of Sarvis's fraudulent misrepresentations during the hiring process. The court agreed. Sarvis had not fully disclosed his personal history, he clearly had an intent to deceive, and the school had justifiably relied on his misrepresentations. Therefore, the school could rescind Sarvis's employment contract.[20] ■

Reliance on the Misrepresentation   The third element of fraud is *justifiable reliance* on the misrepresentation of fact. The deceived party must have a justifiable reason for relying on the misrepresentation, and the misrepresentation must be an important factor (but not necessarily the sole factor) in inducing the party to enter into the contract.

Reliance is not justified if the innocent party knows the true facts or relies on obviously extravagant statements.   **■EXAMPLE 8.16** If a used-car dealer tells you, "This old Cadillac will get over sixty miles to the gallon," you normally would not be justified in relying on this statement. Suppose, however, that Merkel, a bank director, induces O'Connell, a co-director, to sign a statement that the bank has sufficient assets to meet its liabilities by telling O'Connell, "We have plenty of assets to satisfy our creditors." This statement is false. If O'Connell knows the true facts or, as a bank director, should know the true facts, he is not justified in relying on Merkel's statement. If O'Connell does not know the true facts, however, *and has no way of finding them out*, he may be justified in relying on the statement. ■

Injury to the Innocent Party   Most courts do not require a showing of injury when the action is to rescind (cancel) the contract—these courts hold that because rescission

SCIENTER
Knowledge by the misrepresenting party that material facts have been falsely represented or omitted with an intent to deceive.

REMEMBER   An opinion is neither a contract offer, nor a contract term, nor fraud.

Suppose that a city solicited bids from contractors to expand its public transportation system on this strip of land without disclosing the existence of a subsoil condition that would greatly increase the project's cost. Assuming that the city was aware of the situation, would it have had a duty to disclose the condition to bidders? What effect would the city's silence have on the resulting contract?
(Michael McCauslin/Creative Commons)

---

19. Pronounced sy-*en*-ter.
20. *Sarvis v. Vermont State Colleges*, 172 Vt. 76, 772 A.2d 494 (2001).

Coachmen Recreational Vehicle Co. to Arthur and Roswitha Waddell. The Waddells hoped to spend two or three years driving around the country, but almost immediately—and repeatedly—they experienced problems with the RV. Its entry door popped open. Its cooling and heating systems did not work properly. Its batteries did not maintain a charge. Most significantly, its engine overheated when ascending a moderate grade. The Waddells brought it to Wheeler's service department for repairs. Over the next year and a half, the RV spent more than seven months at Wheeler's. In March 1999, the Waddells filed a complaint in a Nevada state court against the dealer to revoke their acceptance of the RV. What are the requirements for a buyer's revocation of acceptance? Were the requirements met in this case? In whose favor should the court rule? Why? [*Waddell v. L.V.R.V., Inc.*, 122 Nev. 125, 125 P.3d 1160 (2006)]

12.8 **A Question of Ethics.** *Scotwood Industries, Inc., sells calcium chloride flake for use in ice melt products. Between July and September 2004, Scotwood delivered thirty-seven shipments of flake to Frank Miller & Sons, Inc. After each delivery, Scotwood billed Miller, which paid thirty-five of the invoices and processed 30 to 50 percent of the flake. In*

August, Miller began complaining about the quality. Scotwood assured Miller that it would remedy the situation. Finally, in October, Miller told Scotwood, "[T]his is totally unacceptable. We are willing to discuss Scotwood picking up the material." Miller claimed that the flake was substantially defective because it was chunked. Calcium chloride maintains its purity for up to five years but chunks if it is exposed to and absorbs moisture, making it unusable. In response to Scotwood's suit to collect payment on the unpaid invoices, Miller filed a counterclaim in a federal district court for breach of contract, seeking to recover based on revocation of acceptance, among other things. [Scotwood Industries, Inc. v. Frank Miller & Sons, Inc., 435 F.Supp.2d 1160 (D.Kans. 2006)]

1 What is revocation of acceptance? How does a buyer effectively exercise this option? Do the facts in this case support this theory as a ground for Miller to recover damages? Why or why not?

2 Is there an ethical basis for allowing a buyer to revoke acceptance of goods and recover damages? If so, is there an ethical limit to this right? Discuss.

CRITICAL THINKING AND WRITING ASSIGNMENTS

12.9 **Critical Legal Thinking.** Under what circumstances should courts not allow fully informed contracting parties to agree to limit remedies?

12.10 **Critical Thinking and Writing Assignment for Business.** Suppose that you are a collector of antique cars and you need to purchase spare parts for a 1938 engine. These parts are not made anymore and are scarce. You discover that Beem has the spare parts that you need. To get the contract

with Beem, you agree to pay 50 percent of the purchase price in advance. You send the payment on May 1, and Beem receives it on May 2. On May 3, Beem, having found another buyer willing to pay substantially more for the parts, informs you that he will not deliver as contracted. That same day, you learn that Beem is insolvent. Discuss fully any possible remedies that would enable you to take possession of these parts.

ONLINE ACTIVITIES

PRACTICAL INTERNET EXERCISES

Go to this text's Web site at **academic.cengage.com/blaw/blt**, select "Chapter 12," and click on "Practical Internet Exercises." There you will find the following Internet research exercises that you can perform to learn more about the topics covered in this chapter.

PRACTICAL INTERNET EXERCISE 12-1 MANAGEMENT PERSPECTIVE—The Right to Reject Goods

PRACTICAL INTERNET EXERCISE 12-2 LEGAL PERSPECTIVE—International Performance Requirements

BEFORE THE TEST

Go to this text's Web site at **academic.cengage.com/blaw/blt**, select "Chapter 12," and click on "Interactive Quizzes." You will find a number of interactive questions relating to this chapter.

CHAPTER 13
Warranties, Product Liability, and Consumer Law

❝I'll warrant him heart-whole.❞

William Shakespeare,
1564–1616
(English dramatist and poet)

LEARNING OBJECTIVES

AFTER READING THIS CHAPTER, YOU SHOULD BE ABLE TO ANSWER THE FOLLOWING QUESTIONS:

1 What factors determine whether a seller's or lessor's statement constitutes an express warranty or mere "puffing"?

2 What implied warranties arise under the UCC?

3 Can a manufacturer be held liable to any person who suffers an injury proximately caused by the manufacturer's negligently made product?

4 What defenses to liability can be raised in a product liability lawsuit?

5 What are the major federal statutes providing for consumer protection?

Warranty is an age-old concept. In sales and lease law, a warranty is an assurance by one party of the existence of a fact on which the other party can rely. Just as William Shakespeare's character in the play *As You Like It* warranted his friend "heart-whole" in the chapter-opening quotation, so sellers and lessors warrant to those who purchase or lease their goods that the goods are as represented or will be as promised.

The Uniform Commercial Code (UCC) has numerous rules governing product warranties as they occur in sales and lease contracts. Those rules are the subject matter of the first part of this chapter. A natural addition to the discussion is *product liability:* Who is liable to consumers, users, and bystanders for physical harm and property damage caused by a particular good or its use? Product liability encompasses the contract theory of warranty, as well as the tort theories of negligence and strict liability (discussed in Chapter 4).

Consumer protection law consists of all statutes, agency rules, and common law judicial rulings that serve to protect the interests of consumers. State and federal consumer laws regulate certain business activities, such as how a business may advertise, engage in mail-order and telemarketing transactions, and package and label their products. In addition, numerous local, state, and federal agencies exist to aid consumers in settling their grievances with sellers and manufacturers. In the last part of this chapter, we examine some of the sources and some of the major issues of consumer protection.

WARRANTIES

Most goods are covered by some type of warranty designed to protect consumers. Article 2 (on sales) and Article 2A (on leases) of the UCC designate several types of warranties that can arise in a sales or lease contract, including warranties of title, express warranties, and implied warranties.

Warranties of Title

Title warranty arises automatically in most sales contracts. The UCC imposes three types of warranties of title.

Good Title   In most sales, sellers warrant that they have good and valid title to the goods sold and that transfer of the title is rightful [UCC 2–312(1)(a)]. **■EXAMPLE 13.1** Sharon steals goods from Miguel and sells them to Carrie, who does not know that the goods are stolen. If Miguel reclaims the goods from Carrie, which he has a right to do, Carrie can then sue Sharon for breach of warranty. When Sharon sold Carrie the goods, Sharon *automatically* warranted to her that the title conveyed was valid and that its transfer was rightful. Because this was not in fact the case, Sharon breached the warranty of title imposed by UCC 2–312(1)(a) and became liable to the buyer for the appropriate damages. ■

No Liens   A second warranty of title provided by the UCC protects buyers who are *unaware* of any encumbrances, or **liens** (claims, charges, or liabilities—see Chapter 16), against goods at the time the contract is made [UCC 2–312(1)(b)]. This warranty protects buyers who, for example, unknowingly purchase goods that are subject to a creditor's security interest (an interest in the goods that secures payment or performance, to be discussed in Chapter 16). If a creditor legally repossesses the goods from a buyer *who had no actual knowledge of the security interest,* the buyer can recover from the seller for breach of warranty. (A buyer who actually knows that a security interest exists has no recourse against the seller.)

   Article 2A affords similar protection for lessees. Section 2A–211(1) provides that during the term of the lease, no claim of any third party will interfere with the lessee's enjoyment of the leasehold interest.

LIEN
An encumbrance on a property to satisfy a debt or protect a claim for payment of a debt.

No Infringements   A merchant-seller is also deemed to warrant that the goods delivered are free from any copyright, trademark, or patent claims of a third person [UCC 2–312(3), 2A–211(2)].[1] If this warranty is breached and the buyer is sued by the party holding copyright, trademark, or patent rights in the goods, the buyer must notify the seller of the litigation within a reasonable time to enable the seller to decide whether to defend the lawsuit. If the seller states in a writing (or record) that she or he has decided to defend and agrees to bear all expenses, then the buyer must turn over control of the litigation to the seller; otherwise, the buyer is barred from any remedy against the seller for liability established by the litigation [UCC 2–607(3)(b), 2–607(5)(b)].

   In situations that involve leases rather than sales, Article 2A requires the same notice of infringement litigation [UCC 2A–516(3)(b), 2A–516(4)(b)]. There is an exception for leases to individual consumers for personal, family, or household purposes. A consumer who fails to notify the lessor within a reasonable time does not lose his or her remedy against the lessor for any liability established in the litigation [UCC 2A–516(3)(b)].

---

1. Recall from Chapter 11 that a *merchant* is defined in UCC 2–104(1) as a person who deals in goods of the kind involved in the sales contract or who, by occupation, presents himself or herself as having knowledge or skill peculiar to the goods involved in the transaction.

Disclaimer of Title Warranty   In an ordinary sales transaction, the title warranty can be disclaimed or modified only by *specific language* in the contract [UCC 2–312(2)]. For example, sellers can assert that they are transferring only such rights, title, and interest as they have in the goods. In a lease transaction, the disclaimer must be specific, be in a writing (or record), and be conspicuous [UCC 2A–214(4)].

Express Warranties

EXPRESS WARRANTY
A seller's or lessor's oral or written promise or affirmation of fact, ancillary to an underlying sales or lease agreement, as to the quality, description, or performance of the goods being sold or leased.

A seller or lessor can create an **express warranty** by making representations concerning the quality, condition, description, or performance potential of the goods. Under UCC 2–313 and 2A–210, express warranties arise when a seller or lessor indicates any of the following:

1 That the goods conform to any *affirmation* (declaration that something is true) or *promise* of fact that the seller or lessor makes to the buyer or lessee about the goods. Such affirmations or promises are usually made during the bargaining process. Statements such as "these drill bits will penetrate stainless steel—and without dulling" are express warranties.

2 That the goods conform to any *description* of them. For example, a label that reads "Crate contains one 150-horsepower diesel engine" or a contract that calls for the delivery of a "camel's-hair coat" creates an express warranty.

3 That the goods conform to any *sample or model* of the goods shown to the buyer or lessee.

Basis of the Bargain   To create an express warranty, a seller or lessor does not have to use formal words such as *warrant* or *guarantee* [UCC 2–313(2), 2A–210(2)]. It is only necessary that a reasonable buyer or lessee would regard the representation of fact as part of the basis of the bargain [UCC 2–313(1), 2A–210(1)]. Just what constitutes the basis of the bargain is hard to say. The UCC does not define the concept, and it is a question of fact in each case whether a representation was made at such a time and in such a way that it induced the buyer or lessee to enter into the contract. (For more information on how sellers can create—or avoid creating—warranties, see the *Application* feature at the end of this chapter.)

Businesspersons engaged in selling or leasing goods should be careful about the words they use with customers, in writing and orally. Express warranties can be found in a seller's or lessor's advertisement, brochure, or promotional materials, in addition to being made orally or in an express warranty provision in a contract. Avoiding unintended warranties is crucial in preventing legal disputes, and all employees should be instructed on how the promises they make to buyers during a sale can create warranties.

Statements of Opinion and Value   Only statements of fact create express warranties. If the seller or lessor makes a statement that relates to the supposed value or worth of the goods, or makes a statement of opinion or recommendation about the goods, the seller or lessor is not creating an express warranty [UCC 2–313(2), 2A–210(2)].

■**EXAMPLE 13.2** A seller claims that "this is the best used car to come along in years; it has four new tires and a 250-horsepower engine just rebuilt this year." The seller has made several *affirmations of fact* that can create a warranty: the automobile has an engine; it has a 250-horsepower engine; it was rebuilt this year; there are four tires on the automobile; and the tires are new. The seller's *opinion* that the vehicle is "the best used car to come along in years," however, is known as "puffing" or "puffery" and creates no warranty. (*Puffing* is the expression of opinion by a seller or lessor that is not made as a representation of fact.) ▣

A statement relating to the value of the goods, such as "this is worth a fortune" or "anywhere else you'd pay $10,000 for it," usually does not create a warranty. If the seller or lessor is an expert and gives an opinion as an expert to a layperson, though, then a warranty may be created.

It is not always easy to determine whether a statement constitutes an express warranty or puffing. The reasonableness of the buyer's or lessee's reliance appears to be the controlling criterion in many cases. For example, a salesperson's statements that a ladder "will never break" and will "last a lifetime" are so clearly improbable that no reasonable buyer should rely on them. Additionally, the context in which a statement is made might be relevant in determining the reasonableness of the buyer's or lessee's reliance. For example, a reasonable person is more likely to rely on a written statement made in an advertisement than on a statement made orally by a salesperson.

Marlboro cigarettes sit on a shelf in a retail store. Suppose that the store clerk tells a customer that these cigarettes "are the best," and the customer buys three cartons. The customer later develops lung cancer from smoking and sues the seller. In this situation, would the seller's statements be enough to create an express warranty? Why or why not?
("Ladyphoenixx"/Creative Commons)

Implied Warranties

An **implied warranty** is one that *the law derives* by implication or inference because of the circumstances of a sale, rather than by the seller's express promise. In an action based on breach of implied warranty, it is necessary to show that an implied warranty existed and that the breach of the warranty proximately caused[2] the damage sustained. We look here at some of the implied warranties that arise under the UCC.

Implied Warranty of Merchantability   Every sale or lease of goods made *by a merchant who deals in goods of the kind sold or leased* automatically gives rise to an **implied warranty of merchantability** [UCC 2–314, 2A–212]. **■EXAMPLE 13.3** A merchant who is in the business of selling ski equipment, for instance, makes an implied warranty of merchantability every time she sells a pair of skis. A neighbor selling his skis at a garage sale does not (because he is not in the business of selling goods of this type). ▣

Merchantable Goods.   Goods that are *merchantable* are "reasonably fit for the ordinary purposes for which such goods are used." They must be of at least average, fair, or medium-grade quality. The quality must be comparable to a level that will pass without objection in the trade or market for goods of the same description. To be merchantable, the goods must also be adequately packaged and labeled as provided by the agreement, and they must conform to the promises or affirmations of fact made on the container or label, if any.

It makes no difference whether the merchant knew or could have discovered that a product was defective (not merchantable). Of course, merchants are not absolute insurers against all accidents arising in connection with the goods. For example, a bar of soap is not unmerchantable merely because a user could slip and fall by stepping on it.

Merchantable Food.   The UCC recognizes the serving of food or drink to be consumed on or off the premises as a sale of goods subject to the implied warranty of merchantability [UCC 2–314(1)]. "Merchantable" food means food that is fit to eat. Courts generally determine whether food is fit to eat on the basis of consumer expectations. The courts assume that consumers should reasonably expect on occasion to find bones in fish fillets, cherry pits in cherry pie, or a nutshell in a package of shelled nuts, for example—because

IMPLIED WARRANTY
A warranty that arises by law because of the circumstances of a sale, rather than by the seller's express promise.

IMPLIED WARRANTY OF MERCHANTABILITY
A warranty that goods being sold or leased are reasonably fit for the general purpose for which they are sold or leased, are properly packaged and labeled, and are of proper quality. The warranty automatically arises in every sale or lease of goods made by a merchant who deals in goods of the kind sold or leased.

---

2. Proximate, or legal, cause exists when the connection between an act and an injury is strong enough to justify imposing liability—see Chapter 4.

such substances are natural incidents of the food. In contrast, consumers would not reasonably expect to find an inchworm in a can of peas or a piece of glass in a soft drink—because these substances are not natural to the food product.[3] In the following classic case, the court had to determine whether a fish bone was a substance that one should reasonably expect to find in fish chowder.

---

3. See, for example, *Ruvolo v. Homovich*, 149 Ohio App.3d 701, 778 N.E.2d 661 (2002).

CASE 13.1 Webster v. Blue Ship Tea Room, Inc.

LANDMARK AND CLASSIC CASES

Supreme Judicial Court of Massachusetts, 347 Mass. 421, 198 N.E.2d 309 (1964).

HISTORICAL AND CULTURAL SETTING

Chowder, a soup or stew made with fresh fish, possibly originated in the fishing villages of Brittany (a French province to the west of Paris) and was probably carried to Canada and New England by Breton fishermen. In the nineteenth century and earlier, recipes for chowder did not call for the removal of the fish bones. Chowder recipes in the first half of the twentieth century were the same as in previous centuries, sometimes specifying that the fish head, tail, and backbone were to be broken in pieces and boiled, with the "liquor thus produced . . . added to the balance of the chowder."[a] By the middle of the twentieth century, there was a considerable body of case law concerning implied warranties and foreign and natural substances in food. It was perhaps inevitable that sooner or later, a consumer injured by a fish bone in chowder would challenge the merchantability of chowder containing fish bones.

FACTS Blue Ship Tea Room, Inc., was located in Boston in an old building overlooking the ocean. Priscilla Webster, who had been born and raised in New England, went to the restaurant and ordered fish chowder. The chowder was milky in color. After three or four spoonfuls, she felt something lodged in her throat. As a result, she underwent two esophagoscopies; in the second esophagoscopy, a fish bone was found and removed. Webster filed a lawsuit against the restaurant in a Massachusetts state court for breach of the implied warranty of merchantability. The jury rendered a verdict for Webster, and the restaurant appealed to the state's highest court.

ISSUE Does serving fish chowder that contains a bone constitute a breach of an implied warranty of merchantability on the part of the restaurant?

---

a. Fannie Farmer, *The Boston Cooking School Cook Book* (Boston: Little, Brown, 1937), p. 166.

DECISION No. The Supreme Judicial Court of Massachusetts held that Webster could not recover against Blue Ship Tea Room because no breach of warranty had occurred.

REASON The court, citing UCC Section 2–314, stated that "a warranty that goods shall be merchantable is implied in a contract for their sale if the seller is a merchant with respect to goods of that kind. Under this section the serving for value of food or drink to be consumed either on the premises or elsewhere is a sale. * * * Goods to be merchantable must at least be * * * fit for the ordinary purposes for which such goods are used." The question here was whether a fish bone made the chowder unfit for eating. In the judge's opinion, "the joys of life in New England include the ready availability of fresh fish chowder. We should be prepared to cope with the hazards of fish bones, the occasional presence of which in chowders is, it seems to us, to be anticipated, and which, in the light of a hallowed tradition, do not impair their fitness or merchantability."

IMPACT OF THIS CASE ON TODAY'S LAW *This classic case, phrased in memorable language, was an early application of the UCC's implied warranty of merchantability to food products. The case established the rule that consumers should expect to find, on occasion, elements of food products that are natural to the product (such as fish bones in fish chowder). Courts today still apply this rule.*

RELEVANT WEB SITES *To locate information on the Web concerning the* Webster *decision, go to this text's Web site at* **academic.cengage.com/blaw/blt**, *select "Chapter 13," and click on "URLs for Landmarks."*

Implied Warranty of Fitness for a Particular Purpose   The **implied warranty of fitness for a particular purpose** arises when any seller or lessor (merchant or nonmerchant) knows the particular purpose for which a buyer or lessee will use the goods *and* knows that the buyer or lessee is relying on the skill and judgment of the seller or lessor to select suitable goods [UCC 2–315, 2A–213].

Particular versus Ordinary Purpose.   A "particular purpose" of the buyer or lessee differs from the "ordinary purpose for which goods are used" (merchantability). Goods can be merchantable but unfit for a particular purpose. **EXAMPLE 13.4** Suppose that you need a gallon of paint to match the color of your living room walls—a light shade somewhere between coral and peach. You take a sample to your local hardware store and request a gallon of paint of that color. Instead, you are given a gallon of bright blue paint. Here, the salesperson has not breached any warranty of implied merchantability—the bright blue paint is of high quality and suitable for interior walls—but he or she has breached an implied warranty of fitness for a particular purpose. ■

Knowledge and Reliance Requirements.   A seller or lessor is not required to have actual knowledge of the buyer's or lessee's particular purpose, so long as the seller or lessor "has reason to know" the purpose. For an implied warranty to be created, however, the buyer or lessee must have *relied* on the skill or judgment of the seller or lessor in selecting or furnishing suitable goods.

EXAMPLE 13.5 Bloomberg leases a computer from Future Tech, a lessor of technical business equipment. Bloomberg tells the clerk that she wants a computer that will run a complicated new engineering graphics program at a realistic speed. Future Tech leases Bloomberg an Architex One computer with a CPU speed of only 2 gigahertz, even though a speed of at least 3.2 gigahertz would be required to run Bloomberg's graphics program at a "realistic speed." Bloomberg, after discovering that it takes forever to run her program, wants her money back. Here, because Future Tech has breached the implied warranty of fitness for a particular purpose, Bloomberg normally will be able to recover. The clerk knew specifically that Bloomberg wanted a computer with enough speed to run certain software. Furthermore, Bloomberg relied on the clerk to furnish a computer that would fulfill this purpose. Because Future Tech did not do so, the warranty was breached. ■

Warranties Implied from Prior Dealings or Trade Custom   Implied warranties can also arise (or be excluded or modified) as a result of course of dealing or usage of trade [UCC 2–314(3), 2A–212(3)]. In the absence of evidence to the contrary, when both parties to a sales or lease contract have knowledge of a well-recognized trade custom, the courts will infer that both parties intended for that trade custom to apply to their contract. **EXAMPLE 13.6** Suppose that it is an industrywide custom to lubricate new cars before the cars are delivered to a buyer. Latoya buys a new car from Bender Chevrolet. After the purchase, Latoya discovers that Bender failed to lubricate the car before delivering it to her. In this situation, Latoya can hold the dealer liable for damages resulting from the breach of an implied warranty. (This, of course, would also be negligence on the part of the dealer.) ■

Overlapping Warranties

Sometimes, two or more warranties are made in a single transaction. An implied warranty of merchantability, an implied warranty of fitness for a particular purpose, or both can exist in addition to an express warranty. For example, when a sales contract for a new car states that "this car engine is warranted to be free from defects for 36,000 miles or thirty-six months, whichever occurs first," there is an express warranty against all defects and an implied warranty that the car will be fit for normal use.

IMPLIED WARRANTY OF FITNESS FOR A PARTICULAR PURPOSE
A warranty that goods sold or leased are fit for a particular purpose. The warranty arises when any seller or lessor knows the particular purpose for which a buyer or lessee will use the goods and knows that the buyer or lessee is relying on the skill and judgment of the seller or lessor to select suitable goods.

The rule under the UCC is that express and implied warranties are construed as *cumulative* if they are consistent with one another [UCC 2–317, 2A–215]. In other words, courts interpret two or more warranties as being in agreement with each other unless this construction is unreasonable. If it is unreasonable, then a court will hold that the warranties are inconsistent and apply the following rules to interpret which warranty is most important:

1 *Express* warranties displace inconsistent *implied* warranties, except for implied warranties of fitness for a particular purpose.

2 Samples take precedence over inconsistent general descriptions.

3 Exact or technical specifications displace inconsistent samples or general descriptions.

BE AWARE Express and implied warranties do not necessarily displace each other. More than one warranty can cover the same goods in the same transaction.

Warranty Disclaimers

The UCC generally permits warranties to be disclaimed or limited by specific and unambiguous language, provided that this is done in a manner that protects the buyer or lessee from surprise. Because each type of warranty is created in a special way, the manner in which a seller or lessor can disclaim warranties varies depending on the type of warranty.

Express Warranties   As already stated, any affirmation of fact or promise, description of the goods, or use of samples or models by a seller or lessor creates an express warranty. Obviously, then, express warranties can be excluded if the seller or lessor carefully refrains from making any promise or affirmation of fact relating to the goods, describing the goods, or using a sample or model.

In addition, a written (or recorded) disclaimer in language that is clear and conspicuous, and called to a buyer's or lessee's attention, can negate all oral express warranties not included in the sales or lease contract [UCC 2–316(1), 2A–214(1)]. This allows the seller or lessor to avoid false allegations that oral warranties were made, and it ensures that only representations made by properly authorized individuals are included in the bargain.

Note, however, that a buyer or lessee must be made aware of any warranty disclaimers or modifications *at the time the contract is formed.* In other words, any oral or written warranties—or disclaimers—made during the bargaining process as part of a contract's formation cannot be modified at a later time by the seller or lessor.

ON THE WEB

For an example of a warranty disclaimer, go to

www.bizguardian.com/terms.php.

Implied Warranties   Generally speaking, implied warranties are much easier for a seller or lessor to disclaim. Under the UCC, unless circumstances indicate otherwise, all implied warranties are disclaimed by the expressions "as is," "with all faults," and other similar language that in common understanding call the buyer's or lessee's attention to the fact that there are no implied warranties [UCC 2–316(3)(a), 2A–214(3)(a)]. (Note, however, that some states have passed consumer protection statutes forbidding "as is" sales or making it illegal to disclaim warranties of merchantability on consumer goods.)

■EXAMPLE 13.7 Sue Hallett saw an advertisement offering a "lovely, eleven-year-old mare" with extensive jumping ability for sale. After visiting Mandy Morningstar's ranch and examining the horse twice, Hallett contracted to buy it for $2,950. The contract she signed described the horse as an eleven-year-old mare, but indicated that the horse was being sold "as is." Shortly after the purchase, a veterinarian determined that the horse was actually sixteen years old and in no condition for jumping. Hallett immediately notified her bank and stopped payment on the check she had written to pay for the horse. Hallett also tried to return the horse and cancel the contract with Morningstar, but Morningstar refused and filed a suit against Hallett, claiming breach of contract. The trial court found in favor of Morningstar because Hallett had examined the horse and was satisfied with its condition at the time she signed the "as is" sales contract. The appellate court reversed, however, finding that the statement in the contract describing the horse as eleven years old constituted an express warranty, which Morningstar breached. The appellate court reasoned that although the "as is" clause effectively disclaimed any implied warranties (of merchantability and fitness for a particular purpose, such as jumping), it did not disclaim the express warranty concerning the horse's age.[4] ◼

Disclaimer of the Implied Warranty of Merchantability. The UCC also permits a seller or lessor to specifically disclaim an implied warranty of merchantability [UCC 2–316(2), 2A–214(2)]. A merchantability disclaimer must specifically mention the word *merchantability*. The disclaimer need not be written, but if it is, the writing (or record) must be conspicuous [UCC 2–316(2), 2A–214(4)]. Under the UCC, a term or clause is conspicuous when it is written or displayed in such a way that a reasonable person would notice it. Conspicuous terms include words set in capital letters, in a larger font size, or in a different color so as to be set off from the surrounding text.

■**EXAMPLE 13.8** Forbes, a merchant, sells Maves a particular lawn mower selected by Forbes with the characteristics clearly requested by Maves. At the time of the sale, Forbes orally tells Maves that he does not warrant the merchantability of the mower, as it is last year's model and has been used for demonstration purposes. If the mower proves to be defective and does not work, Maves can hold Forbes liable for breach of the warranty of fitness for a particular purpose but not for breach of the warranty of merchantability. Forbes's oral disclaimer mentioning the word *merchantability* is a proper disclaimer. ◼

WATCH OUT Courts generally view warranty disclaimers unfavorably, especially when consumers are involved.

Disclaimer of the Implied Warranty of Fitness. To specifically disclaim an implied warranty of fitness for a particular purpose, the disclaimer *must* be in a writing (or record) and must be conspicuous. The word *fitness* does not have to be mentioned; it is sufficient if, for example, the disclaimer states, "THERE ARE NO WARRANTIES THAT EXTEND BEYOND THE DESCRIPTION ON THE FACE HEREOF."

Buyer's or Lessee's Examination or Refusal to Inspect If a buyer or lessee actually examines the goods (or a sample or model) as fully as desired before entering into a contract, or if the buyer or lessee refuses to examine the goods on the seller's or lessor's demand that he or she do so, *there is no implied warranty with respect to defects that a reasonable examination would reveal or defects that are actually found* [UCC 2–316(3)(b), 2A–214(2)(b)].

■**EXAMPLE 13.9** Suppose that Joplin buys a lamp at Gershwin's Home Store. No express warranties are made. Gershwin requests that Joplin inspect the lamp before buying it, but she refuses. Had Joplin inspected the lamp, she would have noticed that the base of the lamp was obviously cracked and the electrical cord was pulled loose. If the lamp later cracks or starts a fire in Joplin's home and she is injured, she normally will not be able to hold Gershwin's liable for breach of the warranty of merchantability. Because Joplin refused to examine the lamp when asked by Gershwin, Joplin will be deemed to have assumed the risk that it was defective. ◼

Warranty Disclaimers and Unconscionability The UCC sections dealing with warranty disclaimers do not refer specifically to unconscionability as a factor. Ultimately, however, the courts will test warranty disclaimers with reference to the UCC's unconscionability standards [UCC 2–302, 2A–108]. Such things as lack of bargaining position, "take-it-or-leave-it" choices, and a buyer's or lessee's failure to understand or know of a warranty disclaimer will become relevant to the issue of unconscionability.

---

4. *Morningstar v. Hallett*, 858 A.2d 125 (Pa.Super.Ct. 2004).

Magnuson-Moss Warranty Act

The Magnuson-Moss Warranty Act of 1975[5] was designed to prevent deception in warranties by making them easier to understand. The Federal Trade Commission (FTC) is the main agency that enforces this federal law. Additionally, the attorney general or a consumer who has been injured can bring an action to enforce the act if informal procedures for settling disputes prove to be ineffective. The act modifies UCC warranty rules to some extent when consumer transactions are involved. The UCC, however, remains the primary codification of warranty rules for commercial transactions.

Under the Magnuson-Moss Act, no seller or lessor is required to give an express written warranty for consumer goods sold. If a seller or lessor chooses to make an express written warranty, however, and the goods are priced at more than $25, the warranty must be labeled as "full" or "limited." In addition, the warrantor must make certain disclosures fully and conspicuously in a single document in "readily understood language." This disclosure must state the names and addresses of the warrantor(s), what specifically is warranted, procedures for enforcing the warranty, any limitations on warranty relief, and that the buyer has legal rights.

Full Warranty   Although a *full warranty* may not cover every aspect of the consumer product sold, what it does cover ensures some type of consumer satisfaction in the event that the product is defective. A full warranty requires free repair or replacement of any defective part; if the product cannot be repaired within a reasonable time, the consumer has the choice of a refund or a replacement without charge. Frequently, there is no time limit on a full warranty. Any limitation on consequential damages must be *conspicuously* stated. Additionally, the warrantor need not perform warranty services if the problem with the product was caused by the consumer's unreasonable use of the product.

Limited Warranty   A *limited warranty* arises when the written warranty fails to meet one of the minimum requirements of a full warranty. The fact that only a limited warranty is being given must be conspicuously stated. If the only distinction between a limited warranty and a full warranty is a time limitation, the Magnuson-Moss Warranty Act allows the warrantor to identify the warranty as a full warranty by such language as "full twelve-month warranty."

Implied Warranties   Implied warranties do not arise under the Magnuson-Moss Warranty Act; they continue to be created according to UCC provisions. Implied warranties may not be disclaimed under the Magnuson-Moss Warranty Act, however. Although a warrantor can impose a time limit on the duration of an implied warranty, it must correspond to the duration of the express warranty.[6]

> **REMEMBER** When a buyer or lessee is a consumer, a limitation on consequential damages for personal injuries resulting from nonconforming goods is *prima facie* unconscionable.

PRODUCT LIABILITY

Those who make, sell, or lease goods can be held liable for physical harm or property damage caused by those goods to a consumer, user, or bystander. This is called **product liability.** Product liability claims may be based on the warranty theories just discussed, as well as on the theories of negligence, misrepresentation, and strict liability. We look here at product liability based on negligence and misrepresentation.

> **PRODUCT LIABILITY**
> The legal liability of manufacturers, sellers, and lessors of goods to consumers, users, and bystanders for injuries or damages that are caused by the goods.

Negligence

Chapter 4 defined *negligence* as the failure to exercise the degree of care that a reasonable, prudent person would have exercised under the circumstances. If a manufacturer

> **RECALL** The elements of negligence include a duty of care, a breach of the duty, and an injury to the plaintiff proximately caused by the breach.

---

5. 15 U.S.C. Sections 2301–2312.

6. The time limit on an implied warranty occurring by virtue of the warrantor's express warranty must, of course, be reasonable, conscionable, and set forth in clear and conspicuous language on the face of the warranty.

fails to exercise "due care" to make a product safe, a person who is injured by the product may sue the manufacturer for negligence.

Due Care Must Be Exercised   The manufacturer must exercise due care in designing the product, selecting the materials, using the appropriate production process, assembling the product, and placing adequate warnings on the label informing the user of dangers of which an ordinary person might not be aware. The duty of care also extends to the inspection and testing of any purchased products that are used in the final product sold by the manufacturer.

Privity of Contract Not Required   A product liability action based on negligence does not require *privity of contract* between the injured plaintiff and the defendant manufacturer. As discussed in Chapter 9, *privity of contract* refers to the relationship that exists between the promisor and the promisee of a contract; privity is the reason that only the parties to a contract can enforce that contract. In the context of product liability law, privity is not required. This means that a person who was injured by a product need not be the one who actually purchased the product—that is, need not be in privity—to maintain a negligence suit against the manufacturer or seller of a defective product. A manufacturer is liable for its failure to exercise due care to *any* person who sustains an injury proximately caused by a negligently made (defective) product.

Relative to the long history of the common law, this exception to the privity requirement is a fairly recent development, dating to the early part of the twentieth century. A leading case in this respect is *MacPherson v. Buick Motor Co.*, which we present as this chapter's *Landmark in the Law* feature on the following page.

Misrepresentation

When a fraudulent misrepresentation has been made to a user or consumer, and that misrepresentation ultimately results in an injury, the basis of liability may be the tort of fraud. For example, the intentional mislabeling of packaged cosmetics or the intentional concealment of a product's defects would constitute fraudulent misrepresentation. The misrepresentation must be of a material fact and the seller must have had the intent to induce the buyer's reliance on the misrepresentation. Misrepresentation on a label or advertisement is enough to show an intent to induce the reliance of anyone who may use the product. In addition, the buyer must have relied on the misrepresentation.

STRICT PRODUCT LIABILITY

Under the doctrine of strict liability (discussed in Chapter 4), people may be liable for the results of their acts regardless of their intentions or their exercise of reasonable care. In addition, liability does not depend on privity of contract. The injured party does not have to be the buyer or a third party beneficiary, as required under contract warranty theory. Indeed, the provisions of the UCC do not govern this type of liability in law because it is a tort doctrine, not a principle of the law relating to sales contracts.

Strict Product Liability and Public Policy

The law imposes strict product liability as a matter of public policy. This public policy rests on the threefold assumption that (1) consumers should be protected against unsafe products; (2) manufacturers and distributors should not escape liability for faulty products simply because they are not in privity of contract with the ultimate user of those products; and (3) manufacturers, sellers, and lessors of products are generally in a better position

ON THE WEB

For an overview of product liability, go to FindLaw for Small Business at

smallbusiness.findlaw.com/business-operations/insurance/liability-product-overview.html.

LANDMARK IN THE LAW — *MacPherson v. Buick Motor Co.* (1916)

In the landmark case of *MacPherson v. Buick Motor Co.*,[a] the New York Court of Appeals—New York's highest court—dealt with the liability of a manufacturer that failed to exercise reasonable care in manufacturing a finished product.

Case Background   The case was brought by Donald MacPherson, who suffered injuries while riding in a Buick automobile that suddenly collapsed because one of the wheels was made of defective wood. The spokes crumbled into fragments, throwing MacPherson out of the vehicle and injuring him.

MacPherson had purchased the car from a Buick dealer, but he brought a lawsuit against the manufacturer, Buick Motor Company. Buick itself had not made the wheel but had bought it from another manufacturer. There was evidence, though, that the defects could have been discovered by a reasonable inspection by Buick and that no such inspection had taken place. MacPherson charged Buick with negligence for putting a human life in imminent danger.

The Issue before the Court and the Court's Ruling   The major issue before the court was whether Buick owed a duty of care to anyone except the immediate purchaser of the car—that is, the Buick dealer. In deciding the issue, Justice Benjamin Cardozo stated that "[i]f the nature of a thing is such that it is reasonably certain to place life and limb in peril when negligently made, it is then a thing of danger. . . . If to the element of danger there is added knowledge that the thing will be used by persons other than the purchaser, and used without new tests, then, irrespective of contract, the manufacturer of this thing of danger is under a duty to make it carefully."

The court concluded that "[b]eyond all question, the nature of an automobile gives warning of probable danger if its construction is defective. This automobile was designed to go 50 miles an hour. Unless its wheels were sound and strong, injury was almost certain." Although Buick had not manufactured the wheel itself, the court held that Buick had a duty to inspect the wheels and that Buick "was responsible for the finished product." Therefore, Buick was liable to MacPherson for the injuries he sustained when he was thrown from the car.

APPLICATION TO TODAY'S WORLD   *This landmark decision was a significant step in creating the legal environment of the modern world. Today, it is common for an automobile manufacturer to be held liable when its negligence causes a product user to be injured. As is often the situation, technological developments necessitated changes in the law. Had the courts continued to require privity of contract in product liability cases, today's legal landscape would be quite different indeed. Certainly, fewer cases would be pending before the courts; and just as certainly, many purchasers of products, including automobiles, would have little recourse for obtaining legal redress for injuries caused by those products.*

RELEVANT WEB SITES   *To locate information on the Web concerning the* MacPherson *decision, go to this text's Web site at* **academic.cengage.com/blaw/blt**, *select "Chapter 13," and click on "URLs for Landmarks."*

a. 217 N.Y. 382, 111 N.E. 1050 (1916).

than consumers to bear the costs associated with injuries caused by their products—costs that they can ultimately pass on to all consumers in the form of higher prices.

California was the first state to impose strict product liability in tort on manufacturers. In a landmark 1963 decision, *Greenman v. Yuba Power Products, Inc.*,[7] the California Supreme Court set out the reason for applying tort law rather than contract law in cases involving consumers injured by defective products. According to the court, the "purpose of such liability is to [e]nsure that the costs of injuries resulting from defective products are borne by the manufacturers . . . rather than by the injured persons who are powerless to protect themselves."

Requirements for Strict Liability

Section 402A of the *Restatement (Second) of Torts* indicates how the drafters envisioned that the doctrine of strict liability should be applied. The *Restatement* was issued in 1964, and during the next decade, Section 402A became a widely accepted statement of the liabilities of sellers of goods (including manufacturers, processors, assemblers, packagers, bottlers, wholesalers, distributors, retailers, and lessors).

The bases for an action in strict liability as set forth in Section 402A of the *Restatement (Second) of Torts,* and as the doctrine came to be commonly applied, can be summarized as a series of six requirements, which are listed here. Depending on the jurisdiction, if these requirements are met, a manufacturer's liability to an injured party can be virtually unlimited.

1 The product must be in a *defective condition* when the defendant sells it.

2 The defendant must normally be engaged in the *business of selling* (or otherwise distributing) that product.

3 The product must be *unreasonably dangerous* to the user or consumer because of its defective condition (in most states).

4 The plaintiff must incur *physical harm* to self or property by use or consumption of the product.

5 The defective condition must be the *proximate cause* of the injury or damage.

6 The *goods must not have been substantially changed* from the time the product was sold to the time the injury was sustained.

Proving a Defective Condition   Under these requirements, in any action against a manufacturer, seller, or lessor, the plaintiff does not have to show why or in what manner the product became defective. The plaintiff does, however, have to prove that the product was defective at the time it left the hands of the seller or lessor and that this defective condition makes it "unreasonably dangerous" to the user or consumer. Unless evidence can be presented that will support the conclusion that the product was defective when it was sold or leased, the plaintiff normally will not succeed. If the product was delivered in a safe condition and subsequent mishandling made it harmful to the user, the seller or lessor is not strictly liable.

Unreasonably Dangerous Products   The *Restatement* recognizes that many products cannot possibly be made entirely safe for all consumption, and thus holds sellers or lessors liable only for products that are *unreasonably* dangerous. A court may consider a product so defective as to be an **unreasonably dangerous product** in either of the following situations:

1 The product is dangerous beyond the expectation of the ordinary consumer.

2 A less dangerous alternative was economically feasible for the manufacturer, but the manufacturer failed to produce it.

UNREASONABLY DANGEROUS PRODUCT
In product liability law, a product that is defective to the point of threatening a consumer's health and safety. A product will be considered unreasonably dangerous if it is dangerous beyond the expectation of the ordinary consumer or if a less dangerous alternative was economically feasible for the manufacturer, but the manufacturer failed to produce it.

Sony manufactured defective lithium-ion cell batteries, some of which caught on fire. Dell and other computer companies bought these Sony batteries for use in their laptop computers. To what extent is Sony liable? To what extent are Dell and other laptop makers who purchased these batteries liable? (Photo Courtesy of theinquirer.net)

7. 59 Cal.2d 57, 377 P.2d 897, 27 Cal.Rptr. 697 (1963).

As will be discussed next, a product may be unreasonably dangerous due to a flaw in the manufacturing process, a design defect, or an inadequate warning.

Product Defects—*Restatement (Third) of Torts*

Because Section 402A of the *Restatement (Second) of Torts* did not clearly define such terms as "defective" and "unreasonably dangerous," they were interpreted differently by different courts. In 1997, to address these concerns, the American Law Institute issued the *Restatement (Third) of Torts: Products Liability*. This *Restatement* defines the three types of product defects that have traditionally been recognized in product liability law—manufacturing defects, design defects, and inadequate warnings.

Manufacturing Defects   According to Section 2(a) of the *Restatement (Third) of Torts: Products Liability*, a product "contains a manufacturing defect when the product departs from its intended design even though all possible care was exercised in the preparation and marketing of the product." Basically, a manufacturing defect is a departure from a product unit's design specifications, which results in products that are physically flawed, damaged, or incorrectly assembled. A glass bottle that is made too thin and explodes in a consumer's face is an example of a manufacturing defect. Liability is imposed on the manufacturer (and on the wholesaler and retailer) regardless of whether the manufacturer's quality control efforts were "reasonable." The idea behind holding defendants strictly liable for manufacturing defects is to encourage greater investment in product safety and stringent quality control standards.

For liability to be imposed on the basis of a manufacturing defect, the plaintiff must prove that the defect caused him or her to suffer an injury. On the question of causation in the following case, the plaintiff offered the testimony of a university professor.

CASE 13.2   DeRienzo v. Trek Bicycle Corp.

United States District Court, Southern District of New York, 376 F.Supp.2d 537 (2005).

FACTS   David DeRienzo of Newburgh, New York, owned a 1998 Y5 mountain bike made by Trek Bicycle Corporation. All of the Y5's parts had been replaced except the aluminum frame. DeRienzo was an aggressive rider, who enjoyed urban assault riding, dirt jumping, and mountain biking. On July 4, 2001, he jumped five to eight feet off a hillside, but as he landed, the frame broke and he crashed. Seriously injured, he filed a suit in a federal district court against Trek, claiming in part strict product liability on the basis of a manufacturing defect. He supported this claim with the testimony of Harold Paxton. Paxton is the U.S. Steel University Professor (Emeritus) of Metallurgy and Materials Science at Carnegie Mellon University and a member of related professional organizations. Paxton inspected and photographed the frame's fracture. To confirm his observations, Paxton had the frame taken apart, photographed again, analyzed chemically, and tested mechanically. Trek and its experts consented to these tests and methods. Paxton believed that the frame failed due to a defect—a crack caused by excess weld metal deposited on the inside of the tube during the manufacturing process. Trek filed

a motion for summary judgment, arguing that Paxton had never analyzed an aluminum bike frame before and did not have "the faintest idea" about the mountain biking industry. Trek also cited mistakes by Paxton's technician and misinterpretation of some of the results.

ISSUE   Was Paxton's testimony admissible, and if so, was it sufficient to defeat Trek's motion for summary judgment?

DECISION   Yes. The court ruled that Paxton could testify as an expert and, on the basis of this testimony, denied Trek's motion.

REASON   To be admissible, expert testimony must be scientifically valid and relevant to the case. Scientific validity requires that the expert's technique can be tested, that it has been subject to peer review and acceptance, that it has a known or potential rate of error, and that there are standards controlling the technique. In this case, the court held that Paxton's methods carried "sufficient indicia [indications] of scientific reliability. * * * Most significant in this regard is * * * that Defendant's own metallurgical expert and defense

CASE 13.2–Continued

counsel agreed upon the protocols by which Paxton analyzed the Bike's frame." Also, "Paxton's described procedures tend to indicate to the Court that he carried out a thorough and scientific analysis of the frame, and that these tests formed the basis for his conclusion." Paxton's testimony was offered for a proper purpose—to help the court determine what caused the Y5's frame to fail. As for Trek's objections, Paxton's "extensive education and teaching background in the field of metallurgy generally, as well as his broad and prestigious professional associations, indicate that he is qualified to undertake analysis

of an aluminum bicycle frame." Trek's other criticisms were "forensic quibbles" about which the defendant could cross-examine Paxton if "they come up at trial." The court reasoned further that Paxton's opinion that the frame failed because of a manufacturing defect gave rise to a reasonable inference that the frame's failure caused the accident.

WHY IS THIS CASE IMPORTANT? *This case illustrates that the admissibility of an expert's opinion can be essential in product liability cases to prove that a manufacturing defect exists and that the defect is what caused the plaintiff's injury.*

Design Defects   In contrast to a manufacturing defect, which is a failure of a product to meet the manufacturer's design specifications, a design defect is a flaw in the product's actual design that causes the product to create an unreasonable risk to the user. A product "is defective in design when the foreseeable risks of harm posed by the product could have been reduced or avoided by the adoption of a reasonable alternative design by the seller or other distributor, or a predecessor in the commercial chain of distribution, and the omission of the alternative design renders the product not reasonably safe."[8]

Test for Design Defects.   To successfully assert a design defect, a plaintiff has to show that a reasonable alternative design was available and that the defendant's failure to adopt the alternative design rendered the product unreasonably dangerous. In other words, a manufacturer or other defendant is liable only when the harm was reasonably preventable. **■EXAMPLE 13.10** Gillespie, who cut off several of his fingers while operating a table saw, filed a lawsuit against the maker of the table saw. Gillespie alleged that the blade guards on the saw were defectively designed. At trial, however, an expert testified that the alternative design for blade guards used for table saws could not have been used for the particular cut that Gillespie was performing at the time he was injured. The court found that Gillespie's claim about defective blade guards must fail because there was no proof that the "better" design of guard would have prevented his injury.[9] ■

Factors to Be Considered.   According to the Official Comments accompanying the *Restatement (Third) of Torts*, a court can consider a broad range of factors in deciding claims of design defects. These factors include the magnitude and probability of the foreseeable risks, as well as the relative advantages and disadvantages of the product as designed and as it alternatively could have been designed.

■EXAMPLE 13.11 Four-year-old Andrea suffered serious burns when she got out of bed one night to go to the bathroom and tripped on the electric cord connected to a hot-water vaporizer. Andrea's parents filed a lawsuit against the manufacturer, alleging that the vaporizer was defectively designed because the top heating unit was not secured to the jar that held the hot water. In this situation, the court said the following factors were relevant: (1) the foreseeability that the vaporizer might be accidentally tipped over, (2) the overall safety provided by an alternative design that secured the heating unit to the receptacle holding the water, (3) the consumer's knowledge or lack of knowledge that the water in the glass jar was scalding hot, (4) the added cost of the safer alternative design, and (5) the relative convenience of a vaporizer with a lift-off cap. The court also observed that

Segway, Inc., manufacturer of the Segway® Personal Transporter, voluntarily recalled all of its transporters to fix a software problem that could lead to users falling and injuring themselves. If a person was injured by such a malfunction of the software in the machine, what would the victim have to prove to establish that the device had a design defect?
(Nelson Pavlosky/Creative Commons)

---

8. *Restatement (Third) of Torts: Products Liability*, Section 2(b).
9. *Gillespie v. Sears, Roebuck & Co.*, 386 F.3d 21 (1st Cir. 2004).

because the parents of small children are frequently told to use vaporizers to treat child-hood illnesses, it was foreseeable that the vaporizer units would be operating unattended in children's rooms. It was also foreseeable that small children might trip over the cord and be burned. As several practical and inexpensive alternative designs were available, the court found that the vaporizer that injured Andrea was defectively designed.[10] ▣

Inadequate Warnings A product may also be deemed defective because of inadequate instructions or warnings. A product will be considered defective "when the foreseeable risks of harm posed by the product could have been reduced or avoided by the provision of reasonable instructions or warnings by the seller or other distributor, or a predecessor in the commercial chain of distribution, and the omission of the instructions or warnings renders the product not reasonably safe."[11] Generally, a seller must warn those who purchase its product of the harm that can result from the *foreseeable misuse* of the product as well.

Important factors for a court to consider under the *Restatement (Third) of Torts* include the risks of a product, the "content and comprehensibility" and "intensity of expression" of warnings and instructions, and the "characteristics of expected user groups."[12] A "reasonableness" test is applied to determine if the warnings adequately alert consumers to the product's risks. For example, children will likely respond more readily to bright, bold, simple warning labels, while educated adults might need more detailed information.

There is no duty to warn about risks that are obvious or commonly known. Warnings about such risks do not add to the safety of a product and could even detract from it by making other warnings seem less significant. The obviousness of a risk and a user's decision to proceed in the face of that risk may be a defense in a product liability suit based on a warning defect. (This defense and other defenses in product liability suits will be discussed later in this chapter.)

ETHICAL ISSUE 13.1

If a warning is provided with a product, should its manufacturer or seller be able to assume that the warning will be read and obeyed? Today, manufacturers tend to include a long list of warnings of the potential risks associated with every product. Even products that are relatively safe include warnings. Consumers are so inundated with multiple warnings for every kind of product that most people no longer pay attention to the warnings. Moreover, in some instances the warnings about a product conflict with how consumers have always used that product.

Consider a trampoline, for example. The risks of jumping on a trampoline are not new. Many children are injured on trampolines each year, but this has not decreased their popularity. The manufacturers of trampolines now warn users not to do flips or to have more than one person on a trampoline at a time—both of which have been common practices on trampolines for years. Should a manufacturer be insulated from liability because it provided warning labels in the box to be affixed on the assembled trampoline? Yes, according to the courts in several 2006 cases.[13] As long as the manufacturer provides adequate warnings, it can assume that the user will read and follow its many warnings. In other words, today's products come with many warnings so that manufacturers and sellers can avoid liability for products that might otherwise be considered defective or unreasonably dangerous. Does allowing manufacturers and sellers to avoid liability in this way make sense, given that the whole reason for imposing strict liability is the public policy of protecting consumers and making sure that manufacturers and sellers share at least some of the risks of unsafe products?

▣

---

10. This example is based on the facts of an early case on design defects, *McCormack v. Hankscraft Co.*, 278 Minn. 322, 154 N.W.2d 488 (1967).

11. *Restatement (Third) of Torts: Products Liability*, Section 2(c).

12. *Restatement (Third) of Torts: Products Liability*, Section 2, Comment h.

13. *Crosswhite v. Jumpking, Inc.*, 411 F.Supp.2d 1228 (D.Or. 2006); and *Celmer v. Jumpking, Inc.*, __ F.Supp.2d __ (D.Md. 2006).

Market-Share Liability

Generally, in all cases involving product liability, a plaintiff must prove that the defective product that caused her or his injury was the product of a specific defendant. In a few situations, however, courts have dropped this requirement when a plaintiff cannot prove which of many distributors of a harmful product supplied the particular product that caused the injuries. Under a theory of **market-share liability,** all firms that manufactured and distributed the product during the period in question are held liable for the plaintiff's injuries in proportion to the firms' respective shares of the market for that product during that period.

> **■EXAMPLE 13.12** In one case, a plaintiff who was a hemophiliac received injections of a blood protein known as antihemophiliac factor (AHF) concentrate. The plaintiff later tested positive for the AIDS (acquired immune deficiency syndrome) virus. Because it was not known which manufacturer was responsible for the particular AHF received by the plaintiff, the court held that all of the manufacturers of AHF could be held liable under a market-share theory of liability.[14] ■

Courts in many jurisdictions do not recognize this theory of liability, believing that it deviates too significantly from traditional legal principles.[15] In jurisdictions that do recognize market-share liability, it is usually applied in cases involving drugs or chemicals, when it is difficult or impossible to determine which company made a particular product.

MARKET-SHARE LIABILITY
A theory of sharing liability among all firms that manufactured and distributed a particular product during a certain period of time. This form of liability sharing is used only in some jurisdictions and only when the true source of the harmful product is unidentifiable.

Other Applications of Strict Liability

Virtually all courts extend the strict liability of manufacturers and other sellers to injured bystanders. **■EXAMPLE 13.13** A forklift that Trent is operating will not go into reverse, and as a result, it runs into a bystander. In this situation, the bystander can sue the manufacturer of the defective forklift under strict liability.[16] ■

The rule of strict liability is also applicable to suppliers of component parts. **■EXAMPLE 13.14** General Motors buys brake pads from a subcontractor and puts them in Chevrolets without changing their composition. If those pads are defective, both the supplier of the brake pads and General Motors will be held strictly liable for the injuries caused by the defects. ■

Statutes of Repose

As discussed in Chapter 1, *statutes of limitations* restrict the time within which an action may be brought. Many states have passed laws, called **statutes of repose,** placing outer time limits on some claims so that the defendant will not be left vulnerable to lawsuits indefinitely. These statutes may limit the time within which a plaintiff can file a product liability suit. Typically, a statute of repose begins to run at an earlier date and runs for a longer time than a statute of limitations. For example, a statute of repose may require that claims be brought within twelve years from the date of sale or manufacture of the defective product. No action can be brought if the injury occurs *after* this statutory period has lapsed. In addition, some of these legislative enactments limit the application of the doctrine of strict liability to new goods only.

STATUTE OF REPOSE
Basically, a statute of limitations that is not dependent on the happening of a cause of action. Statutes of repose generally begin to run at an earlier date and run for a longer period of time than statutes of limitations.

---

14. *Smith v. Cutter Biological, Inc.*, 72 Haw. 416, 823 P.2d 717 (1991). See also *Hymowitz v. Eli Lilly and Co.*, 73 N.Y.2d 487, 539 N.E.2d 1069, 541 N.Y.S.2d 941 (1989).

15. For the Illinois Supreme Court's position on market-share liability, see *Smith v. Eli Lilly Co.*, 137 Ill.2d 252, 560 N.E.2d 324, 148 Ill.Dec. 22 (1990).

16. See, for example, *Batts v. Tow-Motor Forklift Co.*, 978 F.2d 1386 (Miss. 1992).

DEFENSES TO PRODUCT LIABILITY

Defendants in product liability suits can raise a number of defenses. One defense, of course, is to show that there is no basis for the plaintiff's claim. For example, in a product liability case based on negligence, if a defendant can show that the plaintiff has *not* met the requirements (such as causation) for an action in negligence, generally the defendant will not be liable. In regard to strict product liability, a defendant can claim that the plaintiff failed to meet one of the requirements for an action in strict liability. If the defendant, for instance, establishes that the goods have been subsequently altered, normally the defendant will not be held liable.[17] Defendants may also assert the defenses discussed next.

Assumption of Risk

Assumption of risk can sometimes be used as a defense in a product liability action. For example, if a buyer fails to heed a product recall by the seller, a court might conclude that the buyer assumed the risk caused by the defect that led to the recall. To establish such a defense, the defendant must show that (1) the plaintiff knew and appreciated the risk created by the product defect and (2) the plaintiff voluntarily assumed the risk, even though it was unreasonable to do so. (See Chapter 4 for a more detailed discussion of assumption of risk.)

Product Misuse

Similar to the defense of voluntary assumption of risk is that of product misuse, which occurs when a product is used for a purpose for which it was not intended. The courts have severely limited this defense, however, and it is now recognized as a defense only when the particular use was not reasonably foreseeable. If the misuse is foreseeable, the seller must take measures to guard against it.

Comparative Negligence (Fault)

Developments in the area of comparative negligence, or fault (discussed in Chapter 4), have also affected the doctrine of strict liability—the most extreme theory of product liability. Whereas previously the plaintiff's conduct was not a defense to strict liability, today many jurisdictions, when apportioning liability and damages, consider the negligent or intentional actions of both the plaintiff and the defendant. This means that a defendant may be able to limit at least some of its liability for injuries caused by its defective product if it can show that the plaintiff's misuse of the product contributed to the injuries.

■EXAMPLE 13.15 Dan Smith, a mechanic in Alaska, was not wearing a hard hat at work when he was asked to start a diesel engine of an air compressor. Because the compressor was an older model, he had to prop open a door to start it. When he got the engine started, the door fell from its position and hit Smith's head. The injury caused him to suffer from seizures and epilepsy. Smith sued the manufacturer, claiming that the engine was defectively designed. The manufacturer argued that Smith had been negligent by failing to wear his hard hat and by propping the door open in an unsafe manner. Smith's attorney claimed that the plaintiff's ordinary negligence could not be used as a defense in product liability cases, but the Alaska Supreme Court disagreed. Alaska, like many other states, allows comparative negligence to be raised as a defense in product liability lawsuits.[18] ■

17. Under some state laws, the failure to properly maintain a product may constitute a subsequent alteration. See, for example, *La Plante v. American Honda Motor Co.,* 27 F.3d 731 (1st Cir. 1994).

18. *Smith v. Ingersoll-Rand Co.,* 14 P.3d 990 (Alaska 2000).

Commonly Known Dangers

The dangers associated with certain products (such as sharp knives and guns) are so commonly known that manufacturers need not warn users of those dangers. If a defendant succeeds in convincing the court that a plaintiff's injury resulted from a *commonly known danger*, the defendant normally will not be liable.

■EXAMPLE 13.16 A classic case on this issue involved a plaintiff who was injured when an elastic exercise rope that she had purchased slipped off her foot and struck her in the eye, causing a detachment of the retina. The plaintiff claimed that the manufacturer should be liable because it had failed to warn users that the exerciser might slip off a foot in such a manner. The court stated that to hold the manufacturer liable in these circumstances "would go beyond the reasonable dictates of justice in fixing the liabilities of manufacturers." After all, stated the court, "[a]lmost every physical object can be inherently dangerous or potentially dangerous in a sense. . . . A manufacturer cannot manufacture a knife that will not cut or a hammer that will not mash a thumb or a stove that will not burn a finger. The law does not require [manufacturers] to warn of such common dangers."[19] ▣

A related defense is the *knowledgeable user* defense. If a particular danger (such as electrical shock) is or should be commonly known by particular users of the product (such as electricians), the manufacturer of electrical equipment need not warn these users of the danger.

CONSUMER PROTECTION LAWS

Sources of consumer protection exist at all levels of government. At the federal level, a number of laws have been passed to define the duties of sellers and the rights of consumers. Exhibit 13–1 indicates many of the areas of consumer law that are regulated by statutes. Federal administrative agencies, such as the Federal Trade Commission (FTC), also provide an important source of consumer protection. Nearly every agency and department of the federal government has an office of consumer affairs, and most states have one or more such offices, including the offices of state attorneys general, to assist consumers.

---

19. *Jamieson v. Woodward & Lothrop,* 247 F.2d 23, 101 D.C.App. 32 (1957).

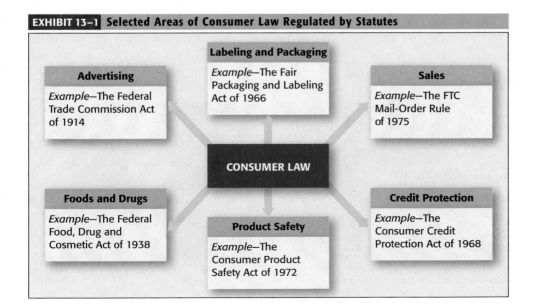

EXHIBIT 13–1 **Selected Areas of Consumer Law Regulated by Statutes**

Labeling and Packaging
Example—The Fair Packaging and Labeling Act of 1966

Advertising
Example—The Federal Trade Commission Act of 1914

Sales
Example—The FTC Mail-Order Rule of 1975

CONSUMER LAW

Foods and Drugs
Example—The Federal Food, Drug and Cosmetic Act of 1938

Product Safety
Example—The Consumer Product Safety Act of 1972

Credit Protection
Example—The Consumer Credit Protection Act of 1968

Because of the wide variation among state consumer protection laws, our primary focus here will be on federal legislation—specifically, on legislation governing deceptive advertising, telemarketing and electronic advertising, labeling and packaging, sales, health protection, product safety, and credit protection. Realize, though, that state laws often provide more sweeping and significant protections for the consumer than do federal laws.

Deceptive Advertising

One of the earliest—and still one of the most important—federal consumer protection laws is the Federal Trade Commission Act of 1914 (mentioned in Chapter 22). The act created the FTC to carry out the broadly stated goal of preventing unfair and deceptive trade practices, including deceptive advertising, within the meaning of Section 5 of the act.

Generally, **deceptive advertising** occurs if a reasonable consumer would be misled by the advertising claim. Vague generalities and obvious exaggerations are permissible. These claims are known as *puffery*—that is, statements about a product that a reasonable person would not believe to be true. When a claim takes on the appearance of literal authenticity, however, it may create problems. Advertising that *appears* to be based on factual evidence but in fact is scientifically untrue will be deemed deceptive. A classic example occurred in a 1944 case in which the claim that a skin cream would restore youthful qualities to aged skin was deemed deceptive.[20]

Some advertisements contain "half-truths," meaning that the presented information is true but incomplete and, therefore, leads consumers to a false conclusion. ■**EXAMPLE 13.17** The maker of Campbell's soups advertised that "most" Campbell's soups were low in fat and cholesterol and thus were helpful in fighting heart disease. What the ad did not say was that Campbell's soups were high in sodium and that high-sodium diets may increase the risk of heart disease. Hence, the FTC ruled that Campbell's claims were deceptive. ■ Advertising featuring an endorsement by a celebrity may be deemed deceptive if the celebrity does not actually use the product.

Bait-and-Switch Advertising   The FTC has issued rules that govern specific advertising techniques. One of the more important rules is contained in the FTC's "Guides on Bait Advertising."[21] The rule is designed to prevent **bait-and-switch advertising**—that is,

---

20. *Charles of the Ritz Distributing Corp. v. Federal Trade Commission*, 143 F.2d 676 (2d Cir. 1944).
21. 16 C.F.R. Section 288.

DECEPTIVE ADVERTISING
Advertising that misleads consumers, either by making unjustified claims concerning a product's performance or by omitting a material fact concerning the product's composition or performance.

BAIT-AND-SWITCH ADVERTISING
Advertising a product at a very attractive price (the "bait") and then, once the consumer is in the store, saying that the advertised product is either not available or is of poor quality. The customer is then urged to purchase ("switched" to) a more expensive item.

These stuffed teddy bears were recalled because the plastic beads inside the toys could come out and create a choking hazard for young children. According to Exhibit 13–1 on page 397, which area of consumer protection law governs such a recall? (Consumer Product Safety Commission/ Getty Images)

advertising a very low price for a particular item that will likely be unavailable to the consumer and then encouraging him or her to purchase a more expensive item. The low price is the "bait" to lure the consumer into the store. The salesperson is instructed to "switch" the consumer to a different, more expensive item. According to the FTC guidelines, bait-and-switch advertising occurs if the seller refuses to show the advertised item, fails to have reasonable quantities of it available, fails to promise to deliver the advertised item within a reasonable time, or discourages employees from selling the item.

Online Deceptive Advertising   Deceptive advertising can occur in the online environment as well. For years, the FTC has actively monitored online advertising and has identified hundreds of Web sites that have made false or deceptive advertising claims. These claims have concerned products ranging from medical treatments for various diseases to exercise equipment and weight-loss aids.

In 2000, the FTC issued guidelines to help online businesses comply with existing laws prohibiting deceptive advertising.[22] The guidelines did not set forth new rules but rather described how existing laws apply to online advertising. Generally, the rules emphasize that any ads—online or offline—must be truthful and not misleading and that any claims made in any ads must be substantiated. Additionally, ads cannot be unfair, which the FTC defines as "likely to cause substantial consumer injury that consumers could not reasonably avoid and that is not outweighed by the benefit to consumers or competition."

The guidelines also call for "clear and conspicuous" disclosure of any qualifying or limiting information. The overall impression of the ad is important in meeting this requirement. The FTC suggests that advertisers should assume that consumers will not read an entire Web page. Therefore, to satisfy the "clear and conspicuous" requirement, advertisers should place the disclosure as close as possible to the claim being qualified or include the disclosure within the claim itself. If such placement is not feasible, the next-best location is on a section of the page to which a consumer can easily scroll. Generally, hyperlinks to a disclosure are recommended only for lengthy disclosures or for disclosures that must be repeated in a variety of locations on the Web page. If the disclosure is an integral part of a claim, however, it should be placed on the same page rather than hyperlinked.

FTC Actions against Deceptive Advertising   The FTC receives complaints from many sources, including competitors of alleged violators, consumers, consumer organizations, trade associations, Better Business Bureaus, government organizations, and state and local officials. If it receives numerous and widespread complaints about a problem, the FTC will investigate. If the FTC concludes that a given advertisement is unfair or deceptive, it sends a formal complaint to the alleged offender. The company may agree to settle the complaint without further proceedings; if not, the FTC can conduct a hearing before an administrative law judge (discussed in Chapter 1) in which the company can present its defense.

If the FTC succeeds in proving that an advertisement is unfair or deceptive, it usually issues a **cease-and-desist order** requiring the company to stop the challenged advertising. It might also require **counteradvertising** in which the company advertises anew—in print, on the Internet, on radio, and on television—to inform the public about the earlier misinformation.

ON THE WEB

A government-sponsored Web site that contains reports on consumer issues, including issues relating to online deceptive advertising and other forms of online fraud, can be accessed at

www.consumer.gov.

CEASE-AND-DESIST ORDER
An administrative or judicial order prohibiting a person or business firm from conducting activities that an agency or court has deemed illegal.

COUNTERADVERTISING
New advertising that is undertaken pursuant to a Federal Trade Commission order for the purpose of correcting earlier false claims that were made about a product.

---

22. *Advertising and Marketing on the Internet: Rules of the Road,* September 2000. This guide is available at **www.ftc.gov/bcp/conline/pubs/buspubs/ruleroad.htm**.

Telemarketing and Electronic Advertising

The pervasive use of the telephone to market goods and services to homes and businesses led to the passage in 1991 of the Telephone Consumer Protection Act (TCPA).[23] The act prohibits telephone solicitation using an automatic telephone dialing system or a pre-recorded voice. Most states also have laws regulating telephone solicitation. The TCPA also makes it illegal to transmit ads via fax without first obtaining the recipient's permission. (Similar issues have arisen with respect to junk e-mail, called *spam*—see Chapter 4.)

The act is enforced by the Federal Communications Commission (FCC) and also provides for a private right of action. The FCC imposes substantial fines ($11,000 each day) on companies that violate the junk fax provisions of the TCPA and has fined one company as much as $5.4 million for violations.[24] Consumers can recover any actual monetary loss resulting from a violation of the act or receive $500 in damages for each violation, whichever is greater. If a court finds that a defendant willfully or knowingly violated the act, the court has the discretion to treble (triple) the damages awarded. When many consumers file their complaints together as a class-action suit, the damages awarded can be large, as can the defendant's liability for attorneys' fees.

The Telemarketing and Consumer Fraud and Abuse Prevention Act of 1994[25] directed the FTC to establish rules governing telemarketing and to bring actions against fraudulent telemarketers. The FTC's Telemarketing Sales Rule of 1995[26] requires a telemarketer to identify the seller's name; describe the product being sold; and disclose all material facts related to the sale, including the total cost of the goods being sold, any restrictions on obtaining or using the goods, and whether a sale will be considered final and nonrefundable. The act makes it illegal for telemarketers to misrepresent information (including facts about their goods or services and earnings potential, for example). A telemarketer must also remove a consumer's name from its list of potential contacts if the consumer so requests. An amendment to the Telemarketing Sales Rule established the national Do Not Call Registry, which became effective in October 2003. Telemarketers must refrain from calling those consumers who have placed their names on the list.

Labeling and Packaging

A number of federal and state laws deal specifically with the information given on labels and packages. The rules are designed to ensure that labels provide accurate information about the product and to warn about possible dangers from its use or misuse. In general, labels must be accurate, and they must use words that are understood by the ordinary consumer. For example, a box of cereal cannot be labeled "giant" if that would exaggerate the amount of cereal contained in the box. In some instances, labels must specify the raw materials used in the product, such as the percentage of cotton, nylon, or other fibers used in a garment. In other instances, the products must carry a warning. Cigarette packages and advertising, for example, must include one of several warnings about the health hazards associated with smoking.[27]

The Fair Packaging and Labeling Act requires that food product labels identify (1) the product; (2) the net quantity of the contents and, if the number of servings is stated, the size of a serving; (3) the manufacturer; and (4) the packager or distrib-

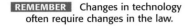

REMEMBER Changes in technology often require changes in the law.

ON THE WEB

You can find current articles concerning consumer issues at the Alexander Law Firm's "Consumer Law Page." Go to **consumerlawpage.com/intro.html**.

Today's consumers are increasingly concerned about eating genetically modified crops and the potential presence of pesticides, hormones, and the causative agent of mad cow disease in foods. Many consumers have thus switched to buying organic foods. How might an organic label be deceptive to consumers?
(Richard Anderson)

---

23. 47 U.S.C. Sections 227 *et seq.*, as modified by the Junk Fax Protection Act of 2005.
24. See *Missouri ex rel. Nixon v. American Blast Fax, Inc.*, 323 F.3d 649 (8th Cir. 2003); *cert.* denied, 540 U.S. 1104, 124 S.Ct. 1043, 157 L.Ed.2d 888 (2004).
25. 15 U.S.C. Sections 6101–6108.
26. 16 C.F.R. Sections 310.1–310.8.
27. 15 U.S.C. Sections 1331 *et seq.*

utor.[28] The act also provides for additional requirements concerning descriptions on packages, savings claims, components of nonfood products, and standards for the partial filling of packages. Food products must bear labels detailing the food's nutrition content, including how much fat the food contains and what kind of fat it is. The Department of Health and Human Services, as well as the FTC, enforces these rules. The Nutrition Labeling and Education Act of 1990 requires standard nutrition facts (including fat content) on food labels; regulates the use of such terms as *fresh* and *low fat*; and, subject to the federal Food and Drug Administration's approval, authorizes certain health claims.

Sales

A number of statutes protect consumers by requiring the disclosure of certain terms in sales transactions and providing rules governing home or door-to-door sales, mail-order transactions, referral sales, and unsolicited merchandise. The Federal Reserve Board of Governors, for example, has issued **Regulation Z,** which governs credit provisions associated with sales contracts (discussed later in this chapter). Many states have also passed laws providing remedies to consumers in home sales. For example, a number of states have passed **"cooling-off" laws** that permit the buyers of goods sold door to door to cancel their contracts within a specified period of time, usually three to five days after the sale. An FTC regulation also requires sellers to give consumers three days to cancel any door-to-door sale, and this rule applies in addition to any state law. Furthermore, states have provided a number of consumer protection measures, such as implied warranties, through the adoption of the Uniform Commercial Code.

REGULATION Z
A set of rules promulgated by the Federal Reserve Board of Governors to implement the provisions of the Truth-in-Lending Act (to be discussed shortly).

"COOLING-OFF" LAWS
Laws that allow buyers a period of time, such as three days, in which to cancel door-to-door sales contracts.

ON THE WEB
To learn more about the FTC's Cooling-Off Rule, go to
www.ftc.gov/bcp/edu/pubs/consumer/products/buy01.shtm.

Telephone and Mail-Order Sales The FTC's Mail or Telephone Order Merchandise Rule of 1993, which amended the FTC's Mail-Order Rule of 1975,[29] provides specific protections for consumers who purchase goods over the phone or through the mails. The 1993 rule extended the 1975 rule to include sales in which orders are transmitted using computers, fax machines, or any similar means involving a telephone. Among other things, the rule requires mail-order merchants to ship orders within the time promised in their catalogues or advertisements, to notify consumers when orders cannot be shipped on time, and to issue a refund within a specified period of time when a consumer cancels an order.

In addition, under the Postal Reorganization Act of 1970[30] a consumer who receives *unsolicited* merchandise sent by U.S. mail can keep it, throw it away, or dispose of it in any manner that she or he sees fit. The recipient will not be obligated to the sender. **EXAMPLE 13.18** Serena receives a copy of the "Cookbook of the Month" from a company via the U.S. mail, even though she did not order the cookbook. She gives it to her friend, Vaya, who loves to cook. The following month, Serena receives a bill for $49.99 from the company that sent the cookbook. Under the 1970 act, because the cookbook was sent to her unsolicited through the U.S. mail, Serena is not obligated to pay the bill. ■

Online Sales Protecting consumers from fraudulent and deceptive sales practices conducted via the Internet has proved to be a challenging task. Nonetheless, the FTC and other federal agencies have brought a number of enforcement actions against those who perpetrate online fraud. Additionally, the laws mentioned in previous chapters, such as the federal statute prohibiting wire fraud (see Chapter 6), apply to online transactions.

28. 15 U.S.C. Sections 4401–4408.
29. 16 C.F.R. Sections 435.1–435.2.
30. 39 U.S.C. Section 3009.

Some states have amended their consumer protection statutes to cover Internet transactions as well. For example, the California legislature revised its Business and Professional Code to include transactions conducted over the Internet or by "any other electronic means of communication." Previously, that code covered only telephone, mail-order catalogue, radio, and television sales. Now any entity selling over the Internet in California must explicitly create an on-screen notice indicating its refund and return policies, where its business is physically located, its legal name, and a number of other details. Various states are also setting up information sites to help consumers protect themselves.

Health and Safety Protection

The laws discussed earlier regarding the labeling and packaging of products go a long way toward promoting consumer health and safety. There is a significant distinction, however, between regulating the information dispensed about a product and regulating the actual content of the product. The classic example is tobacco products. Producers of tobacco products are required to warn consumers about the hazards associated with the use of their products, but the sale of tobacco products has not been subjected to significant restrictions or banned outright despite the obvious dangers to health. We now examine various laws that regulate the actual products made available to consumers.

BE AWARE The Food and Drug Administration is authorized to obtain, among other things, orders for the recall and seizure of certain products.

Food and Drugs   The first federal legislation regulating food and drugs was enacted in 1906 as the Pure Food and Drugs Act.[31] That law, as amended in 1938, exists now as the Federal Food, Drug and Cosmetic Act (FFDCA).[32] The act protects consumers against adulterated and misbranded foods and drugs. In its present form, the act establishes food standards, specifies safe levels of potentially hazardous food additives, and sets classifications of food and food advertising.

Most of these statutory requirements are monitored and enforced by the Food and Drug Administration (FDA). Under an extensive set of procedures established by the FDA, drugs must be shown to be effective as well as safe before they may be marketed to the public, and the use of some food additives suspected of being carcinogenic is prohibited. A 1976 amendment to the FFDCA[33] authorizes the FDA to regulate medical devices, such as pacemakers and other health devices or equipment, and to withdraw from the market any such device that is mislabeled.

ON THE WEB

The Web site of the Consumer Product Safety Commission offers a business information page that provides the text of regulations and laws, Federal Register Notices, and other information. Go to

www.cpsc.gov/businfo/businfo.html.

Consumer Product Safety   In 1972, Congress enacted the Consumer Product Safety Act,[34] which created the first comprehensive scheme of regulation over matters concerning consumer safety. The act also established the Consumer Product Safety Commission (CPSC) and gave it far-reaching authority over consumer safety.

The CPSC's Authority.   The CPSC conducts research on the safety of individual products and maintains a clearinghouse on the risks associated with various products. The Consumer Product Safety Act authorizes the CPSC to set standards for consumer products and to ban the manufacture and sale of any product that the commission deems to be potentially hazardous to consumers. The CPSC also has authority to remove from the market any products it believes to be imminently hazardous and to require manufacturers to report on any products already sold or intended for sale if the products have proved to be hazardous. Additionally, the CPSC administers other product-safety legislation,

---

31. 21 U.S.C. Sections 1–5, 7–15.
32. 21 U.S.C. Section 301.
33. 21 U.S.C. Sections 352(o), 360(j), 360(k), and 360c–360k.
34. 15 U.S.C. Section 2051.

including the Child Protection and Toy Safety Act of 1969[35] and the Federal Hazardous Substances Act of 1960.[36]

The CPSC's authority is sufficiently broad to allow it to ban any product that the commission believes poses merely an "unreasonable risk" to the consumer. Products banned by the CPSC have included various types of fireworks, cribs, and toys, as well as many products containing asbestos or vinyl chloride.

Notification Requirements. The Consumer Product Safety Act imposes notification requirements on distributors of consumer products. Distributors must immediately notify the CPSC when they receive information that a product "contains a defect which . . . creates a substantial risk to the public" or "an unreasonable risk of serious injury or death."

■EXAMPLE 13.19 A corporation, now known as Aroma Housewares Company, had been distributing a particular model of juicer for just over a year when it began receiving letters from customers. They complained that during operation the juicer had suddenly exploded, sending pieces of glass and razor-sharp metal across the room. The company received twenty-three letters from angry consumers about the exploding juicer but waited more than six months before notifying the CPSC that the product posed a significant risk to the public. In a case filed by the federal government, the court held that when a company first receives information regarding a threat, the company is required to report the problem within twenty-four hours to the CPSC. The court also found that even if the company had to investigate the allegations, it should not have taken more than ten days to verify the information and report the problem. The court therefore held that the company had violated the law and ordered it to pay damages.[37] ■

Credit Protection

Considering the extensive use of credit by U.S. consumers, credit protection is one of the most important aspects of consumer protection legislation. A key statute regulating the credit and credit-card industries is the Truth-in-Lending Act (TILA), the name commonly given to Title 1 of the Consumer Credit Protection Act (CCPA),[38] which was passed by Congress in 1968.

Truth in Lending The TILA is basically a *disclosure law*. It is administered by the Federal Reserve Board and requires sellers and lenders to disclose credit terms or loan terms so that individuals can shop around for the best financing arrangements. TILA requirements apply only to persons who, in the ordinary course of business, lend funds, sell on credit, or arrange for the extension of credit. Thus, sales or loans made between two consumers do not come under the protection of the act. Additionally, this law protects only debtors who are *natural* persons (as opposed to the artificial "person" of a corporation); it does not extend to other legal entities.

The disclosure requirements are found in Regulation Z, which was promulgated by the Federal Reserve Board. If the contracting parties are subject to the TILA, the requirements of Regulation Z apply to any transaction involving an installment sales contract that calls for payment to be made in more than four installments. Transactions subject to Regulation Z typically include installment loans, retail and installment sales, car loans,

NOTE The Federal Reserve Board is part of the Federal Reserve System, which influences the lending and investing activities of commercial banks and the cost and availability of credit.

---

35. 15 U.S.C. Section 1262(e).
36. 15 U.S.C. Sections 1261–1273.
37. *United States v. Miram Enterprises, Inc.*, 185 F.Supp.2d 1148 (S.D.Ca. 2002).
38. 15 U.S.C. Sections 1601–1693r. The act was amended in 1980 by the Truth-in-Lending Simplification and Reform Act.

home-improvement loans, and certain real estate loans if the amount of financing is less than $25,000.

Under the provisions of the TILA, all of the terms of a credit instrument must be clearly and conspicuously disclosed. The TILA provides for contract rescission (cancellation) if a creditor fails to follow the exact procedures required by the act.[39]

Equal Credit Opportunity. In 1974, Congress enacted, as an amendment to the TILA, the Equal Credit Opportunity Act (ECOA).[40] The ECOA prohibits the denial of credit solely on the basis of race, religion, national origin, color, gender, marital status, or age. The act also prohibits credit discrimination on the basis of whether an individual receives certain forms of income, such as public-assistance benefits.

Under the ECOA, a creditor may not require the signature of an applicant's spouse, or a cosigner, on a credit instrument if the applicant qualifies under the creditor's standards of creditworthiness for the amount requested. **■EXAMPLE 13.20** Tonja, an African American, applied for financing with a used-car dealer. The dealer reviewed Tonja's credit report and, without submitting the application to the lender, decided that she would not qualify. Instead of informing Tonja that she did not qualify, the dealer told her that she needed a cosigner on the loan to purchase the car. According to a federal appellate court in 2004, the dealership qualified as a creditor in this situation because it unilaterally denied credit. Thus, the dealer could be held liable under the ECOA.[41] ■

Credit-Card Rules. The TILA also contains provisions regarding credit cards. One provision limits the liability of a cardholder to $50 per card for unauthorized charges made before the creditor is notified that the card has been lost. Another provision prohibits a credit-card company from billing a consumer for any unauthorized charges if the credit card was improperly issued by the company. **■EXAMPLE 13.21** Suppose that a consumer receives an unsolicited credit card in the mail and the card is later stolen and used by the thief to make purchases. In this situation, the consumer to whom the card was sent will not be liable for the unauthorized charges. ■

Other provisions of the act set out specific procedures for both the credit-card company and its cardholder to use in settling disputes related to credit-card purchases. These procedures would be used if, for example, a cardholder thinks that an error has occurred in billing or wishes to withhold payment for a faulty product purchased by credit card.

Consumer Leases. The Consumer Leasing Act (CLA) of 1988[42] amended the TILA to provide protection for consumers who lease automobiles and other goods. The CLA applies to those who lease or arrange to lease consumer goods in the ordinary course of their business. The act applies only if the goods are priced at $25,000 or less and if the lease term exceeds four months. The CLA and its implementing regulation, Regulation M,[43] require lessors to disclose in writing all of the material terms of the lease.

Fair Credit Reporting In 1970, to protect consumers against inaccurate credit reporting, Congress enacted the Fair Credit Reporting Act (FCRA).[44] The act provides that consumer credit reporting agencies may issue credit reports to users only for specified

---

39. Note, though, that amendments to the TILA enacted in 1995 prevent borrowers from rescinding loans because of minor clerical errors in closing documents [15 U.S.C. Sections 1605, 1631, 1635, 1640, and 1641].
40. 15 U.S.C. Section 1643.
41. *Treadway v. Gateway Chevrolet Oldsmobile, Inc.,* 362 F.3d 971 (7th Cir. 2004).
42. 15 U.S.C. Sections 1667–1667e.
43. 12 C.F.R. Part 213.
44. 15 U.S.C. Sections 1681 *et seq.*

purposes, including the extension of credit, the issuance of insurance policies, compliance with a court order, and compliance with a consumer's request for a copy of her or his own credit report. The act further provides that any time a consumer is denied credit or insurance on the basis of the consumer's credit report, or is charged more than others ordinarily would be for credit or insurance, the consumer must be notified of that fact and of the name and address of the credit reporting agency that issued the credit report.

Under the FCRA, consumers may request the source of any information being given out by a credit agency, as well as the identity of anyone who has received an agency's report. Consumers are also permitted to have access to the information contained about them in a credit reporting agency's files. If a consumer discovers that the agency's files contain inaccurate information about his or her credit standing, the agency, on the consumer's written request, must investigate the matter and delete any unverifiable or erroneous information within a reasonable period of time. The agency's investigation should include contacting the creditor whose information the consumer disputes and should involve a systematic examination of its records.

The FCRA protects consumers from inaccurate information in credit reports by requiring that lenders and other creditors report correct, relevant, and up-to-date information in a confidential and responsible manner. The FCRA allows an award of punitive damages for a "willful" violation. Did the circumstances in the following case warrant an award of punitive damages? That was the question before the court.

CASE 13.3 **Saunders v. Equifax Information Services, L.L.C.**

United States District Court, Eastern District of Virginia, Richmond Division, 469 F.Supp.2d 343 (2007).

FACTS Rex Saunders obtained an auto loan from Branch Banking & Trust Company of Virginia (BB & T). Contrary to its usual procedure, BB & T did not give Saunders a payment coupon book and rebuffed his attempts to make payments on the loan. In fact, BB & T told him that he did not have a loan from the firm. A copy of the title for the vehicle indicated no loan. Eventually, however, BB & T discovered its mistake and demanded full payment, plus interest and penalties. When payment was not immediately forthcoming, BB & T declared Saunders to be in default and repossessed and sold the car. The lender forwarded adverse credit information about Saunders, with added derogatory details, to credit reporting agencies, without noting that Saunders disputed the information. Saunders filed a suit in a federal district court against BB & T and others, alleging chiefly violations of the Fair Credit Reporting Act (FCRA). On the claims against BB & T, a jury awarded Saunders $1,000 in statutory damages and $80,000 in punitive damages. BB & T asked the court to reduce the punitive award to $4,000. BB & T argued that the credit information was "factually accurate," the mistakes in administering Saunders's loan were not "willful," and the amount of the award was arbitrary.

ISSUE Was Saunders entitled to the award of $80,000 in punitive damages?

DECISION Yes. The court held that BB & T's actions were "willful" violations of the FCRA.

REASON The court recognized the "imprecise manner" in which punitive damages are awarded. The court explained that "the most important *indicium* [indication] of the reasonableness of a punitive damages award is the degree of reprehensibility of the defendant's conduct. * * * [P]unitive damages should only be awarded if the defendant's culpability, after having paid compensatory damages, is so reprehensible [worthy of censure] as to warrant the imposition of further sanctions to achieve punishment or deterrence." Here, "BB & T caused great financial and emotional strain to a consumer by failing to properly 'book' Saunders' loan in violation of BB & T's own internal operating procedures." The jury based its decision on sufficient evidence of misconduct by BB & T, as well as the lender's economic ability, in terms of its substantial net worth of more than $3.2 billion, to pay the amount of the award. Such an assessment has "legitimate punitive and deterrent purpose[s]." Only when the amount can

CASE 13.3—Continues next page

CASE 13.3–Continued

be fairly categorized as "grossly excessive" in relation to these purposes does the award "enter the zone of arbitrariness." The amount of the award in Saunders's favor "enters no such zone of arbitrariness as it reasonably punishes BB & T for particularly egregious [appalling] conduct * * * , not for being an unsavory individual or business."

FOR CRITICAL ANALYSIS–Social Consideration
The jury awarded Saunders only $1,000 in statutory damages, but under the circumstances, this was the maximum allowed under the FCRA. What does the fact that the jury felt compelled to award the maximum allowable amount indicate about its award of punitive damages?

ON THE WEB

The Consumer Action Web site offers useful information and links to consumer protection agencies at the city, county, and state level. Go to

www.consumeraction.gov.

Fair and Accurate Credit Transactions Act   In an effort to combat rampant identity theft (discussed in Chapter 6), Congress passed the Fair and Accurate Credit Transactions (FACT) Act of 2003.[45] The act established a national fraud alert system so that consumers who suspect that they have been or may be victimized by identity theft can place an alert in their credit files. The FACT Act also requires the major credit reporting agencies to provide consumers with a free copy of their credit reports every twelve months. Another provision requires account numbers on credit-card receipts to be shortened (truncated) so that merchants, employees, and others who have access to the receipts cannot obtain a consumer's name and full credit-card number. The act also mandates that financial institutions work with the Federal Trade Commission to identify "red flag" indicators of identity theft and to develop rules for disposing of sensitive credit information.

The FACT Act also gives consumers who have been victimized by identity theft some assistance in rebuilding their credit reputations. For example, credit reporting agencies must stop reporting allegedly fraudulent account information once the consumer establishes that identify theft has occurred. Business owners and creditors are required to provide a consumer with copies of any records that can help the consumer prove that a particular account or transaction is fraudulent (records showing that an account was created by a fraudulent signature, for example). In addition, to help prevent the spread of erroneous credit information, the act allows consumers to report the accounts affected by identity theft directly to the creditors.

Fair Debt-Collection Practices   In 1977, Congress enacted the Fair Debt Collection Practices Act (FDCPA)[46] in an attempt to curb what were perceived to be abuses by collection agencies. The act applies only to specialized debt-collection agencies that regularly attempt to collect debts on behalf of someone else, usually for a percentage of the amount owed. Creditors attempting to collect debts are not covered by the act unless, by misrepresenting themselves, they cause the debtors to believe that they are collection agencies. Attorneys who regularly try to obtain payment of consumer debts through legal proceedings, however, do meet the FDCPA's definition of "debt collector."[47]

The act explicitly prohibits a collection agency from using any of the following tactics:

1 Contacting the debtor at the debtor's place of employment if the debtor's employer objects.

2 Contacting the debtor during inconvenient or unusual times (for example, calling the debtor at three o'clock in the morning) or at any time if an attorney is representing the debtor.

3 Contacting third parties other than the debtor's parents, spouse, or financial adviser about payment of a debt unless a court authorizes such action.

---

45. Pub. L. No. 108-159, 117 Stat. 1952 (December 4, 2003).
46. 15 U.S.C. Section 1692.
47. *Heintz v. Jenkins*, 514 U.S. 291, 115 S.Ct. 1489, 131 L.Ed.2d 395 (1995).

4 Using harassment or intimidation (for example, using abusive language or threatening violence) or employing false and misleading information (for example, posing as a police officer).

5 Communicating with the debtor at any time after receiving notice that the debtor is refusing to pay the debt, except to advise the debtor of further action to be taken by the collection agency.

The enforcement of the act is primarily the responsibility of the Federal Trade Commission. The FDCPA provides that a debt collector who fails to comply with the act is liable for actual damages, plus additional damages not to exceed $1,000[48] and attorneys' fees.

---

48. According to the U.S. Court of Appeals for the Sixth Circuit, the $1,000 limit on damages applies to each lawsuit, not to each violation. See *Wright v. Finance Service of Norwalk, Inc.*, 22 F.3d 647 (6th Cir. 1994).

REVIEWING **Consumer Law**

Leota Sage saw a local motorcycle dealer's advertisement in a newspaper offering a MetroRider EZ electric scooter for $1,699. When she went to the dealership, however, she learned that the EZ model was sold out. The salesperson told Sage that he still had the higher-end MetroRider FX model in stock for $2,199 and would sell her one for $1,999. Sage was disappointed but decided to purchase the FX model. Sage told the sales representative that she wished to purchase the scooter on credit and was directed to the dealer's credit department. As she filled out credit forms, the clerk told Sage, an African American female, that she would need a cosigner. Sage could not understand why she would need a cosigner and asked to speak to the manager. The manager apologized, told her that the clerk was mistaken, and said that he would "speak to" the clerk. The manager completed Sage's credit application, and Sage then rode the scooter home. Seven months later, Sage received a letter from the FTC asking questions about her transaction with the motorcycle dealer and informing her that it had received complaints from other consumers. Using the information presented in the chapter, answer the following questions.

1 Did the dealer engage in deceptive advertising? Why or why not?

2 Suppose that Sage had ordered the scooter through the dealer's Web site but the dealer had been unable to deliver it by the date promised. What would the FTC have required the merchant to do in that situation?

3 Assuming that the clerk required a cosigner based on Sage's race or gender, what act prohibits such credit discrimination?

4 What organization has the authority to ban the sale of scooters based on safety concerns?

APPLICATION **How Do Sellers Create Warranties?***

Warranties are important in both commercial and consumer purchase transactions. There are three types of product warranties: express warranties, implied warranties of mer- chantability, and implied warranties of fitness for a particular purpose. If you are a seller of products, you can make or create any one of these warranties, which are available to both consumers and commercial purchasers. First and foremost, sellers and buyers need to know whether warranties have been created.

* This *Application* is not meant to serve as a substitute for the services of an attorney who is licensed to practice law in your state.

(Continued)

Warranty Creation

Express warranties do not have to be labeled as such, but statements of simple opinion or value generally do not constitute express warranties. Express warranties can be made by descriptions of the goods or by showing a sample or model of the goods. Express warranties can be found in a seller's advertisement, brochure, or promotional materials or can be made orally or in an express writing. A sales representative should use care in describing the merits of a product; otherwise, the seller could be held to an express warranty. If an express warranty is not intended, the sales pitch should not promise too much.

In most sales, because the seller is a merchant, the purchased goods carry the implied warranty of merchantability. If you are a seller, you must also be aware of the importance of the implied warranty of fitness for a particular purpose. Assume that a customer comes to your sales representative, describes the work to be done in detail, and says, "I really need something that can do the job." Your sales representative replies, "This product will do the job," and the customer purchases the recommended product. An implied warranty that the product is fit for that particular purpose has been created.

Warranty Disclaimers

Many sellers, particularly in commercial sales, try to limit or disclaim warranties. The Uniform Commercial Code permits all warranties, including express warranties, to be excluded or negated. Conspicuous statements—such as "THERE ARE NO WARRANTIES WHICH EXTEND BEYOND THE DESCRIPTION ON THE FACE HEREOF" or "THERE ARE NO IMPLIED WARRANTIES OF FITNESS FOR A PARTICULAR PURPOSE OR MERCHANTABILITY WHICH ACCOMPANY THIS SALE"—can be used to disclaim the implied warranties of fitness and merchantability. Used goods are sometimes sold "as is" or "with all faults" so that implied warranties of fitness and merchantability are disclaimed. Whenever these warranties are disclaimed, a purchaser should be aware that the product may not be of even average quality.

CHECKLIST FOR THE SELLER

1 If you wish to limit warranties, do so by means of a carefully worded and prominently placed (conspicuous) written or printed provision that a reasonable person would understand and accept. Instruct your sales associates to point out the disclaimer to consumer-buyers when forming the sales contract.

2 If you are a merchant-seller, remember that in the absence of a disclaimer, almost all sales carry the implied warranty of merchantability.

3 If you do not intend to make an express warranty, do not make a promise or an affirmation of fact concerning the performance or quality of a product you are selling.

KEY TERMS

bait-and-switch advertising 398
cease-and-desist order 399
"cooling-off" laws 401
counteradvertising 399
deceptive advertising 398
express warranty 382

implied warranty 383
implied warranty of fitness
  for a particular purpose 385
implied warranty
  of merchantability 383
lien 381

market-share liability 395
product liability 388
Regulation Z 401
statute of repose 395
unreasonably dangerous
  product 391

CHAPTER SUMMARY Warranties, Product Liability, and Consumer Law

WARRANTIES

Warranties of Title
(See pages 381–382.)

The UCC provides for the following warranties of title [UCC 2–312, 2A–211]:

1. *Good title*—A seller warrants that he or she has the right to pass good and rightful title to the goods.

2. *No liens*—A seller warrants that the goods sold are free of any encumbrances (claims, charges, or liabilities—usually called *liens*). A lessor warrants that the lessee will not be disturbed in her or his possession of the goods by the claims of a third party.

CHAPTER SUMMARY	**Warranties, Product Liability, and Consumer Law—Continued**
Warranties of Title—Continued	3. *No infringements*—A merchant-seller warrants that the goods are free of infringement claims (claims that a patent, trademark, or copyright has been infringed) by third parties. Lessors make similar warranties.
Express Warranties (See pages 382–383.)	Under the UCC, an express warranty arises under the UCC when a seller or lessor indicates, as part of the basis of the bargain, any of the following: 1. An affirmation or promise of fact. 2. A description of the goods. 3. A sample shown as conforming to the contract goods [UCC 2–313, 2A–210].
Implied Warranty of Merchantability (See pages 383–384.)	When a seller or lessor is a merchant who deals in goods of the kind sold or leased, the seller or lessor warrants that the goods sold or leased are properly packaged and labeled, are of proper quality, and are reasonably fit for the ordinary purposes for which such goods are used [UCC 2–314, 2A–212].
Implied Warranty of Fitness for a Particular Purpose (See page 385.)	Arises when the buyer's or lessee's purpose or use is expressly or impliedly known by the seller or lessor, and the buyer or lessee purchases or leases the goods in reliance on the seller's or lessor's selection [UCC 2–315, 2A–213].
Other Implied Warranties (See page 385.)	Other implied warranties can arise as a result of course of dealing or usage of trade [UCC 2–314(3), 2A–212(3)].
Warranty Disclaimers (See pages 386–387.)	Express warranties can be disclaimed in a written disclaimer in language that is clear and conspicuous and called to the buyer's or lessee's attention at the time the contract is formed. A disclaimer of the implied warranty of merchantability must specifically mention the word *merchantability.* It need not be in writing, but if it is written, it must be conspicuous. A disclaimer of the implied warranty of fitness *must* be in writing and be conspicuous, though it need not mention the word *fitness.*
Magnuson-Moss Warranty Act (See page 388.)	Under the Magnuson-Moss Warranty Act, Express written warranties covering consumer goods priced at more than $25, *if made,* must be labeled as one of the following: 1. *Full warranty*—Free repair or replacement of defective parts; refund or replacement for goods if they cannot be repaired in a reasonable time. 2. *Limited warranty*—When less than a full warranty is being offered.
	PRODUCT LIABILITY
Liability Based on Negligence (See pages 388–389.)	1. The manufacturer must use due care in designing the product, selecting materials, using the appropriate production process, assembling and testing the product, and placing adequate warnings on the label or product. 2. Privity of contract is not required. A manufacturer is liable for failure to exercise due care to any person who sustains an injury proximately caused by a negligently made (defective) product.
Liability Based on Misrepresentation (See page 389.)	Fraudulent misrepresentation of a product may result in product liability based on the tort of fraud.
Requirements for Strict Liability (See pages 391–392.)	1. The defendant must sell the product in a defective condition. 2. The defendant must normally be engaged in the business of selling that product. 3. The product must be unreasonably dangerous to the user or consumer because of its defective condition (in most states).

(Continued)

CHAPTER SUMMARY	Warranties, Product Liability, and Consumer Law—Continued
Requirements for Strict Liability— Continued	4. The plaintiff must incur physical harm to self or property by use or consumption of the product. (Courts will also extend strict liability to include injured bystanders.) 5. The defective condition must be the proximate cause of the injury or damage. 6. The goods must not have been substantially changed from the time the product was sold to the time the injury was sustained.
Strict Liability— Product Defects (See pages 392–394.)	A product may be defective in three basic ways: 1. In its manufacture. 2. In its design. 3. In the instructions or warnings that come with it.
Market-Share Liability (See page 395.)	When plaintiffs cannot prove which of many distributors of a defective product supplied the particular product that caused the plaintiffs' injuries, some courts apply market-share liability. All firms that manufactured and distributed the harmful product during the period in question are then held liable for the plaintiffs' injuries in proportion to the firms' respective shares of the market, as directed by the court.
Other Applications of Strict Liability (See page 395.)	1. Manufacturers and other sellers are liable for harms suffered by bystanders as a result of defective products. 2. Suppliers of component parts are strictly liable for defective parts that, when incorporated into a product, cause injuries to users.
Defenses to Product Liability (See pages 396–397.)	1. *Assumption of risk*—The user or consumer knew of the risk of harm and voluntarily assumed it. 2. *Product misuse*—The user or consumer misused the product in a way unforeseeable by the manufacturer. 3. *Comparative negligence (fault)*—Liability may be distributed between the plaintiff and the defendant under the doctrine of comparative negligence if the plaintiff's misuse of the product contributed to the risk of injury. 4. *Commonly known dangers*—If a defendant succeeds in convincing the court that a plaintiff's injury resulted from a commonly known danger, such as the danger associated with using a sharp knife, the defendant will not be liable.
	CONSUMER PROTECTION LAWS

Deceptive Advertising (See pages 398–399.)	1. *Definition of deceptive advertising*—Generally, an advertising claim will be deemed deceptive if it would mislead a reasonable consumer.
	
	2. *Bait-and-switch advertising*—Advertising a lower-priced product (the "bait") when the intention is not to sell the advertised product but to lure consumers into the store and convince them to buy a higher-priced product (the "switch") is prohibited by the FTC.
	
	3. *Online deceptive advertising*—The FTC has issued guidelines to help online businesses comply with existing laws prohibiting deceptive advertising. The guidelines do not set forth new rules but rather describe how existing laws apply to online advertising.
	
	4. *FTC actions against deceptive advertising*—
	
	  a. Cease-and-desist orders—Requiring the advertiser to stop the challenged advertising.
	
	  b. Counteradvertising—Requiring the advertiser to advertise to correct the earlier misinformation.

Telemarketing and Electronic Advertising (See page 400.)	The Telephone Consumer Protection Act of 1991 prohibits telephone solicitation using an automatic telephone dialing system or a prerecorded voice, as well as the transmission of advertising materials via fax without first obtaining the recipient's permission to do so.

CHAPTER SUMMARY Warranties, Product Liability, and Consumer Law—Continued

Labeling and Packaging (See pages 400–401.)	Manufacturers must comply with the labeling or packaging requirements for their specific products. In general, all labels must be accurate and not misleading.
Sales (See pages 401–402.)	1. *Telephone and mail-order sales*—Federal and state statutes and regulations govern certain practices of sellers who solicit over the telephone or through the mails and prohibit the use of the mails to defraud individuals. 2. *Online sales*—Increasingly, the Internet is being used to conduct business-to-consumer transactions. Both state and federal laws protect consumers to some extent against fraudulent and deceptive online sales practices.
Health and Safety Protection (See pages 402–403.)	1. *Food and drugs*—The Federal Food, Drug and Cosmetic Act of 1938, as amended, protects consumers against adulterated and misbranded foods and drugs. The act establishes food standards, specifies safe levels of potentially hazardous food additives, and sets classifications of food and food advertising. 2 *Consumer product safety*—The Consumer Product Safety Act of 1972 seeks to protect consumers from risk of injury from hazardous products. The Consumer Product Safety Commission has the power to remove products that are deemed imminently hazardous from the market and to ban the manufacture and sale of hazardous products.

Credit Protection (See pages 403–407.)	1. *Consumer Credit Protection Act, Title I (Truth-in-Lending Act, or TILA)*—A disclosure law that requires sellers and lenders to disclose credit terms or loan terms in certain transactions, including retail and installment sales and loans, car loans, home-improvement loans, and certain real estate loans. Additionally, the TILA provides for the following:
	
	  a. Equal credit opportunity—Creditors are prohibited from discriminating on the basis of race, religion, marital status, gender, and so on.
	
	  b. Credit-card protection—Credit-card users may withhold payment for a faulty product purchased by credit card, or for an error in billing, until the dispute is resolved; liability of cardholders for unauthorized charges is limited to $50, providing notice requirements are met; consumers are not liable for unauthorized charges made on unsolicited credit cards.
	
	  c. Consumer leases—The Consumer Leasing Act (CLA) of 1988 protects consumers who lease automobiles and other goods priced at $25,000 or less if the lease term exceeds four months.
	
	2. *Fair Credit Reporting Act*—Entitles consumers to request verification of the accuracy of a credit report and to have unverified or false information removed from their files.
	
	3. *Fair Debt Collection Practices Act*—Prohibits debt collectors from using unfair debt-collection practices, such as contacting the debtor at his or her place of employment if the employer objects or at unreasonable times, contacting third parties about the debt, and harassing the debtor, for example.

FOR REVIEW

Answers for the even-numbered questions in this For Review *section can be found in Appendix E at the end of this text.*

1 What factors determine whether a seller's or lessor's statement constitutes an express warranty or mere "puffing"?

2 What implied warranties arise under the UCC?

3 Can a manufacturer be held liable to any person who suffers an injury proximately caused by the manufacturer's negligently made product?

4 What defenses to liability can be raised in a product liability lawsuit?

5 What are the major federal statutes providing for consumer protection?

■

QUESTIONS AND CASE PROBLEMS

HYPOTHETICAL SCENARIOS

13.1 Product Liability. Under what contract theory can a seller be held liable to a consumer for physical harm or property damage that is caused by the goods sold? Under what tort theories can the seller be held liable?

13.2 Product Liability. Carmen buys a television set manufactured by AKI Electronics. She is going on vacation, so she takes the set to her mother's house for her mother to use. Because the set is defective, it explodes, causing considerable damage to her mother's house. Carmen's mother sues AKI for the damages to her house. Discuss the theories under which Carmen's mother can recover from AKI.

13.3 Hypothetical Question with Sample Answer. Maria Ochoa receives two new credit cards on May 1. She had solicited one of them from Midtown Department Store, and the other arrived unsolicited from High-Flying Airlines. During the month of May, Ochoa makes numerous credit-card purchases from Midtown Department Store, but she does not use the High-Flying Airlines card. On May 31, a burglar breaks into Ochoa's home and steals both credit cards, along with other items. Ochoa notifies the Midtown Department Store of the theft on June 2, but she fails to notify High-Flying Airlines. Using the Midtown credit card, the burglar makes a $500 purchase on June 1 and a $200 purchase on June 3. The burglar then charges a vacation flight on the High-Flying Airlines card for $1,000 on June 5. Ochoa receives the bills for these charges and refuses to pay them. Discuss Ochoa's liability in these situations.

For a sample answer to Question 13.3, go to Appendix F at the end of this text.

13.4 Implied Warranties. Sam, a farmer, needs to install a piece of equipment in his barn. The equipment, which weighs two thousand pounds, must be lifted thirty feet into a hayloft. Sam goes to Durham Hardware and tells Durham that he needs some heavy-duty rope to be used on his farm. Durham recommends a one-inch-thick nylon rope, and Sam purchases two hundred feet of it. Sam ties the rope around the piece of equipment, puts the rope through a pulley, and with the aid of a tractor lifts the equipment off the ground. Suddenly, the rope breaks. The equipment crashes to the ground and is extensively damaged. Sam files a suit against Durham for breach of the implied warranty of fitness for a particular purpose. Discuss how successful Sam will be with his suit.

■

CASE PROBLEMS

13.5 Fair Credit Reporting Act. Source One Associates, Inc., is based in Poughquag, New York. Peter Easton, Source One's president, is responsible for its daily operations. Between 1995 and 1997, Source One received requests from persons in Massachusetts seeking financial information about individuals and businesses. To obtain this information, Easton first obtained the targeted individuals' credit reports through Equifax Consumer Information Services by claiming the reports would be used only in connection with credit transactions involving the consumers. From the reports, Easton identified financial institutions at which the targeted individuals held accounts and then called the institutions to learn the account balances by impersonating either officers of the institutions or the account holders. The information was then provided to Source One's customers for a fee. Easton did not know why the customers wanted the information. The state ("Commonwealth") of Massachusetts filed a suit in a Massachusetts state court against Source One and Easton, alleging, among other things, violations of the Fair Credit Reporting Act (FCRA). Did the defendants violate the FCRA? Explain. [*Commonwealth v. Source One Associates, Inc.*, 436 Mass. 118, 763 N.E.2d 42 (2002)]

13.6 Case Problem with Sample Answer. Mary Jane Boerner began smoking in 1945 at the age of fifteen. For a short time, she smoked Lucky Strike–brand cigarettes before switching to the Pall Mall brand, which she smoked until she quit altogether in 1981. Pall Malls had higher levels of carcinogenic tar than other cigarettes and lacked effective filters, which would have reduced the amount of tar inhaled into the lungs. In 1996, Mary Jane developed lung cancer. She and Henry Boerner, her husband, filed a suit in a federal district court against Brown & Williamson Tobacco Co., the maker of Pall Malls. The Boerners claimed, among other things, that Pall Malls contained a design defect. Mary Jane died in 1999. According to Dr. Peter Marvin, her treating physician, she died from the effects of cigarette smoke. Henry continued the suit, offering evidence that Pall Malls featured a filter that actually increased the amount of tar taken into the body. When is a product defective in design? Does this product meet the requirements? Why or why not? [*Boerner v. Brown & Williamson Tobacco Co.*, 394 F.3d 594 (8th Cir. 2005)]

After you have answered Problem 13.6, compare your answer with the sample answer given on the Web site that accompanies this text. Go to academic.cengage.com/blaw/blt**, select "Chapter 13," and click on "Case Problem with Sample Answer."**

13.7 **Implied Warranties.** Shalom Malul contracted with Capital Cabinets, Inc., in August 1999 for new kitchen cabinets made by Holiday Kitchens. The price was $10,900. On Capital's recommendation, Malul hired Barry Burger to install the cabinets for $1,600. Burger finished the job in March 2000, and Malul contracted for more cabinets at a price of $2,300, which Burger installed in April. Within a couple of weeks, the doors on several of the cabinets began to "melt"—the laminate (surface covering) began to pull away from the substrate (the material underneath the surface). Capital replaced several of the doors, but the problem occurred again, affecting a total of six of thirty doors. A Holiday Kitchens representative inspected the cabinets and concluded that the melting was due to excessive heat, the result of the doors being placed too close to the stove. Malul filed a suit in a New York state court against Capital, alleging, among other things, a breach of the implied warranty of merchantability. Were these goods "merchantable"? Why or why not? [*Malul v. Capital Cabinets, Inc.*, 191 Misc.2d 399, 740 N.Y.S.2d 828 (N.Y.City Civ.Ct. 2002)]

13.8 **Debt Collection.** 55th Management Corp. in New York City owns residential property that it leases to various tenants. In June 2000, claiming that one of the tenants, Leslie Goldman, owed more than $13,000 in back rent, 55th retained Jeffrey Cohen, an attorney, to initiate nonpayment proceedings. Cohen filed a petition in a New York state court against Goldman, seeking recovery of the unpaid rent and at least $3,000 in attorneys' fees. After receiving notice of the petition, Goldman filed a suit in a federal district court against Cohen. Goldman contended that the notice of the petition constituted an initial contact that, under the Fair Debt Collection Practices Act (FDCPA), required a validation notice. Because Cohen did not give Goldman a validation notice at the time, or within five days, of the notice of the petition, Goldman argued that Cohen was in violation of the FDCPA. Should the filing of a suit in a state court be considered "communication," requiring a debt collector to provide a validation notice under the FDCPA? Why or why not? [*Goldman v. Cohen*, 445 F.3d 152 (2d Cir. 2006)]

13.9 **Express Warranties.** Videotape is recorded magnetically. The magnetic particles that constitute the recorded image are bound to the tape's polyester base. The binder that holds the particles to the base breaks down over time. This breakdown, which is called sticky shed syndrome, causes the image to deteriorate. The Walt Disney Co. made many of its movies available on tape. Buena Vista Home Entertainment, Inc., sold the tapes, which it described as part of a "Gold Collection" or "Masterpiece Collection." The advertising included such statements as "Give Your Children The Memories Of A Lifetime—Collect Each Timeless Masterpiece!" and "Available For A Limited Time Only!" Charmaine Schreib and others who bought the tapes filed a suit in an Illinois state court against Disney and Buena Vista, alleging, among other things, breach of warranty. The plaintiffs claimed that the defendants' marketing promised the tapes would last for generations. In reality, the tapes were as subject to sticky shed syndrome as other tapes. Did the ads create an express warranty? In whose favor should the court rule on this issue? Explain. [*Schreib v. The Walt Disney Co.*, 219 Ill.2d 597, 852 N.E.2d 249 (2006)]

13.10 **A Question of Ethics.** *One of the products that McDonald's Corp. sells is the Happy Meal, which consists of a McDonald's food entrée, a small order of french fries, a small drink, and a toy. In the early 1990s, McDonald's began to aim its Happy Meal marketing at children ages one to three. In 1995, McDonald's began making nutritional information for its food products available in documents known as "McDonald's Nutrition Facts." Each document lists each food item that the restaurant serves and provides a nutritional breakdown, but the Happy Meal is not included. Marc Cohen filed a suit in an Illinois state court, alleging, among other things, that McDonald's had violated a state law prohibiting consumer fraud and deceptive business practices by failing to adhere to the National Labeling and Education Act of 1990 (NLEA). The court dismissed the suit, and Cohen appealed to a state intermediate appellate court, which affirmed the dismissal, holding that the NLEA preempted the plaintiff's claims. In view of these facts, consider the following questions. [Cohen v. McDonald's Corp., 347 Ill.App.3d 627, 808 N.E.2d 1 (1 Dist. 2004)]*

1 What does the NLEA provide? The NLEA sets out different requirements for products specifically intended for children under the age of four. Does this make sense? Is this ethical? Why or why not?

2 Because the federal government has not established certain requirements for children under the age of four, there are no regulations under the NLEA for reporting these requirements. Should a state court impose such regulations? Explain.

CRITICAL THINKING AND WRITING ASSIGNMENTS

13.11 Critical Legal Thinking. The United States has the strictest product liability laws in the world today. Why do you think many other countries, particularly developing countries, are more lax with respect to holding manufacturers liable for product defects?

13.12 Critical Thinking and Writing Assignment for Business. Many states have enacted laws that go even further than federal law to protect the interests of consumers. These laws vary tremendously from state to state. Generally, is having different laws fair to sellers who may be prohibited from engaging in a practice in one state that is legal in another? How might these different laws affect a business? Is it fair that residents of one state have more protection than residents of another? Or should all consumer protection laws be federally legislated?

13.13 Video Question. Go to this text's Web site at **academic. cengage.com/blaw/blt** and select "Chapter 13." Click on "Video Questions" and view the video titled *Warranties.* Then answer the following questions.

1 Discuss whether the grocery store's label of a "Party Platter for Twenty" creates an express warranty under the Uniform Commercial Code that the platter will actually serve twenty people.

2 List and describe any implied warranties discussed in the chapter that apply to this scenario.

3 How would a court determine whether Oscar had breached any express or implied warranties concerning the quantity of food on the platter?

■

ONLINE ACTIVITIES

PRACTICAL INTERNET EXERCISES

Go to this text's Web site at **academic.cengage.com/blaw/blt**, select "Chapter 13," and click on "Practical Internet Exercises." There you will find the following Internet research exercises that you can perform to learn more about the topics covered in this chapter.

PRACTICAL INTERNET EXERCISE 13-1 LEGAL PERSPECTIVE—Product Liability Litigation

PRACTICAL INTERNET EXERCISE 13-2 MANAGEMENT PERSPECTIVE—Warranties

PRACTICAL INTERNET EXERCISE 13-3 LEGAL PERSPECTIVE—The Food and Drug Administration

BEFORE THE TEST

Go to this text's Web site at **academic.cengage.com/blaw/blt**, select "Chapter 13," and click on "Interactive Quizzes." You will find a number of interactive questions relating to this chapter.

■

CHAPTER 14
Negotiable Instruments

LEARNING OBJECTIVES

AFTER READING THIS CHAPTER, YOU SHOULD BE ABLE
TO ANSWER THE FOLLOWING QUESTIONS:

1 What are the four types of negotiable instruments
with which Article 3 of the UCC is concerned?
Which of these instruments are *orders* to pay, and
which are *promises* to pay?

2 What requirements must an instrument meet to
be negotiable?

3 What are the requirements for attaining HDC
status?

4 What is the key to liability on a negotiable
instrument? What is the difference between
signature liability and warranty liability?

5 Certain defenses are valid against all holders,
including HDCs. What are these defenses called?
Name four defenses that fall within this category.

> **"It took many
> generations for
> people to feel
> comfortable
> accepting paper
> in lieu of gold
> or silver."**
>
> Alan Greenspan, 1926–present
> (Chair of the Board of
> Governors of the Federal
> Reserve System, 1987–2006)

Most commercial transactions would be inconceivable without negotiable instruments. A **negotiable instrument** is a signed writing (record) that contains an unconditional promise or order to pay an exact sum on demand or at a specified future time to a specific person or order, or to bearer. (The term *bearer* refers to a person in possession of an instrument that is payable to bearer or indorsed *in blank,* which will be defined later in this chapter.) Most negotiable instruments are paper documents, which is why they are sometimes referred to as *commercial paper.* The checks you write to pay for groceries, rent, your monthly car payment, insurance premiums, and other items are negotiable instruments.

A negotiable instrument can function as a substitute for cash or as an extension of credit. When a buyer writes a check to pay for goods, the check serves as a substitute for cash. When a buyer gives a seller a promissory note in which the buyer promises to pay the seller the purchase price within sixty days, the seller has essentially extended credit to the buyer for a sixty-day period. For a negotiable instrument to operate *practically* as either a substitute for cash or a credit device, or both, it is essential that the instrument be *easily transferable without danger of being uncollectible.* Each rule described in the following pages can be examined in light of this essential function of negotiable instruments.

Negotiable instruments must meet special requirements relating to form and content. These requirements, which are imposed by Article 3 of the UCC, will be discussed at

NEGOTIABLE INSTRUMENT
A signed writing (record) that
contains an unconditional promise
or order to pay an exact sum on
demand or at an exact future time
to a specific person or order, or to
bearer.

length in this chapter. Article 3 also governs the process of *negotiation* (transferring an instrument from one party to another), as will be discussed. Note that UCC 3–104(b) defines *instrument* as a "negotiable instrument." For that reason, whenever the term *instrument* is used in this book, it refers to a negotiable instrument.

TYPES OF NEGOTIABLE INSTRUMENTS

For an instrument to qualify as a *negotiable instrument*, it must meet the requirements listed as numbers one through six on the facing page. (The requirements for negotiability and the UCC sections pertaining to these requirements are listed and described more fully in Exhibit 14–1 below.)

EXHIBIT 14–1 Requirements for Negotiability

REQUIREMENTS	SECTIONS	BASIC RULES
Must Be in Writing	UCC 3–103(a)(6), (9)	A writing can be on anything that is readily transferable and has a degree of permanence. [See also UCC 1–201(46).]
Must Be Signed by the Maker or Drawer	UCC 1–201(39) 3–103(a)(3), (5) 3–401(b) 3–402	1. The signature can be anyplace on the face of the instrument. 2. It can be in any form (such as a word, mark, or rubber stamp) that purports to be a signature and authenticates the writing. 3. A signature may be made in a representative capacity.
Must Be a Definite Promise or Order	UCC 3–103(a)(6), (9) 3–104(a)	1. A promise must be more than a mere acknowledgment of a debt. 2. The words "I/We promise" or "Pay" meet this criterion.
Must Be Unconditional	UCC 3–106	1. Payment cannot be expressly conditional on the occurrence of an event. 2. Payment cannot be made subject to or governed by another agreement.
Must Be an Order or Promise to Pay a Fixed Amount	UCC 3–104(a) 3–112(b)	An amount may be considered a fixed sum even if it is payable in installments, with a fixed or variable rate of interest, at a stated discount, or at an exchange rate.
Must Be Payable in Money	UCC 3–104(a)(3) 3–107	1. Any medium of exchange recognized as the currency of a government is money. 2. The maker or drawer cannot retain the option to pay the instrument in money or something else.
Must Be Payable on Demand or at a Definite Time	UCC 3–104(a)(2) 3–108(a), (b), (c)	1. Any instrument that is payable on sight, presentation, or issue, or that does not state any time for payment, is a demand instrument. 2. An instrument is still payable at a definite time, even if it is payable on or before a stated date or within a fixed period after sight or if the drawer or maker has an option to extend the time for a definite period. 3. Acceleration clauses do not affect the negotiability of the instrument.
Must Be Payable to Order or to Bearer	UCC 3–104(a)(1), (c) 3–109 3–110(a)	1. An order instrument must identify the payee with reasonable certainty. 2. An instrument that indicates it is not payable to an identified person is payable to bearer. 3. Checks are not required to be payable to order or to bearer.

1 Be in writing.

2 Be signed by the maker or the drawer.

3 Be an unconditional promise or order to pay.

4 State a fixed amount of money.

5 Be payable on demand or at a definite time.

6 Be payable to order or to bearer, unless it is a check.

The UCC specifies four types of negotiable instruments: *drafts, checks, promissory notes,* and *certificates of deposit* (CDs). These instruments, which are summarized briefly in Exhibit 14–2, are frequently divided into the two classifications that we will discuss in the following subsections: *orders to pay* (drafts and checks) and *promises to pay* (promissory notes and CDs).

Negotiable instruments may also be classified as either demand instruments or time instruments. A *demand instrument* is payable on demand; that is, it is payable immediately after it is issued and thereafter for a reasonable period of time. All checks are demand instruments because, by definition, they must be payable on demand. A *time instrument* is payable at a future date.

Drafts and Checks (Orders to Pay)

A **draft** is an unconditional written order to pay rather than a promise to pay. Drafts involve three parties. The party creating the draft (the **drawer**) orders another party (the **drawee**) to pay money, usually to a third party (the **payee**). The most common type of draft is a check, but drafts other than checks may be used in commercial transactions.

Time Drafts and Sight Drafts A *time draft* is payable at a definite future time. A *sight draft* (or demand draft) is payable on sight—that is, when it is presented to the drawee (usually a bank or financial institution) for payment. A sight draft may be payable on acceptance. **Acceptance** is the drawee's written promise to pay the draft when it comes due. The usual manner of accepting an instrument is by writing the word *accepted* across

DRAFT
Any instrument drawn on a drawee that orders the drawee to pay a certain sum of money, usually to a third party (the payee), on demand or at a definite future time.

DRAWER
The party that initiates a draft (such as a check), thereby ordering the drawee to pay.

DRAWEE
The party that is ordered to pay a draft or check. With a check, a bank or a financial institution is always the drawee.

PAYEE
A person to whom an instrument is made payable.

ACCEPTANCE
In negotiable instruments law, the drawee's signed agreement to pay a draft when it is presented.

EXHIBIT 14–2	Basic Types of Negotiable Instruments	
INSTRUMENTS	**CHARACTERISTICS**	**PARTIES**
ORDERS TO PAY		
Draft	An order by one person to another person or to bearer [UCC 3–104(e)].	Drawer—The person who signs or makes the order to pay [UCC 3–103(a)(3)].
Check	A draft drawn on a bank and payable on demand [UCC 3–104(f)].[a] (With certain types of checks, such as cashier's checks, the bank is both the drawer and the drawee—see Chapter 15 for details.)	Drawee—The person to whom the order to pay is made [UCC 3–103(a)(2)]. Payee—The person to whom payment is ordered.
PROMISES TO PAY		
Promissory note	A promise by one party to pay money to another party or to bearer [UCC 3–104(e)].	Maker—The person who promises to pay [UCC 3–103(a)(5)]. Payee—The person to whom the promise is made.
Certificate of deposit	A note issued by a bank acknowledging a deposit of funds made payable to the holder of the note [UCC 3–104(j)].	

a. Under UCC 4–105(1), banks include savings banks, savings and loan associations, credit unions, and trust companies.

the face of the instrument, followed by the date of acceptance and the signature of the drawee. A draft can be both a time and a sight draft; such a draft is payable at a stated time after sight (a draft that states it is payable ninety days after sight, for instance).

Exhibit 14–3 shows a typical time draft. For the drawee to be obligated to honor the order, the drawee must be obligated to the drawer either by agreement or through a debtor-creditor relationship. **■EXAMPLE 14.1** On January 16, Ourtown Real Estate Company orders $1,000 worth of office supplies from Eastman Supply Company, with payment due in ninety days. Also on January 16, Ourtown sends Eastman a draft drawn on its account with the First National Bank of Whiteacre as payment. In this scenario, the drawer is Ourtown, the drawee is Ourtown's bank (First National Bank of Whiteacre), and the payee is Eastman Supply Company. ■

TRADE ACCEPTANCE
A draft that is drawn by a seller of goods ordering the buyer to pay a specified sum to the seller, usually at a stated time in the future. The buyer accepts the draft by signing the face of the draft, thus creating an enforceable obligation to pay the draft when it comes due. On a trade acceptance, the seller is both the drawee and the payee.

Trade Acceptances A **trade acceptance** is a draft that is commonly used in the sale of goods. In this type of draft, the seller is both the drawer and the payee. The buyer to whom credit is extended is the drawee. **■EXAMPLE 14.2** Jackson Street Bistro buys its restaurant supplies from Osaka Industries. When Jackson requests supplies, Osaka creates a draft ordering Jackson to pay Osaka for the supplies within ninety days. Jackson accepts the draft by signing its face and is then obligated to make the payment. If Osaka is in need of cash, it can sell the trade acceptance to a third party in the commercial money market (the market for short-term borrowing that businesses use) before the payment is due. ■ (If the draft orders the buyer's bank to pay, it is called a *banker's acceptance*.)

CHECK
A draft drawn by a drawer ordering the drawee bank or financial institution to pay a certain amount of money to the holder on demand.

Checks As mentioned, the most commonly used type of draft is a **check.** The writer of the check is the drawer, the bank on which the check is drawn is the drawee, and the person to whom the check is payable is the payee. As mentioned earlier, checks are demand instruments because they are payable on demand. (Do other countries always consider checks to be negotiable instruments? For a discussion of this issue, see this chapter's *Beyond Our Borders* feature on page 421.)

Checks will be discussed more fully in Chapter 15, but take note that with certain types of checks, such as *cashier's checks*, the bank is both the drawer and the drawee. The bank customer purchases a cashier's check from the bank—that is, pays the bank the amount of the check—and indicates to whom the check should be made payable. The bank, not the customer, is the drawer of the check, as well as the drawee. The idea behind a cashier's check is

EXHIBIT 14–3 A Typical Time Draft

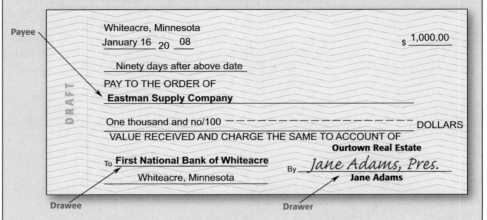

that it functions the same as cash, so there is no question about whether the check will be paid—the bank has committed itself to paying the stated amount on demand.

The following case arose from a party's petition for the discharge of a gambling debt in bankruptcy. Is a casino marker (by which a casino extends credit to a customer) the equivalent of a check? Can a "bad" check alone constitute the making of a false statement (fraud is a ground for denying a discharge in bankruptcy—see Chapter 16)? The court in this case considered these questions.

CASE 14.1   **In re Miller**

United States Bankruptcy Court, Central District of California, 310 Bankr. 185 (2004).

FACTS Obtaining credit at Mandalay Bay casino in Las Vegas, Nevada, is a four-step process. First, the customer applies for credit. Second, the casino verifies that the customer has funds in a bank account to cover the amount. Third, the casino approves the request. Fourth, the customer signs and delivers a marker to the casino, to draw money against the account and buy gambling chips. Richard Miller gambled at Mandalay Bay on at least four occasions in 1999 and 2000. Each time, he obtained credit—for $10,000, $20,000, $30,000, and $25,000, respectively—and each time, he repaid as much of the credit as he used. On his fifth trip, in August 2000, Mandalay granted him $50,000 in credit and accepted four markers—three for $10,000 and one for $20,000—based on the amount in his account with Wells Fargo Bank in Southgate, California. At the end of the month, Mandalay submitted the markers for collection, but the bank returned them unpaid. More than a year later, after paying Mandalay $19,000 of the debt, Miller filed a petition in a federal bankruptcy court, asking for a discharge of the remaining $31,000. Mandalay opposed the discharge, claiming that Miller's markers were fraudulent.

ISSUE Is a casino marker the equivalent of a check?

DECISION Yes. The court discharged the rest of Miller's debt to Mandalay. As for Mandalay's claim, the court held that the delivery of a check alone does not involve the making of a false statement, although this delivery may be part of a larger transaction in which a debtor does make false representations.

REASON To prevail on its claim of fraud, Mandalay needed to show that Miller made an untrue or false statement of fact when he issued his markers in exchange for the casino chips, as would be required if the markers were exchanged for checks. The court recognized that business transactions frequently involve statements but emphasized that these statements are found elsewhere in a transaction, not in a check. Here, Mandalay failed to offer evidence of anything that Miller said or wrote apart from his delivery of the markers. Mandalay presented only the markers, the legal equivalent of checks. In the words of the court, "[d]epositing checks that [are] not supported by sufficient funds * * * [does] not involve making a false statement * * * because a check is literally not a statement. * * * [T]he presentation of a marker, just like a check, does not involve the making of a false statement. Therefore, Miller did not make a false statement or representation by delivering the markers to Mandalay."

WHAT IF THE FACTS WERE DIFFERENT?
Suppose that Mandalay Bay had proved that the debt represented by Miller's markers was induced by fraud. Would the result have been different? Why or why not?

Promissory Notes and Certificates of Deposit (Promises to Pay)

A **promissory note** is a written promise made by one person (the **maker** of the promise to pay) to another (usually a payee). A promissory note, which is often referred to simply as a *note*, can be made payable at a definite time or on demand. It can name a specific payee or merely be payable to bearer (bearer instruments are discussed later in this chapter). **EXAMPLE 14.3** On April 30, Laurence and Margaret Roberts sign a writing unconditionally promising to pay "to the order of" the First National Bank of Whiteacre $3,000 (with

PROMISSORY NOTE
A written promise made by one person (the maker) to pay a fixed amount of money to another person (the payee or a subsequent holder) on demand or on a specified date.

MAKER
One who promises to pay a fixed amount of money to the holder of a promissory note or a certificate of deposit (CD).

8 percent interest) on or before June 29. This writing is a promissory note. ■ A typical promissory note is shown in Exhibit 14–4.

Types of Promissory Notes   Notes are used in a variety of credit transactions and often carry the name of the transaction involved. For example, a note that is secured by personal property, such as an automobile, is called a *collateral note*, because the property pledged as security for the satisfaction of the debt is called collateral (see Chapter 16). A note secured by real estate is called a *mortgage note*. A note payable in installments, such as for payment for a suite of furniture over a twelve-month period, is called an *installment note*.

Certificate of Deposit   A **certificate of deposit (CD)** is a type of note. A CD is issued when a party deposits funds with a bank that the bank promises to repay, with interest, on a certain date [UCC 3–104(j)]. The bank is the maker of the note, and the depositor is the payee. ■**EXAMPLE 14.4** On February 15, Sara Levin deposits $5,000 with the First National Bank of Whiteacre. The bank issues a CD, in which it promises to repay the $5,000, plus 5 percent annual interest, on August 15. ■

Certificates of deposit in small denominations (for amounts up to $100,000) are often sold by savings and loan associations, savings banks, commercial banks, and credit unions. Certificates of deposit for amounts over $100,000 are called large or jumbo CDs. Exhibit 14–5 shows a typical small CD.

Because CDs are time deposits, the purchaser-payee is typically not allowed to withdraw the funds prior to the date of maturity (except in limited circumstances, such as disability or death). If a payee wants to access the funds prior to the maturity date, he or she can sell (negotiate) the CD to a third party.

CERTIFICATE OF DEPOSIT (CD)
A note issued by a bank in which the bank acknowledges the receipt of funds from a party and promises to repay that amount, with interest, to the party on a certain date.

TRANSFER OF INSTRUMENTS

Once issued, a negotiable instrument can be transferred by *assignment* or by *negotiation*. Only a transfer by negotiation can result in the party obtaining the instrument receiving the rights of a holder, as discussed next.

EXHIBIT 14–4 A Typical Promissory Note

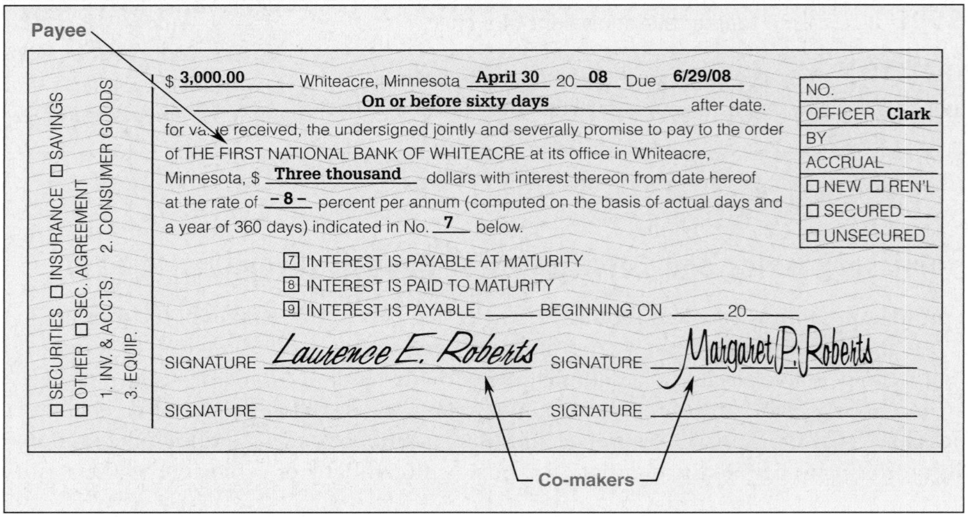

BEYOND OUR BORDERS The Negotiability of Checks in Other Nations

For many people in the United States, checks are the ultimate negotiable instrument. After all, our parents and grandparents negotiated checks. Checks have a long history of being accepted the "same as cash" at most locations in the United States. In other countries, however, checks are used less frequently and sometimes are not even negotiable.

In some European nations, such as Austria, Germany, and the Netherlands, checks are now rarely used. Direct bank transfers and electronic payments (both of which will be discussed in Chapter 15) have replaced checks in these countries. The European Union has a low-cost electronic payment system that is much faster and more efficient than the systems available in the United States. This fact—as well as the increase in identity theft and financial crimes—has contributed to the abandonment of checks elsewhere.

Even in those nations where checks are still used, they are often not actually negotiable. In France, for example, although a segment of the population still uses checks, the payee named on a check cannot indorse the check to a third party. Moreover, the payee on the check cannot walk into any bank in France and cash the check as a payee can in the United States. In France, a check can only be deposited into an account at a bank. More and more shops in France no longer accept check payments at all.

In the United Kingdom, where checks have been used even longer than in the United States, checks are rapidly becoming a thing of the past. Since 2001, businesses' electronic payments have outnumbered their payments by check. In 2006, ASDA, the second largest British supermarket chain and a subsidiary of Wal-Mart, announced that it will not accept checks as a means of payment in the future (beginning in the London area). Similarly, the largest pharmacy chain in the United Kingdom (Boots) is also phasing out checks as a payment method. British utility companies are also discouraging the use of checks by charging higher prices to customers who pay by check.

FOR CRITICAL ANALYSIS *What are the disadvantages of not being able to indorse checks to other parties?*

■

EXHIBIT 14–5 **A Typical Small CD**

Payee (Bearer)

THE FIRST NATIONAL BANK OF WHITEACRE   22-1/960   **13992**
NEGOTIABLE CERTIFICATE OF DEPOSIT

WHITEACRE, MINN. _____ **February 15** _____ 20 **08** _____

THIS CERTIFIES to the deposit in this Bank the sum of $ **5,000.00**

———— **Five thousand and no/100** ————   **DOLLARS**

which is payable to bearer on the __**15th**__ day of __**August**__, 20 __**08**__ against presentation and surrender of this certificate, and bears interest at the rate of __**5**__ % per annum, to be computed (on the basis of 360 days and actual days elapsed) to, and payable at, maturity. No payment may be made prior to, and no interest runs after, that date. Payable at maturity in federal funds, and if desired, at Manufacturers Hanover Trust Company, New York.

THE FIRST NATIONAL BANK OF WHITEACRE

By ___ *John Doe* ___
                              SIGNATURE

Maker

satory and punitive damages that the plaintiff can recover from specific employers—ranging from $50,000 against employers with one hundred or fewer employees to $300,000 against employers with more than five hundred employees.

Discrimination Based on Age

Age discrimination is potentially the most widespread form of discrimination, because anyone—regardless of race, color, national origin, or gender—could be a victim at some point in life. The Age Discrimination in Employment Act (ADEA) of 1967, as amended, prohibits employment discrimination on the basis of age against individuals forty years of age or older. The act also prohibits mandatory retirement for nonmanagerial workers. For the act to apply, an employer must have twenty or more employees, and the employer's business activities must affect interstate commerce. The EEOC administers the ADEA, but the act also permits private causes of action against employers for age discrimination.

Procedures under the ADEA   The burden-shifting procedure under the ADEA is similar to that under Title VII. If a plaintiff can establish that she or he (1) was a member of the protected age group, (2) was qualified for the position from which she or he was discharged, and (3) was discharged under circumstances that give rise to an inference of discrimination, the plaintiff has established a *prima facie* case of unlawful age discrimination. The burden then shifts to the employer, who must articulate a legitimate reason for the discrimination. If the plaintiff can prove that the employer's reason is only a pretext (excuse) and that the plaintiff's age was a determining factor in the employer's decision, the employer will be held liable under the ADEA.

If an employer offers several nondiscriminatory reasons, based on a variety of events, for an act of alleged discrimination, does the employee need to rebut every reason by proving that the events did not occur? That was the question in the following case.

> **REMEMBER**   The Fourteenth Amendment prohibits any state from denying any person "the equal protection of the laws." This prohibition applies to the *federal* government through the due process clause of the Fifth Amendment.

CASE 18.3   **Cash Distributing Co. v. Neely**

Mississippi Supreme Court, 947 So.2d 286 (2007).
www.mssc.state.ms.us[a]

FACTS   Cash Distributing Company is a distributorship for Anheuser-Busch Corporation products, including Budweiser and Michelob beers, with offices in Starkville, Columbus, and Tupelo, Mississippi. In 1973, James Neely began to work for Cash. At the time, the company often relaxed or ignored Anheuser-Busch rules. By the late 1990s, Neely had become the manager of the Columbus office. In 1997, Anheuser-Busch began to require Cash to comply with certain standards. Danny Cash, Cash's chief executive officer (CEO), announced that he intended to strictly enforce the new rules. Part of the

newly required documentation was a tracking form to detect out-of-date beer. Danny also required Neely to, among other things, submit daily call sheets to disclose where he had been and what he had done and to submit regular written employee evaluations. Neely generally refused to provide the new documents. In March 2000, Danny terminated Neely's employment, replacing him with Tony Carley, who was then thirty-eight years old. Neely filed a suit in a Mississippi state court against Cash, alleging a violation of the ADEA, among other things. Neely was awarded $120,000 in back pay. Both parties appealed to a state intermediate appellate court, which reversed the lower court's failure to grant additional remedies to Neely. Cash appealed to the Mississippi Supreme Court.

ISSUE   Can an employee prevail in an ADEA suit without rebutting every nondiscriminatory reason that the employer offers for an act of discrimination?

a. In the center of the page, click on the "Search this Site" link. On the next page, click on "Plain English." When that page opens, in the "Enter the ISYS Plain English query:" box, type "2004-CT-01124-SCT" and click "Search." In the result, click on the item that includes that number to access the opinion. The Mississippi Supreme Court maintains this Web site.

CASE 18.3–Continues next page

ADAPTING THE LAW TO THE ONLINE ENVIRONMENT — New Issues in Online Privacy and Employment Discrimination

As computers come to be used for more and more aspects of both personal and professional life, the line between personal use and work-related use is becoming blurred. As this chapter has explained, employers are legally required to prevent discrimination in the workplace, including a hostile environment created by workers' online activities. That employers have a right—or even an obligation—to monitor their employees' computer use to this end is generally established. Indeed, courts have generally held that employees have no expectation of privacy in their workplace computers when a private employer supplies the equipment. The limits of this privacy exception are still being tested, however, as a number of issues related to computers, privacy, and employment discrimination remain unresolved. A new issue that is just emerging is whether employers can obtain information about job applicants by conducting online searches when asking for the same information on a job application or in an interview might be illegal.

Searches of Workplace Computers

An employee who uses his or her workplace computer to view sexually explicit photographs may create a hostile environment if the photographs can be seen by other employees. Furthermore, if the photographs involve children, the employee's activities may be illegal. Courts have generally held that employers can search a workplace computer for evidence of employee misconduct[a] and that they can also consent to a search by government officials. If the computer is in a locked office, however, does the employee have a greater expectation of privacy? In *United States v. Ziegler*[b] in 2007, the court had to answer this question.

The Internet service provider for Frontline Processing Corporation informed the Federal Bureau of Investigation (FBI) that one of Frontline's computers had been used to access child-pornography Web sites in violation of federal criminal law. The FBI investigated and determined that Jeffrey Ziegler, Frontline's director of operations, had used the computer in his office to search for and view online photos of "very young girls in various states of undress." Frontline agreed to cooperate with the FBI, and at some point corporate employees entered Ziegler's locked office and made a backup copy of the hard drive on his computer without his consent.

Ziegler appealed his subsequent conviction for possessing child pornography on the ground that the search of his computer violated his Fourth Amendment rights against unreasonable search and seizure. The U.S. Court of Appeals for the Ninth Circuit first held that Ziegler had no reasonable expectation of privacy, but on rehearing, the court changed its ruling and held that Ziegler did have a reasonable expectation of privacy in the contents of the computer in his locked office. Because the employer (Frontline) owned the

a. See, for example, *Twymon v. Wells Fargo & Co.*, 462 F.3d 925 (8th Cir. 2006); and *Griffis v. Pinal County*, 213 Ariz. 300, 141 P.3d 780 (2006).
b. 474 F.3d 1184 (9th Cir. 2007).

CASE 18.3–Continued

DECISION Yes. The Mississippi Supreme Court affirmed the lower court's judgment. Neely did not have to prove that the events that Cash claimed led to his dismissal did not actually happen.

REASON Neely did not deny the occurrence of most of the events that Cash claimed were the nondiscriminatory reasons for Neely's discharge. Instead, Neely offered proof that these events were not the real reasons for his termination. For example, Cash claimed that it discharged Neely for "insubordination and his failure to discover and report out-of-date product on a particular occasion." Neely responded that "his operation in Columbus received perfect scores following several evaluations" by Anheuser-Busch. Neely also showed that "out-of-date product was fairly common and that the extremely meticulous audit of his territory," preceding his

discharge, "was unprecedented, * * * a 'witch hunt.'" Neely also claimed that Danny Cash made derogatory comments about his age. For example, in a document titled "Jim Neely Time Line," Danny referred to "too much older supervisors that were riding their time out." The state supreme court concluded, "The jury in this case obviously credited Neely's account of his dismissal and the evidence supporting it over explanations supplied by Cash. This Court has no basis to disturb that decision on appeal. The jury was free to find that even if, as Cash claimed, Neely had been insubordinate, that justification was pretextual based on evidence of unequal treatment [and] age-related statements made by Cash's CEO."

WHAT IF THE FACTS WERE DIFFERENT? *If Neely had admitted that he had committed all of the "wrongful" acts attributed to him by Cash, would the outcome of this case have been different? Why or why not?*

computer, however, the court held that Frontline's consent validated the search. According to the court, a "computer is the type of workplace property that remains within control of the employer 'even if the employee has placed personal items in it.'"

Unresolved Issues

Certainly, the trend is clearly toward limiting employees' expectations of privacy in employer-owned computers in the workplace, but several questions still remain open. What expectations of privacy does an employee have in a laptop computer that is provided by the company but is used by the employee at home or on the road? Similarly, if the employee works at home on an employer-owned computer, to what degree can the employer justify monitoring the employee's online activities? Although computers in remote locations could be used to send harassing e-mail, other employees are unlikely to view offensive material on such computers, so that justification for monitoring Internet use seems less valid.

Other issues have to do with whether employers must tell employees that their computer use will be monitored and the degree to which employers should monitor employees' online activities that are mostly personal. To date, only two states (Connecticut and Delaware) have passed laws specifically requiring private employers to inform employees that their workplace Internet activities will be monitored. Personal blogs raise an even more complex issue: Does an employer have the right to monitor its employees' personal blogs? If an employee's personal blog contains racially or sexually offensive comments about co-workers, what should the employer do? Thus far, in most of the cases involving employees dismissed for computer misuse, the employer had a written

Internet policy and presented evidence that the employee knew about and disregarded the policy. According to recent surveys, however, most organizations do not have policies on employees' blogs.

Even more problematic is another issue that is just emerging. Today, many college students and recent graduates belong to social networking sites such as Facebook.com and MySpace.com where they can post photographs, comments, blogs, or even videos about themselves. Some of this material is suggestive, to say the least. A number of employers have begun to use search engines to search for information on job applicants. A search may turn up not just photos that the applicant intended to be viewed only by close friends but also information about the applicant's marital status, sexual orientation, or political or religious views that the employer could not ask for on a job application or discuss in a job interview. Nevertheless, this information is now readily available to employers. Some colleges and employment counselors are beginning to advise job seekers to make sure that they remove any information they do not want a prospective employer to see, but the issue of whether employers have a right to search for this information is likely to persist.

FOR CRITICAL ANALYSIS *Suppose that an employee writes a message to like-minded persons concerning religious beliefs or political views. Can the employee be fired in that situation? Who decides what is acceptable Internet activity when there is no written policy?*

Replacing Older Workers with Younger Workers   Numerous age discrimination cases have been brought against employers who, to cut costs, replaced older, higher-salaried employees with younger, lower-salaried workers. Whether a firing is discriminatory or simply part of a rational business decision to prune the company's ranks is not always clear. Companies often defend a decision to discharge a worker by asserting that the worker could no longer perform his or her duties or that the worker's skills were no longer needed. The employee must prove that the discharge was motivated, at least in part, by age bias. Proof that qualified older employees are generally discharged before younger employees or that co-workers continually made unflattering age-related comments about the discharged worker may be enough.

The plaintiff need not prove that he or she was replaced by a person outside the protected class—that is, by a person under the age of forty years.[49] Rather, the issue in all ADEA cases is whether age discrimination has, in fact, occurred, regardless of the age of the replacement worker.

State Employees Not Covered by the ADEA   Generally, the states are immune from lawsuits brought by private individuals in federal court—unless a state consents to the suit.

---

49. *O'Connor v. Consolidated Coin Caterers Corp.*, 517 U.S. 308, 116 S.Ct. 1307, 134 L.Ed.2d 433 (1996).

This immunity stems from the United States Supreme Court's interpretation of the Eleventh Amendment (the text of this amendment is included in Appendix B). **■EXAMPLE 18.16** In two Florida cases, professors and librarians contended that their employers—two Florida state universities—denied them salary increases and other benefits because they were getting old and their successors could be hired at lower cost. The universities claimed that as agencies of a sovereign state, they could not be sued in federal court without the state's consent. The cases ultimately reached the United States Supreme Court, which held that the Eleventh Amendment bars private parties from suing state employers for violations of the ADEA.[50] ■

State immunity under the Eleventh Amendment is not absolute, however, as the Supreme Court explained in 2004. In some situations, such as when fundamental rights are at stake, Congress has the power to abrogate (abolish) state immunity to private suits through legislation that unequivocally shows Congress's intent to subject states to private suits.[51] As a general rule, though, the Court has found that state employers are immune from private suits brought by employees under the ADEA (for age discrimination, as noted above), the Americans with Disabilities Act[52] (for disability discrimination), and the Fair Labor Standards Act.[53] In contrast, states are not immune from the requirements of the Family and Medical Leave Act.[54]

Discrimination Based on Disability

The Americans with Disabilities Act (ADA) of 1990 is designed to eliminate discriminatory employment practices that prevent otherwise qualified workers with disabilities from fully participating in the national labor force. Prior to 1990, the major federal law providing protection to those with disabilities was the Rehabilitation Act of 1973. That act covered only federal government employees and those employed under federally funded programs. The ADA extends federal protection against disability-based discrimination to all workplaces with fifteen or more workers (with the exception of state government employers, who are generally immune under the Eleventh Amendment, as was just discussed). Basically, the ADA requires that employers "reasonably accommodate" the needs of persons with disabilities unless to do so would cause the employer to suffer an "undue hardship."

Procedures under the ADA   To prevail on a claim under the ADA, a plaintiff must show that he or she (1) has a disability, (2) is otherwise qualified for the employment in question, and (3) was excluded from the employment solely because of the disability. As in Title VII cases, a claim alleging a violation of the ADA may be commenced only after the plaintiff has pursued the claim through the EEOC. Plaintiffs may sue for many of the same remedies available under Title VII. The EEOC may decide to investigate and perhaps even sue the employer on behalf of the employee. If the EEOC decides not to sue, then the employee is entitled to sue.

Significantly, the United States Supreme Court held in 2002 that the EEOC could bring a suit against an employer for disability-based discrimination even though the employee had agreed to submit any job-related disputes to arbitration (see Chapter 3). The Court reasoned that because the EEOC was not a party to the arbitration agreement, the agreement was not binding on the EEOC.[55]

---

50. *Kimel v. Florida Board of Regents*, 528 U.S. 62, 120 S.Ct. 631, 145 L.Ed.2d 522 (2000).
51. *Tennessee v. Lane*, 541 U.S. 509, 124 S.Ct. 1978, 158 L.Ed.2d 820 (2004).
52. *Board of Trustees of the University of Alabama v. Garrett*, 531 U.S. 356, 121 S.Ct. 955, 148 L.Ed.2d 866 (2001).
53. *Alden v. Maine*, 527 U.S. 706, 119 S.Ct. 2240, 144 L.Ed.2d 636 (1999).
54. *Nevada Department of Human Resources v. Hibbs*, 538 U.S. 721, 123 S.Ct. 1972, 155 L.Ed.2d 953 (2003).
55. *EEOC v. Waffle House, Inc.*, 534 U.S. 279, 122 S.Ct. 754, 151 L.Ed.2d 75 (2002).

Plaintiffs in lawsuits brought under the ADA may seek many of the same remedies available under Title VII. These include reinstatement, back pay, a limited amount of compensatory and punitive damages (for intentional discrimination), and certain other forms of relief. Repeat violators may be ordered to pay fines of up to $100,000.

What Is a Disability? The ADA is broadly drafted to cover persons with a wide range of disabilities. Specifically, the ADA defines *disability* as "(1) a physical or mental impairment that substantially limits one or more of the major life activities of such individuals; (2) a record of such impairment; or (3) being regarded as having such an impairment."

Health conditions that have been considered disabilities under the federal law include blindness, alcoholism, heart disease, cancer, muscular dystrophy, cerebral palsy, paraplegia, diabetes, acquired immune deficiency syndrome (AIDS), testing positive for the human immunodeficiency virus (HIV), and morbid obesity (defined as existing when an individual's weight is two times that of a normal person).[56] The ADA excludes from coverage certain conditions, such as kleptomania (the obsessive desire to steal).

Although the ADA's definition of disability is broad, starting in 1999, the United States Supreme Court has issued a series of decisions narrowing the definition of what constitutes a disability under the act.

Correctable Conditions. In 1999, in *Sutton v. United Airlines, Inc.,*[57] the Supreme Court reviewed a case raising the issue of whether severe myopia, or nearsightedness, which can be corrected with lenses, qualifies as a disability under the ADA. The Supreme Court ruled that it does not. The determination of whether a person is substantially limited in a major life activity is based on how the person functions when taking medication or using corrective devices, not on how the person functions without these measures.

Co-workers discuss business matters. What is a disability under the Americans with Disabilities Act? (Johnny Stockshooter/Image State)

In a similar case in 2002, a federal appellate court held that a pharmacist suffering from diabetes, which could be corrected by insulin, did not have a cause of action against his employer under the ADA.[58] In other cases decided in the early 2000s, the courts have held that plaintiffs with bipolar disorder, epilepsy, and other such conditions do *not* fall under the ADA's protections if the conditions can be corrected.

Repetitive-Stress Injuries. For some time, the courts were divided on the issue of whether carpal tunnel syndrome (or other repetitive-stress injury) constitutes a disability under the ADA. Carpal tunnel syndrome is a condition of pain and weakness in the hand caused by repetitive compression of a nerve in the wrist. In 2002, in a case involving this issue, the Supreme Court unanimously held that it does not. The Court stated that although the employee could not perform the manual tasks associated with her job, the condition did not constitute a disability under the ADA because it did not "substantially limit" the major life activity of performing manual tasks.[59]

Reasonable Accommodation The ADA does not require that employers accommodate the needs of job applicants or employees with disabilities who are not otherwise qualified

---

56. *Cook v. Rhode Island Department of Mental Health,* 10 F.3d 17 (1st Cir. 1993).
57. 527 U.S. 471, 119 S.Ct. 2139, 144 L.Ed.2d 450 (1999).
58. *Orr v. Walmart Stores, Inc.,* 297 F.3d 720 (8th Cir. 2002).
59. *Toyota Motor Manufacturing, Kentucky, Inc. v. Williams,* 534 U.S. 184, 122 S.Ct. 681, 151 L.Ed.2d 615 (2002).

for the work. If a job applicant or an employee with a disability, with reasonable accommodation, can perform essential job functions, however, the employer must make the accommodation. Required modifications may include installing ramps for a wheelchair, establishing more flexible working hours, creating or modifying job assignments, and creating or improving training materials and procedures.

Generally, employers should give primary consideration to employees' preferences in deciding what accommodations should be made. What happens if a job applicant or employee does not indicate to the employer how her or his disability can be accommodated so that the employee can perform essential job functions? In this situation, the employer may avoid liability for failing to hire or retain the individual on the ground that the applicant or employee has failed to meet the "otherwise qualified" requirement.[60]

Undue Hardship.   Employers who do not accommodate the needs of persons with disabilities must demonstrate that the accommodations will cause "undue hardship." Generally, the law offers no uniform standards for identifying what is an undue hardship other than the imposition of a "significant difficulty or expense" on the employer. In other words, the focus is on the resources and circumstances of the particular employer in relation to the cost or difficulty of providing a specific accommodation.

Usually, the courts decide whether an accommodation constitutes an undue hardship on a case-by-case basis. **■EXAMPLE 18.17** Bryan Lockhart, who uses a wheelchair, works for a cell phone company that provides parking to its employees. Lockhart informs the company supervisors that the parking spaces are so narrow that he is unable to extend the ramp on his van that allows him to get in and out of the vehicle. Lockhart therefore requests that the company reasonably accommodate his needs by paying a monthly fee for him to use a larger parking space in an adjacent lot. In this situation, a court would likely find that it would not be an undue hardship for the employer to pay for additional parking for Lockhart. **■**

Job Applications and Preemployment Physical Exams.   Employers must modify their job-application process so that those with disabilities can compete for jobs with those who do not have disabilities. **■EXAMPLE 18.18** A job announcement that includes only a phone number would discriminate against potential job applicants with hearing impairments. Thus, the job announcement must also provide an address. **■**

Employers are restricted in the kinds of questions they may ask on job-application forms and during preemployment interviews (see the *Application* feature at the end of this chapter for guidelines on this topic). Furthermore, they cannot require persons with disabilities to submit to preemployment physicals unless such exams are required of all other applicants. Employers can condition an offer of employment on the applicant's successfully passing a medical examination, but can disqualify the applicant only if the medical problems they discover would render the applicant unable to perform the job.

Dangerous Workers.   Employers are not required to hire or retain workers who, because of their disabilities, pose a direct threat to the health or safety of their co-workers or the public.[61] This danger must be substantial and immediate; it cannot be speculative. In the wake of the AIDS epidemic, many employers have been concerned about hiring or con-

ON THE WEB

The Equal Employment Opportunity Commission posts a manual that provides guidance on reasonable accommodation and undue hardship under the ADA. Go to

www.eeoc.gov/policy/docs/ accommodation.html.

DON'T FORGET   Preemployment screening procedures must be applied equally in regard to all job applicants.

---

60. See, for example, *Beck v. University of Wisconsin Board of Regents,* 75 F.3d 1130 (7th Cir. 1996); and *White v. York International Corp.,* 45 F.3d 357 (10th Cir. 1995).

61. The United States Supreme Court has also upheld regulations that permit an employer to refuse to hire a worker when the job would pose a threat to that person's own health. *Chevron USA, Inc. v. Echazabal,* 536 U.S. 73, 122 S.Ct. 2045, 153 L.Ed.2d 82 (2002).

tinuing to employ a worker who has AIDS under the assumption that the worker might pose a direct threat to the health or safety of others in the workplace. Courts have generally held, however, that AIDS is not so contagious as to disqualify employees in most jobs. Therefore, employers must reasonably accommodate job applicants or employees who have AIDS or who test positive for HIV, the virus that causes AIDS.

Substance Abusers. Drug addiction is a disability under the ADA because drug addiction is a substantially limiting impairment. Those who are using illegal drugs at the present time are not protected by the act, however. The ADA protects only persons with *former* drug addictions—those who have completed a supervised drug-rehabilitation program or are in a supervised rehabilitation program. Individuals who have used drugs casually in the past are not protected under the act. They are not considered addicts and therefore do not have a disability (addiction).

People suffering from alcoholism are protected by the ADA. Employers cannot legally discriminate against employees simply because they are suffering from alcoholism and must treat them in the same way they treat other employees. In other words, an employee with alcoholism who comes to work late because she or he was drinking the night before cannot be disciplined any differently than someone else who is late for another reason. Of course, employers have the right to prohibit the use of alcohol in the workplace and can require that employees not be under the influence of alcohol while working. Employers can also fire or refuse to hire a person with alcoholism if he or she poses a substantial risk of harm either to himself or herself or to others and the risk cannot be reduced by reasonable accommodation.

Health-Insurance Plans. Workers with disabilities must be given equal access to any health insurance provided to other employees. Employers can exclude from coverage preexisting health conditions and certain types of diagnostic or surgical procedures, though. An employer can also put a limit, or cap, on health-care payments under its particular group health policy—as long as such caps are "applied equally to all insured employees" and do not "discriminate on the basis of disability." Whenever a group health-care plan makes a disability-based distinction in its benefits, the plan violates the ADA. The employer must then be able to justify the distinction by proving one of the following:

1 That limiting coverage of certain ailments is required to keep the plan financially sound.

2 That coverage of certain ailments would cause such a significant increase in premium payments or their equivalent that the plan would be unappealing to a significant number of workers.

3 That the disparate treatment is justified by the risks and costs associated with a particular disability.

Hostile-Environment Claims under the ADA As discussed earlier in this chapter, under Title VII of the Civil Rights Act of 1964, an employee may base certain types of employment-discrimination causes of action on a hostile-environment theory. Using this theory, a worker may successfully sue her or his employer, even if the worker was not fired or otherwise discriminated against.

Although the ADA does not expressly provide for hostile-environment claims, a number of courts have allowed such actions. Only a few plaintiffs have been successful, however.[62]

62. See, for example, *Shaver v. Independent Stave Co.*, 350 F.3d 716 (8th Cir. 2003); *Johnson v. North Carolina Department of Health and Human Services*, 454 F.Supp.2d 467 (M.D.N.C. 2006); and *Lucenti v. Potter*, 432 F.Supp.2d 347 (S.D.N.Y. 2006).

For a claim to succeed, the conduct complained of must be sufficiently severe or pervasive to permeate the workplace and alter the conditions of employment such that a reasonable person would find the environment hostile or abusive. **■EXAMPLE 18.19** Lester Wenigar was a fifty-seven-year-old man with a low IQ and limited mental capacity who worked at a farm doing manual labor and serving as a night watchman. His employer frequently shouted at him and called him names, did not allow him to take breaks, and provided him with substandard living quarters (a storeroom over a garage without any heat or windows). In this situation, because the employer's conduct was severe and offensive, a court would likely find that the working conditions constituted a hostile environment under the ADA.[63] ■

DEFENSES TO EMPLOYMENT DISCRIMINATION

The first line of defense for an employer charged with employment discrimination is, of course, to assert that the plaintiff has failed to meet his or her initial burden of proving that discrimination occurred. As noted, plaintiffs bringing cases under the ADA sometimes find it difficult to meet this initial burden because they must prove that their alleged disabilities are disabilities covered by the ADA. Furthermore, plaintiffs in ADA cases must prove that they were otherwise qualified for the job and that their disabilities were the sole reason they were not hired or were fired.

Once a plaintiff succeeds in proving that discrimination occurred, the burden shifts to the employer to justify the discriminatory practice. Often, employers attempt to justify the discrimination by claiming that it was the result of a business necessity, a bona fide occupational qualification, or a seniority system. In some cases, as noted earlier, an effective antiharassment policy and prompt remedial action when harassment occurs may shield employers from liability for sexual harassment under Title VII.

Business Necessity

BUSINESS NECESSITY
A defense to allegations of employment discrimination in which the employer demonstrates that an employment practice that discriminates against members of a protected class is related to job performance.

An employer may defend against a claim of disparate-impact (unintentional) discrimination by asserting that a practice that has a discriminatory effect is a **business necessity.** **■EXAMPLE 18.20** If requiring a high school diploma is shown to have a discriminatory effect, an employer might argue that a high school education is necessary for workers to perform the job at a required level of competence. If the employer can demonstrate to the court's satisfaction that a definite connection exists between a high school education and job performance, the employer will normally succeed in this business necessity defense. ■

Bona Fide Occupational Qualification

BONA FIDE OCCUPATIONAL QUALIFICATION (BFOQ)
Identifiable characteristics reasonably necessary to the normal operation of a particular business. These characteristics can include gender, national origin, and religion, but not race.

Another defense applies when discrimination against a protected class is essential to a job—that is, when a particular trait is a **bona fide occupational qualification (BFOQ)**. Race, however, can never be a BFOQ. Generally, courts have restricted the BFOQ defense to instances in which the employee's gender is essential to the job.[64] **■EXAMPLE 18.21** A women's clothing store might legitimately hire only female sales attendants if part of an attendant's job involves assisting clients in the store's dressing rooms. Similarly, the Federal Aviation Administration can legitimately impose age limits for airline pilots—but an airline cannot impose weight limits only on female flight attendants. ■

---

63. *Wenigar v. Johnson*, 712 N.W.2d 190 (Minn.App. 2006). This case involved a hostile-environment claim under the Minnesota disability statute rather than the ADA, but the court relied on another court's decision under the ADA.
64. A classic example is *United Auto Workers v. Johnson Controls, Inc.*, 499 U.S. 187, 111 S.Ct. 1196, 113 L.Ed.2d 158 (1991), in which the Supreme Court held that a policy adopted to protect unborn children of female employees from the harmful effects of lead exposure was an unacceptable BFOQ.

Seniority Systems

An employer with a history of discrimination might have no members of protected classes in upper-level positions. Even if the employer now seeks to be unbiased, it may face a lawsuit in which the plaintiff asks a court to order that minorities be promoted ahead of schedule to compensate for past discrimination. If no present intent to discriminate is shown, however, and if promotions or other job benefits are distributed according to a fair **seniority system** (in which workers with more years of service are promoted first or laid off last), the employer has a good defense against the suit.

According to the United States Supreme Court in 2002, this defense may also apply to alleged discrimination under the ADA. If an employee with a disability requests an accommodation (such as an assignment to a particular position) that conflicts with an employer's seniority system, the accommodation will generally not be considered "reasonable" under the act.[65]

SENIORITY SYSTEM
In regard to employment relationships, a system in which those who have worked longest for the employer are first in line for promotions, salary increases, and other benefits. They are also the last to be laid off if the workforce must be reduced.

After-Acquired Evidence of Employee Misconduct

In some situations, employers have attempted to avoid liability for employment discrimination on the basis of "after-acquired evidence"—that is, evidence that the employer discovers after a lawsuit is filed—of an employee's misconduct. **■EXAMPLE 18.22** Suppose that an employer fires a worker, who then sues the employer for employment discrimination. During pretrial investigation, the employer learns that the employee made material misrepresentations on his or her employment application—misrepresentations that, had the employer known about them, would have served as a ground to fire the individual. ■

According to the United States Supreme Court, after-acquired evidence of wrongdoing cannot be used to shield an employer entirely from liability for employment discrimination. It may, however, be used to limit the amount of damages for which the employer is liable.[66]

---

65. *U.S. Airways, Inc. v. Barnett,* 535 U.S. 391, 122 S.Ct. 1516, 152 L.Ed.2d 589 (2002).
66. *McKennon v. Nashville Banner Publishing Co.,* 513 U.S. 352, 115 S.Ct. 879, 130 L.Ed.2d 852 (1995).

REVIEWING **Employment Law**

Rick Saldona began working as a traveling salesperson for Aimer Winery in 1977. Sales constituted 90 percent of Saldona's work time. Saldona worked an average of fifty hours per week but received no overtime pay. In June 2007, Saldona's new supervisor, Caesar Braxton, claimed that Saldona had been inflating his reported sales calls and required Saldona to submit to a polygraph test. Saldona reported Braxton to the U.S. Department of Labor, which prohibited Aimer from requiring Saldona to take a polygraph test for this purpose. In August 2007, Saldona's wife, Venita, fell from a ladder and sustained a head injury while employed as a full-time agricultural harvester. Saldona delivered to Aimer's human resources department a letter from his wife's physician indicating that she would need daily care for several months, and Saldona took leave until December 2007. Aimer had sixty-three employees at that time. When Saldona returned to Aimer, he was informed that his position had been eliminated because his sales territory had been combined with an adjacent territory. Using the information presented in the chapter, answer the following questions.

1 Would Saldona have been legally entitled to receive overtime pay at a higher rate? Why or why not?

2 What is the maximum length of time Saldona would have been allowed to take leave to care for his injured spouse?

3 Under what circumstances would Aimer have been allowed to require an employee to take a polygraph test?

4 Would Aimer likely be able to avoid reinstating Saldona under the *key employee* exception? Why or why not?

Many employers have been held liable under the Americans with Disabilities Act (ADA) of 1990 simply because they asked the wrong questions when interviewing job applicants with disabilities. If you are an employer, you can do several things to avoid violating the ADA.

Become Familiar with the EEOC Guidelines

As a preliminary step, you should become familiar with the guidelines on job interviews issued by the Equal Employment Opportunity Commission (EEOC). These guidelines indicate the kinds of questions that employers may—and may not—ask job applicants with disabilities. Often, the line between permissible and impermissible questions is a fine one. Consider these examples:

- *Ability to perform the job.* As an employer, you may ask a job applicant, "Can you do the job?" You may also ask whether the applicant can perform specific tasks related to the job. You may not ask the candidate, "How would you do the job?"—*unless* the disability is obvious, the applicant brings up the subject during the interview, or you ask the question of all applicants.

- *Absenteeism.* You may ask, "Can you meet our attendance requirements?" or "How many days were you absent last year?" You may not ask, "How many days were you sick last year?"

- *Drug use.* Generally, employers may ask about current or past use of illegal drugs but not about drug addiction. Therefore, as an employer, you may ask, "Have you ever used illegal drugs?" or "Have you done so in the last six months?" You may not ask, "How often did you use illegal drugs?" or "Have you been treated for drug abuse?"

- *Alcohol use.* Generally, employers may ask about a candidate's drinking habits but not about alcoholism. Therefore, you may ask, "Do you drink alcohol?" or "Have you been arrested for driving while intoxicated?" but you may not ask, "How often do you drink?"

- *History of job-related injuries.* Employers may not ask a job candidate with a disability any questions about the appli-

cant's previous job-related injuries or about workers' compensation claims submitted in the past.

Once you have made a job offer, though, you may ask the applicant questions concerning his or her disability, including questions about previous workers' compensation claims or about the extent of a drinking problem. You may also ask for medical documents verifying the nature of the applicant's disability. Generally, however, you should ask such questions only if you ask them of all applicants or if they are follow-up questions concerning information about the applicant's disability that she or he already disclosed during a job interview.

Obtain Legal Assistance and Instruct Staff Members

To avoid liability under the ADA, the wisest thing you can do is consult with an attorney. You should inform the attorney of the kinds of questions you typically ask job applicants during interviews or following employment offers. Then, you should work with the attorney in modifying these questions so that they are consistent with the EEOC's guidelines on permissible and impermissible questions. Finally, you should make sure that anyone on your staff who interviews job applicants receives thorough instructions on what questions may and may not be asked of candidates with disabilities. You might also remind your staff that under the ADA, the words and phraseology the interviewer uses may result in a violation of the ADA regardless of the interviewer's intentions.

CHECKLIST FOR THE EMPLOYER

1 Familiarize yourself with the EEOC's guidelines indicating what questions are and are not permissible when interviewing job applicants with disabilities.

2 Work with an attorney to create a list of particular types of questions that are and are not permissible under the EEOC's guidelines with respect to job candidates with disabilities.

3 Make sure that all persons in your firm who interview job applicants are thoroughly instructed as to the types of questions that they may and may not ask when interviewing job applicants with disabilities.

* This *Application* is not meant to substitute for the services of an attorney who is licensed to practice law in your state.

dealers selling the product. To this end, it may institute territorial restrictions or attempt to prohibit wholesalers or retailers from reselling the product to certain classes of buyers, such as competing retailers.

A firm may have legitimate reasons for imposing such territorial or customer restrictions. **■EXAMPLE 22.4** A computer manufacturer may wish to prevent a dealer from cutting costs and undercutting rivals by selling computers without promotion or customer service, while relying on nearby dealers to provide these services. In this situation, the cost-cutting dealer reaps the benefits (sales of the product) paid for by other dealers who undertake promotion and arrange for customer service. By not providing customer service, the cost-cutting dealer may also harm the manufacturer's reputation. ■

Territorial and customer restrictions are judged under the rule of reason. In *United States v. Arnold, Schwinn & Co.*,[5] a case decided in 1967, a bicycle manufacturer, Schwinn, was assigning specific territories to its wholesale distributors and authorizing certain retail dealers only if they agreed to advertise Schwinn bikes and give them the same prominence as other brands. The United States Supreme Court held that these vertical territorial and customer restrictions were *per se* violations of Section 1 of the Sherman Act. Ten years later, however, in *Continental T.V., Inc. v. GTE Sylvania, Inc.*,[6] a case involving similar restrictions imposed on retailers by a television manufacturer, the Supreme Court overturned the *Schwinn* decision. In the *Continental* decision, the Court held that such vertical restrictions should be judged under the rule of reason, and this rule is still applied in most vertical restraint cases.[7] The *Continental* decision marked a definite shift from rigid characterization of these kinds of vertical restraints to a more flexible, economic analysis of the restraints under the rule of reason.

Resale Price Maintenance Agreements   An agreement between a manufacturer and a distributor or retailer in which the manufacturer specifies what the retail prices of its products must be is referred to as a **resale price maintenance agreement.** This type of agreement may violate Section 1 of the Sherman Act. Though once considered a *per se* violation, such vertical price fixing is now judged under the rule of reason because the practice may increase competition and benefit consumers.[8]

**RESALE PRICE
MAINTENANCE AGREEMENT**
An agreement between a
manufacturer and a retailer in
which the manufacturer specifies
what the retail prices of its products
must be.

Refusals to Deal   As discussed previously, joint refusals to deal (group boycotts) are subject to close scrutiny under Section 1 of the Sherman Act. A single manufacturer acting unilaterally, though, is generally free to deal, or not to deal, with whomever it wishes. In vertical arrangements, even though a manufacturer cannot set retail prices for its products, it can refuse to deal with retailers or dealers that cut prices to levels substantially below the manufacturer's suggested retail prices. In *United States v. Colgate & Co.*,[9] for example, the United States Supreme Court held that a manufacturer's advance announcement that it would not sell to price cutters was not a violation of the Sherman Act.

Nevertheless, in some instances, a unilateral refusal to deal will violate antitrust laws. These instances involve offenses proscribed under Section 2 of the Sherman Act and occur only if (1) the firm refusing to deal has—or is likely to acquire—monopoly power and (2) the refusal is likely to have an anticompetitive effect on a particular market.

---

5. 388 U.S. 365, 87 S.Ct. 1856, 18 L.Ed.2d 1249 (1967).

6. 433 U.S. 36, 97 S.Ct. 2549, 53 L.Ed.2d 568 (1977).

7. Note that there is some disagreement in the case law on when a vertical restraint should be considered unreasonable. See, for example, *State of New York by Abrams v. Anheuser-Busch*, 811 F.Supp. 848 (E.D.N.Y. 1993), which calls into doubt one of the holdings of the *Continental* case.

8. *State Oil Co. v. Khan*, 522 U.S. 3, 118 S.Ct. 275, 139 L.Ed.2d 199 (1997).

9. 250 U.S. 300, 39 S.Ct. 465, 63 L.Ed. 992 (1919).

ADAPTING THE LAW TO THE ONLINE ENVIRONMENT — Can Realtor® Associations Limit Listings on Their Web Sites?

Like almost every other product, homes are now being sold via the Internet on hundreds of thousands of Web sites. The most extensive listings of homes for sale, though, are found on the multiple listing services (MLS) sites that are available for every locality in the United States. An MLS site is developed through a cooperative agreement by real estate brokers in a particular market area to pool information about the properties they have for sale. Today, the majority of residential real estate sales involve the use of MLS. Although MLS sites offer convenience by combining listings from many brokers, the sites have also raised antitrust concerns by restricting how certain brokers may use the sites. The Federal Trade Commission (FTC) and the U.S. Department of Justice have brought antitrust actions against both local real estate associations and the National Association of Realtors®, a national trade association for real estate brokers and agents, for attempting to restrict the use of MLS databases.

Boards of Realtors® Have Attempted to Limit Listings on Their Web Sites

In a given market area, the MLS listings are put together by the members of a local real estate association, typically called a Board of Realtors®, for the members' exclusive use. In many areas, Boards of Realtors® have attempted to restrict the homes that can be listed on the official MLS Web site. In particular, the boards have tried to prevent discount brokers from listing the homes they have for sale.

The FTC's Bureau of Competition filed a complaint for violation of antitrust laws against the Board of Realtors® in Austin, Texas, which had a rule prohibiting discount brokers from listing on its MLS site. After several months of negotiations, the FTC prevented the Austin board from adopting and enforcing "any rule that treats different types of real estate listing agreements differently." The FTC is now pursuing similar negotiations in other cities including Cleveland, Columbus, Detroit, and Indianapolis.

The NAR Tries to Restrict Virtual Brokers

The National Association of Realtors (NAR) represents more than 1 million individual member brokers and their affiliated agents and sales associates. Its policies govern the conduct of its members throughout the United States. In the 1990s, many members of the NAR began to create password-protected Web sites through which prospective home buyers could search the MLS database. The password would be given only to potential buyers who had registered as customers of the broker. The brokers who worked through these virtual office Web sites, or VOWs, came to be known as VOW-operating brokers. Because they had no need of a physical office, their operating

---

SECTION 2 OF THE SHERMAN ACT

Section 1 of the Sherman Act proscribes certain concerted, or joint, activities that restrain trade. In contrast, Section 2 condemns "every person who shall monopolize, or attempt to monopolize." Thus, two distinct types of behavior are subject to sanction under Section 2: *monopolization* and *attempts to monopolize*. One tactic that may be involved in either offense is **predatory pricing.** Predatory pricing involves an attempt by one firm to drive its competitors from the market by selling its product at prices substantially *below* the normal costs of production. Once the competitors are eliminated, the firm will attempt to recapture its losses and go on to earn higher profits by driving prices up far above their competitive levels.

PREDATORY PRICING
The pricing of a product below cost with the intent to drive competitors out of the market.

Monopolization

MONOPOLIZATION
The possession of monopoly power in the relevant market and the willful acquisition or maintenance of that power, as distinguished from growth or development as a consequence of a superior product, business acumen, or historic accident.

In *United States v. Grinnell Corp.,*[10] the United States Supreme Court defined the offense of **monopolization** as involving the following two elements: "(1) the possession of monopoly power in the relevant market and (2) the willful acquisition or maintenance of [that] power as distinguished from growth or development as a consequence of a superior

---

10. 384 U.S. 563, 86 S.Ct. 1698, 16 L.Ed.2d 778 (1966).

expenses were lower than those of traditional brokers. Soon both Cendant and RE/MAX, the largest and second-largest U.S. real estate franchisors, respectively, expressed concern that VOW-operating brokers would put downward pressure on brokers' commissions.

In response, the NAR developed a new policy for Web listings. The policy included an opt-out provision "that forbade any broker participating in a multiple listing service from conveying a listing to his or her customers via the Internet without the permission of the listing broker." In other words, a traditional broker could prevent her or his listings in the MLS database from being displayed on the Web site of a VOW-operating broker.

The U.S. Department of Justice Enters the Fray

The Antitrust Division of the U.S. Department of Justice, however, contended that the opt-out policy was anticompetitive and harmful to consumers. When the Justice Department indicated that it would bring an antitrust action against the NAR, the association modified its policy and eliminated the selective opt-out provision aimed specifically at VOW-operating brokers. Nevertheless, the revised policy still allowed brokers to prevent their listings from being displayed on any competitor's Web site. Thus, under the new policy, traditional brokers could still prevent VOW-operating brokers from providing the same MLS information via the Internet that traditional brokers could provide in person. The policy also permitted MLS sites to lower the quality of the data feed they provide brokers, thereby restraining brokers from using Internet-based features to enhance the services they offer customers.

In response, the Justice Department filed a suit in federal district court against the NAR, asserting that the association's policies had violated Section 1 of the Sherman Act by preventing real estate brokers from offering better services as well as lower costs to online consumers. The department contends that the NAR's policies constitute a "contract, combination, and conspiracy between NAR and its members which unreasonably restrains competition in brokerage service markets throughout the United States to the detriment of American consumers." In 2006, finding that the Justice Department had shown sufficient evidence of anticompetitive effects to allow the suit to go forward, the court denied the NAR's motion to dismiss the case.[a]

 **FOR CRITICAL ANALYSIS** *Why couldn't discount brokers simply create their own Web sites to list the houses they have for sale?*

a. *United States v. National Association of Realtors*, 2006 WL 3434263 (N.D.Ill. 2006).

---

product, business acumen, or historic accident." A violation of Section 2 requires that both these elements—monopoly power and an intent to monopolize—be established.

Monopoly Power   The Sherman Act does not define *monopoly*. In economic parlance, monopoly refers to control of a single market by a single entity. It is well established in antitrust law, however, that a firm may be deemed a monopolist even though it is not the sole seller in a market. Additionally, size alone does not determine whether a firm is a monopoly. For example, a "mom and pop" grocery located in an isolated desert town is a monopolist if it is the only grocery serving that particular market. Size in relation to the market is what matters because monopoly involves the power to affect prices.

Market Power.   *Monopoly power*, as mentioned earlier in this chapter, exists when a firm has an extremely large amount of market power. If a firm has sufficient market power to control prices and exclude competition, that firm has monopoly power. As difficult as it is to define market power precisely, it is even more difficult to measure it. In determining the extent of a firm's market power, courts often use the so-called **market-share test**,[11] which measures the firm's percentage share of the "relevant market." A firm may be considered

MARKET-SHARE TEST
The primary measure of monopoly power. A firm's market share is the percentage of a market that the firm controls.

---

11. Other measures of market power have been devised, but the market-share test is the most widely used.

to have monopoly power if its share of the relevant market is 70 percent or more. This is merely a rule of thumb, though; it is not a binding principle of law. In some instances, a smaller share may be held to constitute monopoly power.[12]

Relevant Market. The relevant market consists of two elements: (1) a relevant product market and (2) a relevant geographic market. What should the relevant product market include? No doubt, it must include all products that, although produced by different firms, have identical attributes, such as sugar. Products that are not identical, however, may sometimes be substituted for one another. Coffee may be substituted for tea, for example. In defining the relevant product market, the key issue is the degree of interchangeability between products. If one product is a sufficient substitute for another, the two products are considered to be part of the same product market.

The second component of the relevant market is the geographic extent of the market. For products that are sold nationwide, the geographic boundaries of the market encompass the entire United States. If a producer and its competitors sell in only a limited area (one in which customers have no access to other sources of the product), the geographic market is limited to that area. A national firm may thus compete in several distinct areas and have monopoly power in one area but not in another.

The geographic size of a relevant market was at issue in the following case.

---

12. This standard was first articulated by Judge Learned Hand in *United States v. Aluminum Co. of America*, 148 F.2d 416 (2d Cir. 1945). A 90 percent share was held to be clear evidence of monopoly power. Anything less than 64 percent, said Judge Hand, made monopoly power doubtful, and anything less than 30 percent was clearly not monopoly power.

CASE 22.1   Heerwagen v. Clear Channel Communications

United States Court of Appeals, Second Circuit, 435 F.3d 219 (2006).

FACTS Clear Channel Communications, Inc., owns nearly 1,200 U.S. radio stations and has interests in 240 radio stations overseas. It also promotes or produces more than 26,000 live entertainment events per year; owns more than 135 live entertainment venues; and controls 900 music-related Web sites, 19 television stations, and more than 700,000 outdoor-advertising displays. In 2001, Clear Channel accounted for 70 percent of U.S. concert ticket revenue. Its combined ownership of media and concert halls enabled it to book and sell nationwide tours for performers without involving other parties. Malinda Heerwagen lived in Chicago, Illinois. Over a five-year period beginning in 1997, she attended ten rock concerts in Chicago, including performances by U2, the Grateful Dead, the Rolling Stones, and Paul McCartney. In 2002, on behalf of "[a]ll persons * * * who purchased tickets to any live rock concert in the United States" from Clear Channel, Heerwagen filed a suit in a federal district court. She claimed that Clear Channel had used anticompetitive practices to acquire and maintain monopoly power in a national ticket market for live rock concerts in violation of Section 2 of the Sherman Act, thereby forcing audiences to pay inflated prices for tickets. The court denied Heerwagen's petition. She appealed to the U.S. Court of Appeals for the Second Circuit.

ISSUE Is the relevant market for tickets to live rock concerts national?

DECISION No. The U.S. Court of Appeals for the Second Circuit affirmed the lower court's ruling, which was based on the conclusion that "the market at issue here is local."

REASON During the relevant five-year period, Heerwagen did not go to a live rock concert outside Chicago, nor did she check out the ticket prices of performances elsewhere. The U.S. Court of Appeals for the Second Circuit reasoned that, as Heerwagen's own experience demonstrated, "there is little cross-elasticity of demand for live rock concert tickets between geographic areas. A purchaser of a concert ticket is hardly likely to look outside of her own area, even if the price for

CASE 22.1–Continued

tickets has increased inside her region and decreased for the same tour in other places. Tours are promoted nationally, but a higher price in Boston will not lead Boston purchasers to buy tickets for the same concert held in New York." Evidence of this fact, which was presented to the lower court, "accords with common sense in the calculus for the availability of substitutes. The cost to attend a concert in a remote geographic region would be substantially greater than whatever increment a concert promoter might add to the cost

of a concert ticket. Hence, from the standpoint of the individual concertgoer the two concert tickets are not substitutes for one another."

FOR CRITICAL ANALYSIS–Economic Consideration
Around the United States, prices vary for tickets to live rock concerts by the same performing artists. What might this indicate about any one promoter's power to control prices and exclude competition nationally?

The Intent Requirement Monopoly power, in and of itself, does not constitute the offense of monopolization under Section 2 of the Sherman Act. The offense also requires an *intent* to monopolize. A dominant market share may be the result of business acumen or the development of a superior product. It may simply be the result of historic accident. In these situations, the acquisition of monopoly power is not an antitrust violation. Indeed, it would be contrary to society's interest to condemn every firm that acquired a position of power because it was well managed and efficient and marketed a product desired by consumers.

If a firm possesses market power as a result of carrying out some purposeful act to acquire or maintain that power through anticompetitive means, then it is in violation of Section 2. In most monopolization cases, intent may be inferred from evidence that the firm had monopoly power and engaged in anticompetitive behavior.

■EXAMPLE 22.5 Navigator, the first popular graphical Internet browser, used Java technology that was able to run on a variety of platforms. When Navigator was introduced, Microsoft perceived a threat to its dominance of the operating-system market. Microsoft developed a competing browser, Internet Explorer, and then began to require computer makers that wanted to install Windows to also install Explorer and exclude Navigator. In addition, Microsoft included codes in Windows that would cripple the operating system if Explorer was deleted, and it also paid Internet service providers to distribute Explorer and exclude Navigator. Because of this pattern of exclusionary conduct, a court found that Microsoft was guilty of monopolization in violation of Section 2 of the Sherman Act. The court reasoned that Microsoft's pattern of conduct could be rational only if the firm knew that it possessed monopoly power.[13] ■

KEEP IN MIND Section 2 of the Sherman Act essentially condemns the act of monopolizing, not the possession of monopoly power.

Because exclusionary conduct can have legitimate efficiency-enhancing effects, it can be difficult to determine when conduct will be viewed as anticompetitive and a violation of Section 2 of the Sherman Act. Thus, a business that possesses monopoly power must be careful that its actions cannot be inferred to be evidence of intent to monopolize. Even if your business does not have a dominant market share, you would be wise to take precautions. Make sure that you can articulate clear, legitimate reasons for the particular conduct or contract and that you do not provide any direct evidence (damaging e-mails, for example) of an intent to exclude competitors. A court will be less likely to infer the intent to monopolize if the specific conduct was aimed at increasing output and

**PREVENTING
LEGAL DISPUTES**

---

13. *United States v. Microsoft Corp.*, 253 F.3d 34 (D.D.C. 2001). Microsoft has faced numerous antitrust claims and has settled a number of lawsuits in which it was accused of antitrust violations and anticompetitive tactics.

lowering per-unit costs, improving product quality, or protecting a patented technology or innovation. Exclusionary conduct and agreements that have no redeeming qualities are much more likely to be deemed illegal.

Attempts to Monopolize

ATTEMPTED MONOPOLIZATION
Any actions by a firm to eliminate competition and gain monopoly power.

Section 2 also prohibits **attempted monopolization** of a market. Any action challenged as an attempt to monopolize must have been specifically intended to exclude competitors and garner monopoly power. In addition, the attempt must have had a "dangerous" probability of success—only *serious* threats of monopolization are condemned as violations. The probability cannot be dangerous unless the alleged offender possesses some degree of market power.

ETHICAL ISSUE 22.1

Are we destined for more monopolies in the future? Knowledge and information form the building blocks of the so-called new economy. Some observers believe that the nature of this new economy means that we will see an increasing number of monopolies similar to Microsoft. Consider that the justification for all antitrust law is that monopoly leads to restricted output and hence higher prices for consumers. That is how a monopolist maximizes profits relative to a competitive firm. In the knowledge-based sector, however, firms face *economies of scale* (defined as decreases in long-run average costs resulting from increases in output), so they will do the exact opposite of a traditional monopolist—they will increase output and reduce prices. That is exactly what Microsoft has done over the years—the prices of its operating system and applications have fallen, particularly when corrected for inflation.

This characteristic of knowledge-based monopolies may mean that antitrust authorities will have to have greater tolerance for these monopolies to allow them to benefit from full economies of scale. After all, consumers are the ultimate beneficiaries of such economies of scale. In the early 1900s, economist Joseph Schumpeter argued in favor of allowing monopolies. According to his theory of "creative destruction," monopolies stimulate innovation and economic growth because firms that capture monopoly profits have a greater incentive to innovate. Those that do not survive—the firms that are "destroyed"—leave room for the more efficient firms that will survive.

THE CLAYTON ACT

In 1914, Congress attempted to strengthen federal antitrust laws by enacting the Clayton Act. The Clayton Act was aimed at specific anticompetitive or monopolistic practices that the Sherman Act did not cover. The substantive provisions of the act deal with four distinct forms of business behavior, which are declared illegal but not criminal. With regard to each of the four provisions, the act's prohibitions are qualified by the general condition that the behavior is illegal only if it substantially tends to lessen competition or create monopoly power. The major offenses under the Clayton Act are set out in Sections 2, 3, 7, and 8 of the act.

Section 2—Price Discrimination

PRICE DISCRIMINATION
Setting prices in such a way that two competing buyers pay two different prices for an identical product or service.

Section 2 of the Clayton Act prohibits **price discrimination,** which occurs when a seller charges different prices to competitive buyers for identical goods or services. Because businesses frequently circumvented Section 2 of the act, Congress strengthened this section by amending it with the passage of the Robinson-Patman Act in 1936.

As amended, Section 2 prohibits price discrimination that cannot be justified by differences in production costs or transportation costs, or cost differences due to other reasons. To violate Section 2, the seller must be engaged in interstate commerce, and the effect of the price discrimination must be to substantially lessen competition or create a competitive injury. In other words, a seller is prohibited from reducing a price to one buyer below the price charged to that buyer's competitor. Even offering goods to different customers at the same price but with different delivery arrangements may violate Section 2 in some circumstances.[14]

An exception is made if the seller can justify the price reduction by demonstrating that the lower price was charged temporarily and in good faith to meet another seller's equally low price to the buyer. To be predatory, a seller's pricing policies must also include a reasonable prospect that the seller will recoup its losses.[15]

Section 3—Exclusionary Practices

Under Section 3 of the Clayton Act, sellers or lessors cannot sell or lease goods "on the condition, agreement or understanding that the . . . purchaser or lessee thereof shall not use or deal in the goods . . . of a competitor or competitors of the seller." In effect, this section prohibits two types of vertical agreements involving exclusionary practices—exclusive-dealing contracts and tying arrangements.

Exclusive-Dealing Contracts A contract under which a seller forbids a buyer to purchase products from the seller's competitors is called an **exclusive-dealing contract.** A seller is prohibited from making an exclusive-dealing contract under Section 3 if the effect of the contract is "to substantially lessen competition or tend to create a monopoly."

■EXAMPLE 22.6 In *Standard Oil Co. of California v. United States,*[16] a leading case decided by the United States Supreme Court in 1949, the then-largest gasoline seller in the nation made exclusive-dealing contracts with independent stations in seven western states. The contracts involved 16 percent of all retail outlets, with sales amounting to approximately 7 percent of all retail sales in that market. The Court noted that the market was substantially concentrated because the seven largest gasoline suppliers all used exclusive-dealing contracts with their independent retailers and together controlled 65 percent of the market. Looking at market conditions after the arrangements were instituted, the Court found that market shares were extremely stable and that entry into the market was apparently restricted. Thus, the Court held that Section 3 of the Clayton Act had been violated because competition was "foreclosed in a substantial share" of the relevant market. ■

Note that since the Supreme Court's 1949 decision in the *Standard Oil* case, a number of subsequent decisions have called the holding in this case into doubt.[17] Today, it is clear that to violate antitrust law, an exclusive-dealing agreement (or tying arrangement, discussed next) must qualitatively and substantially harm competition. To prevail, a plaintiff must present affirmative evidence that the performance of the agreement will foreclose competition and harm consumers.

Suppose that the owner of this gas station agrees to buy gas only from Shell Oil Company. Does this agreement necessarily violate the Clayton Act? Why or why not? ("Iotae/Aaron"/Creative Commons)

EXCLUSIVE-DEALING CONTRACT
An agreement under which a seller forbids a buyer to purchase products from the seller's competitors.

---

14. *Bell v. Fur Breeders Agricultural Cooperative,* 3 F.Supp.2d 1241 (D. Utah 1998).
15. See, for example, *Brooke Group, Ltd. v. Brown & Williamson Tobacco Corp.,* 509 U.S. 209, 113 S.Ct. 2578, 125 L.Ed.2d 168 (1993), in which the United States Supreme Court held that a seller's price-cutting policies could not be predatory "[g]iven the market's realities"—the size of the seller's market share and the expanding output by other sellers, as well as additional factors.
16. 337 U.S. 293, 69 S.Ct. 1051, 93 L.Ed. 1371 (1949).
17. See, for example, *Illinois Tool Works, Inc. v. Independent Ink, Inc.,* 547 U.S. 28, 126 S.Ct. 1281, 164 L.Ed.2d 26 (2006), also presented as Case 22.2; *Stop & Shop Supermarket Co. v. Blue Cross & Blue Shield of Rhode Island,* 373 F.3d 57 (1st Cir. 2004); *Yeager's Fuel, Inc. v. Pennsylvania Power & Light Co.,* 953 F.Supp. 617 (E.D.Pa. 1997); and *Tampa Electric Co. v. Nashville Coal Co.,* 365 U.S. 320, 81 S.Ct. 632, 5 L.Ed.2d 580 (1961).

TYING ARRANGEMENT
An agreement between a buyer and a seller in which the buyer of a specific product or service becomes obligated to purchase additional products or services from the seller.

Tying Arrangements   When a seller conditions the sale of a product (the tying product) on the buyer's agreement to purchase another product (the tied product) produced or distributed by the same seller, a **tying arrangement**, or *tie-in sales agreement*, results. The legality of a tie-in agreement depends on many factors, particularly the purpose of the agreement and its likely effect on competition in the relevant markets (the market for the tying product and the market for the tied product).

■EXAMPLE 22.7   In 1936, the United States Supreme Court held that International Business Machines and Remington Rand had violated Section 3 of the Clayton Act by requiring the purchase of their own machine cards (the tied product) as a condition for leasing their tabulation machines (the tying product). Because only these two firms sold completely automated tabulation machines, the Court concluded that each possessed market power sufficient to "substantially lessen competition" through the tying arrangements.[18] ■

Section 3 of the Clayton Act has been held to apply only to commodities, not to services. Tying arrangements, however, can also be considered agreements that restrain trade in violation of Section 1 of the Sherman Act. Thus, cases involving tying arrangements of services have been brought under Section 1 of the Sherman Act. Although earlier cases condemned tying arrangements as illegal *per se*, courts now evaluate tying agreements under the rule of reason.

When an arrangement ties patented and unpatented products, can the relevant market and the patent holder's power in that market be presumed without proof? That was the question in the following case.

---

18. *International Business Machines Corp. v. United States,* 298 U.S. 131, 56 S.Ct. 701, 80 L.Ed. 1085 (1936).

CASE 22.2   Illinois Tool Works, Inc. v. Independent Ink, Inc.

Supreme Court of the United States, 547 U.S. 28, 126 S.Ct. 1281, 164 L.Ed.2d 26 (2006).
www.findlaw.com/casecode/supreme.html[a]

FACTS   Illinois Tool Works, Inc., in Glenview, Illinois, owns Trident, Inc. The firms make printing systems that include three components: a patented inkjet printhead, a patented ink container that attaches to the printhead, and specially designed, but unpatented, ink. They sell the systems to original equipment manufacturers (OEMs) that incorporate the systems into printers that are sold to other companies to use in printing bar codes on packaging materials. As part of each deal, the OEMs agree to buy ink exclusively from Illinois and Trident and not to refill the patented containers with ink of any other kind. Independent Ink, Inc., in Gardena, California, sells ink with the same chemical composition as Illinois and Trident's product at lower prices. Independent filed a suit in a federal district court against Illinois and Trident, alleging, among other things, that they were engaged in illegal tying in violation of the Sherman Act. Independent filed a motion for summary judgment, arguing that because the defendants owned patents in their

products, market power could be presumed. The court issued a summary judgment in the defendants' favor, holding that market power could not be presumed. The U.S. Court of Appeals for the Federal Circuit reversed this judgment. Illinois and Trident appealed to the United States Supreme Court.

ISSUE   Does a party claiming a violation of antitrust law in a deal tying patented and unpatented products have to offer proof of the relevant market and the patent holder's power in that market?

DECISION   Yes. The United States Supreme Court vacated the judgment of the appellate court and remanded the case to the trial court to give Independent "a fair opportunity" to offer evidence of the relevant market and the defendants' power within it. The Supreme Court ruled that a plaintiff that alleges an illegal tying arrangement involving a patented product must prove that the defendant has market power in the tying product.

REASON   The Court pointed out that the presumption that a company automatically possesses market power in a

---

a. In the "Browsing" section, click on "2006 Decisions." When that page opens, scroll to the name of the case and click on it to read the opinion.

CASE 22.2–Continued

patented product arose outside the area of antitrust law as part of the patent misuse doctrine. The assumption was that "by tying the purchase of unpatented goods to the sale of [a] patented good, the patentee was restraining competition or securing a limited monopoly of an unpatented material." The patent misuse doctrine "presumed the requisite economic power over the tying product such that the patentee could extend its economic control to unpatented products." Over the years, however, Congress "chipp[ed] away at the assumption in the patent misuse context" and finally amended the patent laws to eliminate the presumption in that context. "[G]iven the fact that the patent misuse doctrine provided the basis for the market power presumption, it would be anomalous to preserve the presumption in antitrust after Congress has

eliminated its foundation." Instead, tying arrangements involving patented products should be evaluated according to such factors as those that apply in a rule-of-reason analysis.

WHY IS THIS CASE IMPORTANT TO BUSINESSPERSONS? *This case effectively reversed more than forty years of case law. Prior to this decision, the mere fact that a patent existed gave rise to a presumption that the patent holder had market power for purposes of a tying claim. In this case, the Court rejected the presumption of market power and required the plaintiff to provide affirmative evidence of market power over the tied product in all future tying claims. Further, by recognizing that tying arrangements can have legitimate business justifications, the Court signaled a shift in its view of tying claims.*

Section 7–Mergers

Under Section 7 of the Clayton Act, a person or business organization cannot hold stock and/or assets in another entity "where the effect . . . may be to substantially lessen competition." Section 7 is the statutory authority for preventing mergers or acquisitions that could result in monopoly power or a substantial lessening of competition in the marketplace. Section 7 applies to horizontal mergers and vertical mergers, both of which we discuss in the following subsections.

A crucial consideration in most merger cases is the **market concentration** of a product or business. Determining market concentration involves allocating percentage market shares among the various companies in the relevant market. When a small number of companies control a large share of the market, the market is concentrated. For example, if the four largest grocery stores in Chicago accounted for 80 percent of all retail food sales, the market clearly would be concentrated in those four firms. Competition, however, is not necessarily diminished solely as a result of market concentration, and other factors will be considered in determining whether a merger will violate Section 7. One factor of particular importance in evaluating the effects of a merger is whether the merger will make it more difficult for potential competitors to enter the relevant market.

MARKET CONCENTRATION
The degree to which a small number of firms control a large percentage share of a relevant market; determined by calculating the percentages held by the largest firms in that market.

Horizontal Mergers Mergers between firms that compete with each other in the same market are called **horizontal mergers.** If a horizontal merger creates an entity with anything other than a small percentage market share, the merger will be presumed illegal. This is because the United States Supreme Court has held that Congress, in amending Section 7 of the Clayton Act in 1950, intended to prevent mergers that increase market concentration.[19] When analyzing the legality of a horizontal merger, the courts also consider three other factors: overall concentration of the relevant product market, the relevant market's history of tending toward concentration, and whether the apparent design of the merger is to establish market power or to restrict competition.

The Federal Trade Commission and the U.S. Department of Justice have established guidelines indicating which mergers will be challenged. Under the guidelines, the first

HORIZONTAL MERGER
A merger between two firms that are competing in the same marketplace.

---

19. *Brown Shoe v. United States*, 370 U.S. 294, 82 S.Ct. 1502, 8 L.Ed.2d 510 (1962).

factor to be considered is the degree of concentration in the relevant market. Other factors to be considered include the ease of entry into the relevant market, economic efficiency, the financial condition of the merging firms, and the nature and price of the product or products involved. If a firm is a leading one—having at least a 35 percent share and twice the share of the next leading firm—any merger with a firm having as little as a 1 percent share will be closely scrutinized.

Vertical Mergers   A **vertical merger** occurs when a company at one stage of production acquires a company at a higher or lower stage of production. An example of a vertical merger is a company merging with one of its suppliers or retailers. In the past, courts focused almost exclusively on "foreclosure" in assessing vertical mergers. Foreclosure occurs because competitors of the merging firms lose opportunities to sell or buy products from the merging firms.

> **■EXAMPLE 22.8** In *United States v. E. I. du Pont de Nemours & Co.,*[20] du Pont was challenged for acquiring a considerable amount of General Motors (GM) stock. In holding that the transaction was illegal, the United States Supreme Court noted that the stock acquisition would enable du Pont to prevent other sellers of fabrics and finishes from selling to GM, which then accounted for 50 percent of all auto fabric and finishes purchases. ■

Today, whether a vertical merger will be deemed illegal generally depends on several factors, such as whether the merger would produce a firm controlling an undue percentage share of the relevant market. The courts also analyze whether the merger would result in a significant increase in the concentration of firms in that market, the barriers to entry into the market, and the apparent intent of the merging parties.[21] Mergers that do not prevent competitors of either merging firm from competing in a segment of the market will not be condemned as "foreclosing" competition and are legal.

Section 8—Interlocking Directorates

Section 8 of the Clayton Act deals with *interlocking directorates*—that is, the practice of having individuals serve as directors on the boards of two or more competing companies simultaneously. Specifically, no person may be a director in two or more competing corporations at the same time if either of the corporations has capital, surplus, or undivided profits aggregating more than $24,001,000 or competitive sales of $2,400,100 or more. The Federal Trade Commission (FTC) adjusts the threshold amounts each year. (The amounts given here are those announced by the FTC in 2007.)

ENFORCEMENT OF ANTITRUST LAWS

The federal agencies that enforce the federal antitrust laws are the U.S. Department of Justice (DOJ) and the Federal Trade Commission (FTC). The FTC was established by the Federal Trade Commission Act of 1914. Section 5 of that act condemns all forms of anticompetitive behavior that are not covered under other federal antitrust laws.

Only the DOJ can prosecute violations of the Sherman Act, which can be either criminal or civil offenses. Either the DOJ or the FTC can enforce the Clayton Act, but violations of that statute are not crimes and can be pursued only through civil proceedings. The DOJ or the FTC may ask the courts to impose various remedies, including **divestiture** (making a company give up one or more of its operating functions) and dissolution. A

VERTICAL MERGER
The acquisition by a company at one level in a marketing chain of a company at a higher or lower level in the chain (such as a company merging with one of its suppliers or retailers).

CONTRAST   Section 5 of the Federal Trade Commission Act is broader than the other antitrust laws. It covers virtually all anticompetitive behavior, including conduct that does not violate either the Sherman Act or the Clayton Act.

DIVESTITURE
The act of selling one or more of a company's divisions or parts, such as a subsidiary or plant; often mandated by the courts in merger or monopolization cases.

---

20. 353 U.S. 586, 77 S.Ct. 872, 1 L.Ed.2d 1057 (1957).
21. *United States v. Dairy Farmers of America, Inc.,* 426 F.3d 850 (6th Cir. 2005); *United States v. Philadelphia National Bank,* 374 U.S. 321, 83 S.Ct. 1715, 10 L.Ed.2d 915 (1963).

meatpacking firm, for example, might be forced to divest itself of control or ownership of butcher shops. (To find out how you can avoid antitrust problems, see the *Application* feature at the end of this chapter.)

The FTC has the sole authority to enforce violations of Section 5 of the Federal Trade Commission Act. FTC actions are effected through administrative orders, but if a firm violates an FTC order, the FTC can seek court sanctions for the violation.

Private Actions

A private party who has been injured as a result of a violation of the Sherman Act or the Clayton Act can sue for damages and attorneys' fees. In some instances, private parties may also seek injunctive relief to prevent antitrust violations. The courts have determined that the ability to sue depends on the directness of the injury suffered by the would-be plaintiff. Thus, a person wishing to sue under the Sherman Act must prove (1) that the antitrust violation either caused or was a substantial factor in causing the injury that was suffered and (2) that the unlawful actions of the accused party affected business activities of the plaintiff that were protected by the antitrust laws.

Treble Damages

In recent years, more than 90 percent of all antitrust actions have been brought by private plaintiffs. One reason for this is that successful plaintiffs may recover **treble damages**— three times the damages that they have suffered as a result of the violation. Such recoveries by private plaintiffs for antitrust violations have been rationalized as encouraging people to act as "private attorneys general" who will vigorously pursue antitrust violators on their own initiative. In a situation involving a price-fixing agreement, normally each competitor is jointly and severally liable for the total amount of any damages, including treble damages if they are imposed.

TREBLE DAMAGES
Damages that, by statute, are three times the amount that the fact finder determines is owed.

EXEMPTIONS FROM ANTITRUST LAWS

There are many legislative and constitutional limitations on antitrust enforcement. Most statutory and judicially created exemptions to the antitrust laws apply to the following areas or activities:

1 *Labor.* Section 6 of the Clayton Act generally permits labor unions to organize and bargain without violating antitrust laws. Section 20 of the Clayton Act specifies that strikes and other labor activities are not violations of any law of the United States. A union can lose its exemption, however, if it combines with a nonlabor group rather than acting simply in its own self-interest.

2 *Agricultural associations and fisheries.* Section 6 of the Clayton Act (along with the Capper-Volstead Act of 1922) exempts agricultural cooperatives from the antitrust laws. The Fisheries Cooperative Marketing Act of 1976 exempts from antitrust legislation individuals in the fishing industry who collectively catch, produce, and prepare for market their products. Both exemptions allow members of such co-ops to combine and set prices for a particular product, but do not allow them to engage in exclusionary practices or restraints of trade directed at competitors.

3 *Insurance.* The McCarran-Ferguson Act of 1945 exempts the insurance business from the antitrust laws whenever state regulation exists. This exemption does not cover boycotts, coercion, or intimidation on the part of insurance companies.

Congress named an act after baseball player Curt Flood. Why?
(Courtesy of the National Baseball Hall of Fame)

NOTE State actions include the regulation of public utilities, whose rates may be set by the states in which they do business.

4 *Foreign trade.* Under the provisions of the Webb-Pomerene Act, of 1918, U.S. exporters may engage in cooperative activity to compete with similar foreign associations. This type of cooperative activity may not, however, restrain trade within the United States or injure other U.S. exporters. The Export Trading Company Act of 1982 broadened the Webb-Pomerene Act by permitting the Department of Justice to certify properly qualified export trading companies. Any activity within the scope described by the certificate is exempt from public prosecution under the antitrust laws.

5 *Professional baseball.* In 1922, the United States Supreme Court held that professional baseball was not within the reach of federal antitrust laws because it did not involve "interstate commerce."[22] Some of the effects of this decision, however, were modified by the Curt Flood Act of 1998. Essentially, the act allows players the option of suing team owners for anticompetitive practices if, for example, the owners collude to "blacklist" players, hold down players' salaries, or force players to play for specific teams.[23]

6 *Oil marketing.* The Interstate Oil Compact of 1935 allows states to determine quotas on oil that will be marketed in interstate commerce.

7 *Cooperative research and production.* Cooperative research among small-business firms is exempt under the Small Business Act of 1958, as amended. Research or production of a product, process, or service by joint ventures consisting of competitors is exempt under special federal legislation, including the National Cooperative Research Act of 1984 and the National Cooperative Production Amendments of 1993.

8 *Joint efforts by businesspersons to obtain legislative or executive action.* This is often referred to as the *Noerr-Pennington* doctrine.[24] For example, DVD producers may jointly lobby Congress to change the copyright laws without being held liable for attempting to restrain trade. Though selfish rather than purely public-minded conduct is permitted, there is an exception: an action will not be protected if it is clear that the action is "objectively baseless in the sense that no reasonable [person] could reasonably expect success on the merits" and it is an attempt to make anticompetitive use of government processes.[25]

9 *Other exemptions.* Other activities exempt from antitrust laws include activities approved by the president in furtherance of the defense of our nation (under the Defense Production Act of 1950, as amended); state actions, when the state policy is clearly articulated and the policy is actively supervised by the state;[26] and activities of regulated industries (such as the communication and banking industries) when federal commissions, boards, or agencies (such as the Federal Communications Commission and the Federal Maritime Commission) have primary regulatory authority.

The issue in the following case was whether a National Football League eligibility rule fell within the labor exemption from the antitrust laws.

---

22. *Federal Baseball Club of Baltimore, Inc. v. National League of Professional Baseball Clubs,* 259 U.S. 200, 42 S.Ct. 465, 66 L.Ed. 898 (1922).

23. Note that in 2003, a federal appellate court held that because baseball was exempt from federal antitrust laws, it was also exempt from the reach of state antitrust laws due to the supremacy clause. *Major League Baseball v. Crist,* 331 F.3d 1177 (11th Cir. 2003).

24. See *Eastern Railroad Presidents Conference v. Noerr Motor Freight, Inc.,* 365 U.S. 127, 81 S.Ct. 523, 5 L.Ed.2d 464 (1961); and *United Mine Workers of America v. Pennington,* 381 U.S. 657, 85 S.Ct. 1585, 14 L.Ed.2d 626 (1965).

25. *Professional Real Estate Investors, Inc. v. Columbia Pictures Industries, Inc.,* 508 U.S. 49, 113 S.Ct. 1920, 123 L.Ed.2d 611 (1993).

26. See *Parker v. Brown,* 317 U.S. 341, 63 S.Ct. 307, 87 L.Ed. 315 (1943).

employee in the terms and conditions of employment because of any lawful act done by the employee—

(1) to provide information, cause information to be provided, or otherwise assist in an investigation regarding any conduct which the employee reasonably believes constitutes a violation of section 1341, 1343, 1344, or 1348, any rule or regulation of the Securities and Exchange Commission, or any provision of Federal law relating to fraud against shareholders, when the information or assistance is provided to or the investigation is conducted by—

(A) a Federal regulatory or law enforcement agency;

(B) any Member of Congress or any committee of Congress; or

(C) a person with supervisory authority over the employee (or such other person working for the employer who has the authority to investigate, discover, or terminate misconduct); or

(2) to file, cause to be filed, testify, participate in, or otherwise assist in a proceeding filed or about to be filed (with any knowledge of the employer) relating to an alleged violation of section 1341, 1343, 1344, or 1348, any rule or regulation of the Securities and Exchange Commission, or any provision of Federal law relating to fraud against shareholders.

(b) Enforcement action.—

(1) In general.—A person who alleges discharge or other discrimination by any person in violation of subsection (a) may seek relief under subsection (c), by—

(A) filing a complaint with the Secretary of Labor; or

(B) if the Secretary has not issued a final decision within 180 days of the filing of the complaint and there is no showing that such delay is due to the bad faith of the claimant, bringing an action at law or equity for de novo review in the appropriate district court of the United States, which shall have jurisdiction over such an action without regard to the amount in controversy.

(2) Procedure.—

(A) In general.—An action under paragraph (1)(A) shall be governed under the rules and procedures set forth in section 42121(b) of title 49, United States Code.

(B) Exception.—Notification made under section 42121(b)(1) of title 49, United States Code, shall be made to the person named in the complaint and to the employer.

(C) Burdens of proof.—An action brought under paragraph (1)(B) shall be governed by the legal burdens of proof set forth in section 42121(b) of title 49, United States Code.

(D) Statute of limitations.—An action under paragraph (1) shall be commenced not later than 90 days after the date on which the violation occurs.

(c) Remedies.—

(1) In general.—An employee prevailing in any action under subsection (b)(1) shall be entitled to all relief necessary to make the employee whole.

(2) Compensatory damages.—Relief for any action under paragraph (1) shall include—

(A) reinstatement with the same seniority status that the employee would have had, but for the discrimination;

(B) the amount of back pay, with interest; and

(C) compensation for any special damages sustained as a result of the discrimination, including litigation costs, expert witness fees, and reasonable attorney fees.

(d) Rights retained by employee.—Nothing in this section shall be deemed to diminish the rights, privileges, or remedies of any employee under any Federal or State law, or under any collective bargaining agreement.

EXPLANATORY COMMENTS: *Section 806 is one of several provisions that were included in the Sarbanes-Oxley Act to encourage and protect whistleblowers—that is, employees who report their employer's alleged violations of securities law to the authorities. This section applies to employees, agents, and independent contractors who work for publicly traded companies or testify about such a company during an investigation. It sets up an administrative procedure at the U.S. Department of Labor for individuals who claim that their employer retaliated against them (fired or demoted them, for example) for blowing the whistle on the employer's wrongful conduct. It also allows the award of civil damages—including back pay, reinstatement, special damages, attorneys' fees, and court costs—to employees who prove that they suffered retaliation. Since this provision was enacted, whistleblowers have filed numerous complaints with the U.S. Department of Labor under this section.*

SECTION 807

Securities fraud[10]

Whoever knowingly executes, or attempts to execute, a scheme or artifice—

(1) to defraud any person in connection with any security of an issuer with a class of securities registered under section 12 of the Securities Exchange Act of 1934 (15 U.S.C. 78l) or that is required to file reports under section 15(d) of the Securities Exchange Act of 1934 (15 U.S.C. 78o(d)); or

(2) to obtain, by means of false or fraudulent pretenses, representations, or promises, any money or property in connection with the purchase or sale of any security of an issuer with a class of securities registered under section 12 of the Securities Exchange Act of 1934 (15 U.S.C. 78l) or that is required to file reports under section 15(d) of the Securities Exchange Act of 1934 (15 U.S.C. 78o(d)); shall be fined under this title, or imprisoned not more than 25 years, or both.

＊　　＊　　＊　　＊

EXPLANATORY COMMENTS: *Section 807 adds a new provision to the federal criminal code that addresses securities fraud. Prior to 2002, federal securities law had already made it a crime—under Section 10(b) of the Securities Exchange Act of 1934 and SEC Rule 10b-5, both of which are discussed in Chapter 21—to intentionally defraud someone in connection with a purchase or sale of securities, but the offense was not listed in the federal criminal code. Also, paragraph 2 of Section 807 goes beyond what is prohibited under securities law by making it a crime to obtain by means of false or fraudulent pretenses any money or property from the purchase or sale of securities. This new provision allows violators to be punished by up to twenty-five years in prison, a fine, or both.*

---

10. Codified at 18 U.S.C. Section 1348.

SECTION 906

Failure of corporate officers to certify financial reports[11]

(a) Certification of periodic financial reports.—Each periodic report containing financial statements filed by an issuer with the Securities Exchange Commission pursuant to section 13(a) or 15(d) of the Securities Exchange Act of 1934 (15 U.S.C. 78m(a) or 78o(d)) shall be accompanied by a written statement by the chief executive officer and chief financial officer (or equivalent thereof) of the issuer.

(b) Content.—The statement required under subsection (a) shall certify that the periodic report containing the financial statements fully complies with the requirements of section 13(a) or 15(d) of the Securities Exchange Act of 1934 (15 U.S.C. 78m or 78o(d)) and that information contained in the periodic report fairly presents, in all material respects, the financial condition and results of operations of the issuer.

(c) Criminal penalties.—Whoever—

(1) certifies any statement as set forth in subsections (a) and (b) of this section knowing that the periodic report accompanying the statement does not comport with all the requirements set forth in

this section shall be fined not more than $1,000,000 or imprisoned not more than 10 years, or both; or

(2) willfully certifies any statement as set forth in subsections (a) and (b) of this section knowing that the periodic report accompanying the statement does not comport with all the requirements set forth in this section shall be fined not more than $5,000,000, or imprisoned not more than 20 years, or both.

EXPLANATORY COMMENTS: *As previously discussed, under Section 302 a corporation's CEO and CFO are required to certify that they believe the quarterly and annual reports their company files with the SEC are accurate and fairly present the company's financial condition. Section 906 adds "teeth" to these requirements by authorizing criminal penalties for those officers who intentionally certify inaccurate SEC filings. Knowing violations of the requirements are punishable by a fine of up to $1 million, ten years' imprisonment, or both. Willful violators may be fined up to $5 million, sentenced to up to twenty years' imprisonment, or both. Although the difference between a knowing and a willful violation is not entirely clear, the section is obviously intended to remind corporate officers of the serious consequences of certifying inaccurate reports to the SEC.*

---

11. Codified at 18 U.S.C. Section 1350.

APPENDIX E
Answers to Even-Numbered For Review Questions

CHAPTER 1

2A.   *Precedent*

Judges attempt to be consistent, and when possible, they base their decisions on the principles suggested by earlier cases. They seek to decide similar cases in a similar way and consider new cases with care, because they know that their conflicting decisions make new law. Each interpretation becomes part of the law on the subject and serves as a legal precedent—a decision that furnishes an example or authority for deciding subsequent cases involving similar legal principles or facts. A court will depart from the rule of a precedent when it decides that the rule should no longer be followed. If a court decides that a precedent is simply incorrect or that technological or social changes have rendered the precedent inapplicable, the court might rule contrary to the precedent.

4A.   *Commercial activities*

To prevent states from establishing laws and regulations that would interfere with trade and commerce among the states, the Constitution expressly delegated to the national government the power to regulate interstate commerce. The commerce clause (Article I, Section 8, of the U.S. Constitution) expressly permits Congress "[t]o regulate Commerce with foreign Nations, and among the several States, and with the Indian Tribes."

CHAPTER 2

2A.   *Ensuring legal and ethical behavior*

Ethical leadership is important to create and maintain an ethical workplace. Management can set standards, and apply those standards to themselves and their firm's employees.

4A.   *Ethical standards*

Duty-based ethical standards are derived from religious precepts or philosophical principles. Outcome-based ethics focus on the consequences of an action, not on the nature of the action or on a set of preestablished moral values or religious beliefs.

CHAPTER 3

2A.   *Jurisdiction*

To hear a case, a court must have jurisdiction over the person against whom the suit is brought or over the property involved in the suit. The court must also have jurisdiction over the subject matter. Generally, courts apply a "sliding-scale" standard to determine when

it is proper to exercise jurisdiction over a defendant whose only connection with the jurisdiction is the Internet.

4A.   *Pleadings, discovery, and electronic filing*

The pleadings include the plaintiff's complaint and the defendant's answer (and the counterclaim and reply). The pleadings inform each party of the other's claims and specify the issues involved in a case. Discovery is the process of obtaining information and evidence about a case from the other party or third parties. Discovery entails gaining access to witnesses, documents, records, and other types of evidence. Electronic discovery differs in its subject (e-media rather than traditional sources of information). Electronic filing involves the filing of court documents in electronic media, typically over the Internet.

CHAPTER 4

2A.   *Purpose and categories of torts*

Generally, the purpose of tort law is to provide remedies for the invasion of legally recognized and protected interests (personal safety, freedom of movement, property, and some intangibles, including privacy and reputation). The two broad categories of torts are intentional and unintentional.

4A.   *Strict liability*

Strict liability is liability without fault. Strict liability for damages proximately caused by an abnormally dangerous or exceptional activity, or the keeping of dangerous animals, is an application of this doctrine. Another significant application of strict liability is in the area of product liability.

CHAPTER 5

2A.   *Trademarks and patents*

As stated in Article I, Section 8, of the Constitution, Congress is authorized "[t]o promote the Progress of Science and useful Arts, by securing for limited Times to Authors and Inventors the exclusive Right to their respective Writings and Discoveries." Laws protecting patents and trademarks, as well copyrights, are designed to protect and reward inventive and artistic creativity.

4A.   *Trade secrets*

Trade secrets are business processes and information that are not or cannot be patented, copyrighted, or trademarked. Trade secrets consist of generally anything that makes an individual company unique and that would have value to a competitor. The Uniform Trade Secrets Act, the Economic Espionage Act, and the common law offer trade secrets protection.

CHAPTER 6

2A. *Types of crime and white-collar crime*
Traditionally, crimes have been grouped into the following categories: violent crime (crimes against persons), property crime, public order crime, white-collar crime, and organized crime. White-collar crime is an illegal act or series of acts committed by an individual or business entity using some nonviolent means, usually in the course of a legitimate occupation.

4A. *Constitutional safeguards and criminal process*
Under the Fourth Amendment, before searching or seizing private property, law enforcement officers must obtain a search warrant, which requires probable cause. Under the Fifth Amendment, no one can be deprived of "life, liberty, or property without due process of law." The Fifth Amendment also protects persons against double jeopardy and self-incrimination. The Sixth Amendment guarantees the right to a speedy trial, the right to a jury trial, the right to a public trial, the right to confront witnesses, and the right to counsel. All evidence obtained in violation of the Fourth, Fifth, and Sixth Amendments must be excluded from the trial, as well as all evidence derived from the illegally obtained evidence. Individuals who are arrested must be informed of certain constitutional rights, including their Fifth Amendment right to remain silent and their Sixth Amendment right to counsel. The Eighth Amendment prohibits excessive bails and fines, and cruel and unusual punishment. The basic steps in the criminal process include an arrest, the booking, the initial appearance, a preliminary hearing, a grand jury or magistrate's review, the arraignment, a plea bargain (if any), and the trial or guilty plea.

CHAPTER 7

2A. *Types of contracts*
The various types of contracts include bilateral, unilateral, express, implied, formal, informal, quasi, valid, void, voidable, and unenforceable.

4A. *Acceptance of an offer*
An acceptance is a voluntary act on the part of the offeree that shows assent, or agreement, to the terms of an offer. The acceptance must be unequivocal and must be timely communicated to the offeror.

CHAPTER 8

2A. *Intoxication*
If a person who is sufficiently intoxicated to lack mental capacity enters into a contract, the contract is voidable at the option of that person. It must be proved that the person's reason and judgment were impaired to the extent that he or she did not comprehend the legal consequences of entering into the contract.

4A. *Elements of fraudulent misrepresentation*
Fraudulent misrepresentation has three elements: (1) misrepresentation of a material fact must occur, (2) there must be an intent to deceive, and (3) the innocent party must justifiably rely on the mis-

representation. Also, to collect damages, a party must have been injured as a result of the misrepresentation.

CHAPTER 9

2A. *Intended beneficiary*
A beneficiary will be considered an intended beneficiary if a reasonable person in the position of the beneficiary would believe that the promisee intended to confer on the beneficiary the right to bring suit to enforce the contract. Other factors include whether performance is rendered directly to the third party, whether the third party has the right to control the details of performance, and whether the third party is expressly designated as a beneficiary in the contract.

4A. *Equitable remedies*
When fraud, mistake, duress, or failure of consideration is present, rescission is available. The failure of one party to perform under a contract entitles the other party to rescind the contract. Specific performance might be granted as a remedy when damages is an inadequate remedy and the subject matter of the contract is unique. Reformation allows a contract to be rewritten to reflect the parties' true intentions. It applies most often when fraud or mutual mistake occurs.

CHAPTER 10

2A. *Shrink-wrap and click-on agreements*
A shrink-wrap agreement is an agreement whose terms are expressed inside a box in which the goods are packaged. Generally, courts have enforced the terms of shrink-wrap agreements the same as the terms of other contracts, applying the traditional common law of contracts.

4A. *Partnering agreement*
A partnering agreement is an agreement between a seller and a buyer who often do business on the terms and conditions that apply to all of their transactions conducted electronically. Such an agreement reduces the likelihood of a dispute and provides for the resolution of any dispute that does arise.

CHAPTER 11

2A. *Additional terms*
Under the UCC, a contract can be formed even if the acceptance includes an offeree's additional or different terms. If one of the parties is a nonmerchant, the contract does not include the additional terms. If both parties are merchants, the additional terms automatically become part of the contract unless (1) the original offer expressly limits acceptance to the terms of the offer, (2) the new or changed terms *materially* alter the contract, or (3) the offeror objects to the new or changed terms within a reasonable period of time. (If the additional terms expressly require the offeror's assent, the offeree's expression is not an acceptance, but a counteroffer.) Under some circumstances, a court might strike the additional terms.

4A. *Passage of risk without movement of goods*
If the goods are held by a seller, and the seller is a merchant, the risk of loss passes to the buyer when the buyer actually takes physical possession of the goods. If the seller is not a merchant, the risk of loss to goods held by the seller passes to the buyer on tender of delivery. When a bailee is holding the goods, the risk of loss passes to the buyer when (1) the buyer receives a negotiable document of title for the

goods, (2) the bailee acknowledges the buyer's right to possess the goods, or (3) the buyer receives a nonnegotiable document of title and has had a reasonable time to present the document to the bailee and demand the goods.

CHAPTER 12

2A. *Perfect tender rule*

Under the perfect tender rule, the seller or lessor has an obligation to ship or tender conforming goods, and if goods or tender of delivery fail in any respect, the buyer or lessee has the right to accept the goods, reject the entire shipment, or accept part and reject part. Exceptions to the perfect tender rule may be established by agreement. When tender is rejected because of nonconforming goods and the time for performance has not yet expired, the seller or lessor can notify the buyer or lessee promptly of the intention to cure and can then do so within the contract time for performance. Once the time for performance has expired, the seller or lessor can, for a reasonable time, exercise the right to cure if he or she had, at the time of delivery, reasonable grounds to believe that the nonconforming tender would be acceptable to the buyer or lessee. When an agreed-on manner of delivery becomes impracticable or unavailable through no fault of either party, a seller may choose a commercially reasonable substitute. In an installment contract, a buyer or lessee can reject an installment only if the nonconformity substantially impairs the value of the installment and cannot be cured. Delay in delivery or nondelivery in whole or in part is not a breach when performance is commercially impracticable. If an unexpected event totally destroys goods identified at the time the contract is formed through no fault of either party and before risk passes to the buyer or lessee, the parties are excused from performance. If a party has reasonable grounds to believe that the other party will not perform, he or she may in writing demand assurance of performance from the other party. Until such assurance is received, he or she may suspend further performance. Finally, when required cooperation is not forthcoming, the cooperative party can suspend her or his own performance without liability.

4A. *Remedies for breach*

Depending on the circumstances at the time of a buyer's breach, a seller may have the right to cancel the contract, withhold delivery, resell or dispose of the goods subject to the contract, recover the purchase price (or lease payments), recover damages, stop delivery in transit, or reclaim the goods. Similarly, on a seller's breach, a buyer may have the right to cancel the contract, recover the goods, obtain specific performance, obtain cover, replevy the goods, recover damages, reject the goods, withhold delivery, resell or dispose of the goods, stop delivery, or revoke acceptance.

CHAPTER 13

2A. *Implied warranties*

Implied warranties that arise under the UCC include the implied warranty of merchantability, the implied warranty of fitness for a particular purpose, and implied warranties that may arise from, or be excluded or modified by, course of dealing, course of performance, or usage of trade.

4A. *Defenses*

Defenses to product liability include plaintiff's assumption of risk, product misuse, and comparative negligence, as well as the attribu-

tion of injuries to commonly known dangers. Also, as in any suit, a defendant can avoid liability by showing that the elements of the cause of action have not been properly pleaded or proved.

CHAPTER 14

2A. *Requirements for negotiability*

For an instrument to be negotiable, it must (1) be in writing, (2) be signed by the maker or the drawer, (3) be an unconditional promise or order to pay, (4) state a fixed amount of money, (5) be payable on demand or at a definite time, and (6) be payable to order or to bearer, unless it is a check.

4A. *Liability*

The key to liability on a negotiable instrument is a signature. Every party, except a qualified indorser, who signs a negotiable instrument is primarily or secondarily liable for payment of that instrument when it comes due. Signature liability arises from indorsing an instrument. Warranty liability arises from transferring an instrument, whether or not the transferor also indorses it.

CHAPTER 15

2A. *Dishonor*

A bank may dishonor a customer's check without liability to the customer when the customer's account contains insufficient funds to pay the check, providing the bank did not agree to cover overdrafts. A bank may also properly dishonor a stale check, a timely check subject to a valid stop-payment order, a check drawn after the customer's death, and forged or altered checks. If a bank wrongfully dishonors a customer's check, the bank is liable to the customer for damages for the failure to pay.

4A. *EFTs and consumers*

The four most common types of EFT systems used by bank customers are automated teller machines, point-of-sale systems, systems handling direct deposits and withdrawals of funds, and Internet payment systems. The EFTA provides a basic framework for the rights, liabilities, and responsibilities of users of these EFT systems. For consumers, the terms and conditions of EFTs must be disclosed in readily understandable language, a receipt must be provided at an e-terminal at the time of a transfer, periodic statements must describe transfers for each account through which an EFT system provides access, and some preauthorized payments can be stopped within three days before they are made.

CHAPTER 16

2A. *Attachment and writs of execution*

Attachment is a court-ordered seizure and taking into custody of property prior to the securing of a judgment for a past-due debt. To use attachment as a remedy, a creditor (1) files with a court an affidavit, stating that a debtor is in default and the grounds on which attachment is sought, and (2) posts a bond to cover costs, the value of the loss of use of the good by the debtor, and the value of the property. The court directs the sheriff or other officer to seize nonexempt property, which can be sold to satisfy a judgment. A *writ of execution* is a court order directing a sheriff to seize and sell any of the debtor's nonexempt real or personal property within the court's jurisdiction. This is used when a debtor will not or cannot pay a judgment.

4A. *Debtor's estate in bankruptcy and debtor in possession*

In a bankruptcy proceeding, a *debtor's estate in property* consists of all the debtor's legal and equitable interests in property currently held, wherever located, together with certain jointly owned property, property transferred in transactions voidable by the trustee, proceeds and profits from the property of the estate, and certain after-acquired property. Federal law exempts (1) up to $20,200 in equity in the debtor's residence and burial plot; (2) interest in a motor vehicle up to $3,225; (3) interest in household goods and furnishings, wearing apparel, appliances, books, animals, crops, and musical instruments up to $525 in a particular item but limited to $10,775 in total; (4) interest in jewelry up to $1,350; (5) any other property worth up to $1,075, plus any unused part of the $20,200 homestead exemption up to an amount of $10,775; (6) interest in any tools of the debtor's trade, up to $2,025; (7) certain life insurance contracts owned by the debtor; (8) certain interests in accrued dividends or interests under life insurance contracts owned by the debtor; (9) professionally prescribed health aids; (10) the right to receive Social Security and certain welfare benefits, alimony and support payments, and certain pension benefits; and (11) the right to receive certain personal-injury and other awards, up to $20,200.

CHAPTER 17

2A. *Agency relationships*

Agency relationships normally are consensual: they arise by voluntary consent and agreement between the parties.

4A. *Liability to third parties*

A disclosed or partially disclosed principal is liable to a third party for a contract made by an agent who is acting within the scope of her or his authority. If the agent exceeds the scope of authority and the principal fails to ratify the contract, the agent may be liable (and the principal may not). When neither the fact of agency nor the identity of the principal is disclosed, the agent is liable, and if an agent has acted within the scope of his or her authority, the undisclosed principal is also liable. Each party is liable for his or her own torts and crimes. A principal may also be liable for an agent's torts committed within the course or scope of employment. A principal is liable for an agent's crime if the principal participated by conspiracy or other action.

CHAPTER 18

2A. *Hours and wages*

The Fair Labor Standards Act is the most significant federal statute governing working hours and wages.

4A. *Federal employment discrimination acts*

Title VII of the Civil Rights Act of 1964 and its amendments prohibit job discrimination against employees, applicants, and union members on the basis of race, color, national origin, religion, and gender at any stage of employment. The Age Discrimination in Employment Act of 1967 and the Americans with Disabilities Act of 1990 prohibit discrimination on the basis of age and disability, respectively.

CHAPTER 19

2A. *Advantages and disadvantages of business forms*

Advantages of the sole proprietorship include the proprietor receiving all of the profits and the ease and inexpensiveness to start the business. Disadvantages of the sole proprietorship include the exclusive burden on the owner of any losses or liabilities incurred by the business enterprise and the limitation on capital to personal funds and the funds of those who are willing to make loans. One of the advantages of a partnership is that it can be organized fairly easily and inexpensively. Additionally, the partnership itself files only an informational tax return. The main disadvantage of the partnership form of business is that partners are subject to personal liability for partnership obligations. One of the key advantages of a corporation is that the liability of its owners is limited to their investments. A disadvantage of the corporate form is that profits are taxed twice.

4A. *Joint ventures and other business organizational forms*

A *joint venture* is an enterprise in which two or more persons or business entities combine their efforts or their property for a single transaction or project, or a related series of transactions or projects. Other special business organizational forms include a joint stock company, syndicate, and cooperative. A *joint stock company* has many characteristics of a corporation (its ownership is represented by transferable shares of stock, it is usually managed by directors and officers of the company or association, and it can have a perpetual existence), but most of its other features are more characteristic of a partnership, and it is usually treated like a partnership. A *syndicate* is a group of individuals getting together to finance a particular project, such as the building of a shopping center. A *business trust* is created by a written trust agreement that sets forth the interests of the beneficiaries, who receive the profits, and the obligations and powers of the trustees, with whom legal ownership and management of the property of the business rests. A *cooperative* is an association, which may not or may be incorporated, that is organized to provide an economic service to its members (or shareholders), who have limited liability. Cooperatives that are unincorporated are often treated like partnerships, and the members have joint liability for the cooperative's acts.

CHAPTER 20

2A. *Duties of directors and officers*

Directors and officers are fiduciaries of the corporation. The fiduciary duties of the directors and officers include the duty of care and the duty of loyalty.

4A. *Roles and rights of shareholders*

Shareholders have an equitable interest in the firm. They are ultimately responsible for choosing the board of directors. Shareholders must approve fundamental corporate changes before the changes can be effected. Shareholders possess numerous rights, including preemptive rights in the purchase of new stock, dividends from corporate profits, and the right to inspection of corporate books and records. Shareholders also have the right to act on behalf of the firm by filing a shareholder's derivative suit to compel the directors to act to redress a wrong suffered by the corporation.

CHAPTER 21

2A. *Major statutes and the Securities and Exchange Commission*

The major statutes regulating the securities industry are the Securities Act of 1933 and the Securities Exchange Act of 1934, which created the Securities and Exchange Commission (SEC). The SEC's major functions are to (1) require the disclosure of facts concerning offerings of securities listed on national securities exchanges and of certain securities traded over the counter; (2) regulate the trade in securities on the national and regional securities exchanges and in the over-the-counter markets; (3) investigate securities fraud; (4) regulate the activities of securities brokers, dealers, and investment advisers and require their registration; (5) supervise the activities of mutual funds; and (6) recommend administrative sanctions, injunctive remedies, and criminal prosecution against those who violate securities laws.

4A. *State securities laws*

Typically, state laws have disclosure requirements and antifraud provisions patterned after Section 10(b) of the Securities Exchange Act of 1934 and SEC Rule 10b-5. State laws provide for the registration or qualification of securities offered or issued for sale within the state with the appropriate state official. Also, most state securities laws regulate securities brokers and dealers.

CHAPTER 22

2A. *Sherman Act*

Section 1 prohibits agreements that are anticompetitively restrictive—that is, agreements that have the wrongful purpose of restraining competition. Section 2 prohibits the misuse, and attempted misuse, of monopoly power in the marketplace.

4A. *Enforcing agencies*

The federal agencies that enforce the federal antitrust laws are the U.S. Department of Justice and the Federal Trade Commission.

CHAPTER 23

2A. *Gifts and other means of acquisition*

To make an effective gift, the donor must intend to make the gift, the gift must be delivered to the donee, and the donee must accept the gift. Property can also be acquired by purchase, possession, production, accession, and confusion.

4A. *Rights and duties of bailees and bailors*

A bailee has the right to control and possess the property temporarily, which includes the right to recover damages for its loss or damage and to regain possession. A bailee may also have the right to use the property. A bailee has a right to be compensated as provided for in the bailment agreement, a right to be reimbursed for costs and services rendered in the keeping of the bailed property, or both. A bailee may have the right to limit liability as long as the limit is called to the atten-

tion of the bailor and is not against public policy. A bailee has the duty to (1) take reasonable care of the property and (2) surrender to the bailor or dispose of the property in accord with the bailor's instructions at the end of the bailment. The bailor must provide the bailee with goods that are free from known defects that could cause injury to the bailee. In a mutual-benefit bailment, the bailor must notify the bailee of any hidden defects that the bailor could have discovered with reasonable diligence and proper inspection. Also, the implied warranties of merchantability and fitness for a particular purpose apply to a bailment that includes the right to use the bailed goods.

CHAPTER 24

2A. *Limitations*

Limits on property owners' rights may be imposed for public uses (flights over private land, for example) or to respect others' rights (restrictions on owners' exercise of subsurface rights to protect the surface owners' rights, for example).

4A. *Environmental impact statements*

An environmental impact statement (EIS) analyzes (1) the impact on the environment that an action will have, (2) any adverse effects on the environment and alternative actions that might be taken, and (3) irreversible effects the action might generate. For every major federal action that significantly affects the quality of the environment, an EIS must be prepared. An action is "major" if it involves a substantial commitment of resources (monetary or otherwise). An action is "federal" if a federal agency has the power to control it.

CHAPTER 25

2A. *Act of state doctrine*

The *act of state doctrine* is a judicially created doctrine that provides that the judicial branch of one country will not examine the validity of public acts committed by a recognized foreign government within its own territory. This doctrine is often employed in cases involving expropriation or confiscation.

4A. *Antitrust laws*

U.S. courts will apply U.S. antitrust laws extraterritorially when it is shown that an alleged violation has a substantial effect on U.S. commerce.

APPENDIX F
Sample Answers for End-of-Chapter *Hypothetical Questions* with Sample Answer

1.3A. HYPOTHETICAL QUESTION WITH SAMPLE ANSWER

1. The U.S. Constitution—The U.S. Constitution is the supreme law of the land. A law in violation of the Constitution, no matter what its source, will be declared unconstitutional and will not be enforced.
2. The federal statute—Under the U.S. Constitution, when there is a conflict between federal law and state law, federal law prevails.
3. The state statute—State statutes are enacted by state legislatures. Areas not covered by state statutory law are governed by state case law.
4. The U.S. Constitution—State constitutions are supreme within their respective borders unless they conflict with the U.S. Constitution, which is the supreme law of the land.
5. The federal administrative regulation—Under the U.S. Constitution, when there is a conflict between federal law and state law, federal law prevails.

2.2A. HYPOTHETICAL QUESTION WITH SAMPLE ANSWER

This question essentially asks whether good behavior can ever be unethical. The answer to this question depends on which approach to ethical reasoning you are using. Under the outcome-based approach of utilitarianism, it is simply not possible for selfish motives to be unethical if they result in good conduct. A good outcome is moral regardless of the nature of the action itself or the reason for the action. Under a duty-based approach, motive would be more relevant in assessing whether a firm's conduct was ethical. You would need to analyze the firm's conduct in terms of religious truths or to determine whether human beings were being treated with the inherent dignity that they deserve. Although a good motive would not justify a bad act to a religious ethicist, in this situation the actions were good and the motive was questionable (because the firm was simply seeking to increase its profit). Nevertheless, unless one's religion prohibited making a profit, the firm's actions would likely not be considered unethical. Applying Kantian ethics would require you to evaluate the firm's actions in light of what would happen if everyone in society acted that way (categorical imperative). Here, because the conduct was good, it would be positive for society if every firm acted that way. Hence, the profit-seeking motive would be irrelevant in a Kantian analysis. In a debate between motive and conduct, then, conduct is almost always given greater weight in evaluating ethics.

3.2A. HYPOTHETICAL QUESTION WITH SAMPLE ANSWER

Marya can bring suit in all three courts. The trucking firm did business in Florida, and the accident occurred there. Thus, the state of Florida would have jurisdiction over the defendant. Because the firm was headquartered in Georgia and had its principal place of business in that state, Marya could also sue in a Georgia court. Finally, because the amount in controversy exceeds $75,000, the suit could be brought in federal court on the basis of diversity of citizenship.

4.2A. HYPOTHETICAL QUESTION WITH SAMPLE ANSWER

The correct answer is (2). The *Restatement (Second) of Torts* defines negligence as "conduct that falls below the standard established by law for the protection of others against unreasonable risk of harm." The standard established by law is that of a reasonable person acting with due care in the circumstances. Mary was well aware that the medication she took would make her drowsy, and her failure to observe due care (that is, refrain from driving) under the circumstances was negligent. Answer (1) is incorrect because Mary had no reason to believe the golf club was defective, and she could not have prevented the injury by the exercise of due care.

5.2A. HYPOTHETICAL QUESTION WITH SAMPLE ANSWER

1. Making a photocopy of an article in a scholarly journal "for purposes such as * * * scholarship, or research, is not an infringement of copyright" under Section 107 of the Copyright Act.
2. This is an example of trademark infringement. Whenever a trademark is copied to a substantial degree or used in its entirety by one who is not entitled to its use, the trademark has been infringed.
3. This is the most likely example of copyright infringement. Generally, determining whether the reproduction of copyrighted material constitutes copyright infringement is made on a case-by-case basis under the "fair use" doctrine, as expressed in Section 107 of the Copyright Act. Courts look at such factors as the "purpose and character" of a use, such as whether it is "of a commercial nature;" "the amount and substantiality of the portion used in relation to the copyrighted work as a whole;" and "the effect of the use on the potential market" for the copied work. In this question, the DVD store owner is copying copyright-protected works in their entirety for commercial purposes, thereby affecting the market for the works.
4. Taping a television program "for purposes such as * * * teaching * * * is not an infringement of copyright" under Section 107 of the Copyright Act.

6.2A. HYPOTHETICAL QUESTION WITH SAMPLE ANSWER

1. Sarah has wrongfully taken and carried away the personal property of another with the intent to permanently deprive the owner of such property. She has committed the crime of larceny.

2. Sarah has unlawfully and forcibly taken the personal property of another. She has committed the crime of robbery.

3. Sarah has broken and entered a dwelling with the intent to commit a felony. She has committed the crime of burglary. (Most states have dispensed with the requirement that the act take place at night.)

Note the basic differences: Burglary requires breaking and entering into a building without the use of force against a person. Robbery does not involve any breaking and entering, but force is required. Larceny is the taking of personal property without force and without breaking and entering into a building. Generally, because force is used, robbery is considered the most serious of these crimes and carries the most severe penalties. Larceny involves no force or threat to human life; therefore, it carries the least severe penalty of the three. Burglary, because it involves breaking and entering, frequently where people live, carries a lesser penalty than robbery but a greater penalty than larceny.

7.2A. HYPOTHETICAL QUESTION WITH SAMPLE ANSWER

1. Death of either the offeror or the offeree prior to acceptance automatically terminates a revocable offer. The basic legal reason is that the offer is personal to the parties and cannot be passed on to others, not even to the estate of the deceased. This rule applies even if the other party is unaware of the death. Thus, Cherneck's offer terminates on Cherneck's death, and Bollow's later acceptance does not constitute a contract.

2. An offer is automatically terminated by the destruction of the specific subject matter of the offer prior to acceptance. Thus, Bollow's acceptance after the fire does not constitute a contract.

3. When the offer is irrevocable, under an option contract, death of the offeror does not terminate the option contract, and the offeree can accept the offer to sell the equipment, binding the offeror's estate to performance. Performance is not personal to Cherneck, as the estate can transfer title to the equipment. Knowledge of the death is immaterial to the offeree's right of acceptance. Thus, Bollow can hold Cherneck's estate to a contract for the purchase of the equipment.

4. When the offer is irrevocable, under an option contract, death of the offeree also does not terminate the offer. Because the option is a separate contract, the contract survives and passes to the offeree's estate, which can exercise the option by acceptance within the option period. Thus, acceptance by Bollow's estate binds Cherneck to a contract for the sale of the equipment.

8.2A. HYPOTHETICAL QUESTION WITH SAMPLE ANSWER

Contracts in restraint of trade are usually illegal and unenforceable. An exception to this rule applies to a covenant not to compete that is ancillary to certain types of business contracts in which some fair protection is deemed appropriate (such as in the sale of a business). The covenant, however, must be reasonable in terms of time and area to be legally enforceable. If either term is excessive, the court can declare that the restraint goes beyond what is necessary for reasonable protection. In this event, the court can either declare the covenant illegal, or it can reform the covenant to make the terms of time and area reasonable and then enforce it. Suppose the court declares the covenant illegal and unenforceable. Because the covenant is ancillary and severable from the primary contract,

the primary contract is not affected by such a ruling. In the case of Hotel Lux, the primary contract concerns employment; the covenant is ancillary and desirable for the protection of the hotel. The time period of one year may be considered reasonable for a chef with an international reputation. The reasonableness of the three-state area restriction may be questioned, however. If it is found to be reasonable, the covenant probably will be enforced. If it is not found to be reasonable, the court could declare the entire covenant illegal, allowing Perlee to be employed by any restaurant or hotel, including one in direct competition with Hotel Lux. Alternatively, the court could reform the covenant, making its terms reasonable for protecting Hotel Lux's normal customer market area.

9.3A. HYPOTHETICAL QUESTION WITH SAMPLE ANSWER

As a general rule any right(s) flowing from a contract can be assigned. There are, however, exceptions, such as when the contract expressly and specifically prohibits or limits the right of assignment. Because of the principle of freedom of contract, this type of prohibition is enforced—unless it is deemed contrary to public policy. For example, courts have held that a prohibition clause against assignment that restrains the alienation of property is invalid by virtue of being against public policy. Authorities differ on how a case like Aron's should be decided. Some courts would enforce the prohibition completely, holding that Aron's assignment to Erica is completely ineffective without the landlord's consent. Others would permit the assignment to be effective, with the landlord's remedies limited to the normal contract remedies ensuing from Aron's breach.

10.2A. HYPOTHETICAL QUESTION WITH SAMPLE ANSWER

Anne has entered into an enforceable contract to subscribe to *E-Commerce Weekly*. In this problem, the offer to deliver, via e-mail, the newsletter was presented by the offeror with a statement of how to accept—by clicking on the "SUBSCRIBE" button. Consideration was in the promise to deliver the newsletter and at the price that the subscriber agreed to pay. The offeree had an opportunity to read the terms of the subscription agreement before making the contract. Whether or not she actually read those terms does not matter.

11.2A. HYPOTHETICAL QUESTION WITH SAMPLE ANSWER

1. In a destination contract, the risk of loss passes to the buyer when the goods are tendered to the buyer at the specified destination—in this case, San Francisco.

2. In a shipment contract, if the seller is required or authorized to ship goods by carrier, but the contract specifies no locale, the risk of loss passes to the buyer when the goods are duly delivered to the carrier.

3. If the seller is a merchant, risk of loss to goods held by the seller passes to the buyer when the buyer actually takes physical possession of the goods. If the seller is not a merchant, the risk of loss to goods held by the seller passes to the buyer on tender of delivery.

4. When a bailee is holding goods for a person who has contracted to sell them and the goods are to be delivered without being moved, risk of loss passes to the buyer when (1) the buyer receives a negotiable document of title for the goods, (2) the bailee acknowledges the buyer's right to possess the goods, or (3) the buyer receives a non-negotiable document of title and has had a reasonable time to present the document to the bailee and demand the goods. (If the bailee refuses to honor the document, the risk of loss remains with the seller.) If the goods are to be delivered by being moved, but the contract does not specify whether it is a destination or a shipment contract, it is presumed to be a shipment contract. If no locale is specified in the contract, risk of loss passes to the buyer when the seller delivers the goods to the carrier.

12.2A. HYPOTHETICAL QUESTION WITH SAMPLE ANSWER

No. Cummings had not breached the sales contract because the C.O.D. shipment had deprived him of his absolute right, in the absence of agreement, to inspect the goods before accepting them. Had Cummings requested or agreed to the C.O.D. method of shipment, the result would have been different. Because he had not agreed to the C.O.D. shipment, he was fully within his rights to refuse to accept the goods because he could not inspect them prior to acceptance. In this case, it was the seller who had breached the contract by shipping the goods C.O.D. without Cummings's consent.

13.2A. HYPOTHETICAL QUESTION WITH SAMPLE ANSWER

The Truth-in-Lending Act (TILA) deals specifically with lost or stolen credit cards and their unauthorized use. For credit cards *solicited* by the cardholder and then lost or stolen, the act limits the liability of the cardholder to $50 for unauthorized charges made prior to the time the creditor is notified. There is no liability for any unauthorized charges made after the date of notice. In the case of the Midtown Department Store credit card stolen on May 31, the $500 charge made on June 1, which is prior to Ochoa's notice, causes Ochoa to be liable for the $50 limit. For the June 3 charge of $200 made after the notification, Ochoa has no liability. TILA also deals with unsolicited credit cards. Unless a credit cardholder accepts an unsolicited card (such as by using it), the cardholder is not liable for any unauthorized charges. Moreover, the act prohibits the issuance of unsolicited credit cards. No notice by the cardholder of an unsolicited, unaccepted credit card is required to absolve the cardholder from liability for unauthorized charges. Therefore, Ochoa owes $50 to the Midtown Department Store and nothing to High-Flying Airlines.

14.2A. HYPOTHETICAL QUESTION WITH SAMPLE ANSWER

For an instrument to be negotiable, it must meet the following requirements:

1. Be in writing.
2. Be signed by the maker or the drawer.
3. Be an unconditional promise or order to pay.
4. State a fixed amount of money.
5. Be payable on demand or at a definite time.
6. Be payable to order or to bearer, unless it is a check.

The instrument in this case meets the writing requirement in that it is handwritten and on something with a degree of permanence that is transferable. The instrument meets the requirement of being signed by the maker, as Muriel Evans's signature (her name in her handwriting) appears in the body of the instrument. The instrument's payment is not conditional and contains Muriel Evans's definite promise to pay. In addition, the sum of $100 is both a fixed amount and payable in money (U.S. currency). Because the instru-

ment is payable on demand and to bearer (Karen Marvin or any holder), the instrument is negotiable.

15.2A. HYPOTHETICAL QUESTION WITH SAMPLE ANSWER

Under the Home Mortgage Disclosure Act (HMDA) and the Community Reinvestment Act of 1977, which were passed to prevent discrimination in lending practices, a bank is required to define its market area. This area must be established contiguous to the bank's branch offices. It must be mapped using the existing boundaries of the counties or the standard metropolitan areas (SMAs) in which the offices are located. A bank must delineate the community served, and annually review this delineation. The issue here is how a successful Internet-only bank could delineate its community. Does an Internet bank have a physically limited market area or serve a physically distinct community? Will the Federal Reserve Board, the government agency charged with enforcing this law, allow a bank to describe its market area as a "cybercommunity"?

16.2A. HYPOTHETICAL QUESTION WITH SAMPLE ANSWER

Mendez has a security interest in Arabian Knight and is a perfected secured party. He has met all the necessary criteria listed under UCC 9–203 to be a secured creditor. Mendez has given value of $5,000 and has taken possession of the collateral, Arabian Knight, owned by Marsh (who has rights in the collateral). Thus, he has a security interest even though Marsh did not sign a security agreement. Once a security interest attaches, a transfer of possession of the collateral to the secured party can perfect the party's security interest without a filing [UCC 9–310(b)(6); 9–313]. Thus, a security interest was created and perfected at the time Marsh transferred Arabian Knight to Mendez as security for the loan.

17.2A. HYPOTHETICAL QUESTION WITH SAMPLE ANSWER

Agency is usually a consensual relationship in that the principal and agent agree that the agent will have the authority to act for the principal, binding the principal to any contract with a third party. If no agency in fact exists, the purported agent's contracts with third parties are not binding on the principal. In this case, no agency by agreement was created. Brown may claim that an agency by estoppel was created; however, this argument will fail. Agency by estoppel is applicable only when a *principal* causes a third person to believe that another person is the principal's agent. Then the third party's actions in dealing with the agent are in reliance upon the principal's words or actions and the third party's reasonable belief that the agent has authority. This is said to estop the principal from claiming that in fact no agency existed. Acts and declarations of the *agent*, however, do not in and of themselves create an agency by estoppel, because such actions should not reasonably lead a third person to believe that the purported agent has authority. In this case, Wade's declarations and allegations alone led Brown to believe that Wade was an agent. Gett's actions were not involved. It is not reasonable to believe that someone is an agent solely because he or she is a friend of the principal. Therefore, Brown cannot hold Gett liable unless Gett ratifies Wade's contract—which is unlikely, as Wade has disappeared with the rare coin.

18.2A. HYPOTHETICAL QUESTION WITH SAMPLE ANSWER

The Occupational Safety and Health Act (OSHA) requires employers to provide safe working conditions for employees. The act prohibits employers from discharging or discriminating against any employee who refuses to work when the employee believes in good faith that he or she will risk death or great bodily harm by undertaking the employment activity. Denton and Carlo had sufficient reason to believe that the maintenance job required of them by their employer involved great risk, and therefore, under OSHA, their discharge was wrongful. Denton and Carlo can turn to the Occupational Safety and Health Administration, which is part of the U.S. Department of Labor, for assistance.

19.3A. HYPOTHETICAL QUESTION WITH SAMPLE ANSWER

The court would likely consider the terms of any contracts between the parties and whether or not the parties were acting in good faith. One way to avoid conflicts such as those described in this problem is to institute a Web site in conjunction with a franchisor's franchisees. When a Web site directs interested parties to a franchisee, for example, all parties would seem to benefit. Because territorial conflicts can occur not only between a franchisor and its franchisees but also between competing franchisees, some companies have instituted specific "no compete" pledges.

20.2A. HYPOTHETICAL QUESTION WITH SAMPLE ANSWER

If Artel acquires the stocks and assets of Fox Express, a *merger* will take place. Artel will be the surviving corporation, and Fox Express will disappear as a corporation. If Artel and Fox Express combine so that both corporations cease to exist and a new corporation, A&F Enterprises, is formed, a *consolidation* will take place. In either case, title to the property of the corporation that ceases to exist will pass automatically to the surviving or new corporation without a formal transfer being necessary. In addition, in a merger, the debt liabilities of Fox Express become the liabilities of Artel. Artel's articles of incorporation are deemed to be amended to include the terms stated in the articles of merger. If a consolidation takes place, A&F Enterprises will automatically acquire title to the properties of both Artel and Fox Express without a formal transfer being necessary. A&F Enterprises also will assume liability for the debts and obligations of Artel and Fox Express. The articles of consolidation take the place of the articles of incorporation of Artel and Fox Express, and they will be regarded thereafter as the articles of incorporation of A&F Enterprises.

21.2A. HYPOTHETICAL QUESTION WITH SAMPLE ANSWER

No. Under federal securities law, a stock split is exempt from registration requirements. This is because no *sale* of stock is involved. The existing shares are merely being split, and no consideration is received by the corporation for the additional shares created.

22.2A. HYPOTHETICAL QUESTION WITH SAMPLE ANSWER

Yes. The major antitrust law being violated is the Sherman Act, Section 1. Allitron and Donovan are engaged in interstate commerce, and the agreement to divide marketing territories between them is a contract in restraint of trade. The U.S. Department of Justice could seek fines of up to $1 million for each corporation, and the officers or directors responsible could be imprisoned for up to three years. In addition, the U.S. Department of Justice could institute civil proceedings to restrain this conduct.

23.3A. HYPOTHETICAL QUESTION WITH SAMPLE ANSWER

For Curtis to recover against the hotel, he must first prove that a bailment relationship was created between himself and the hotel as to the car or the fur coat, or both. For a bailment to exist, there must be a delivery of the personal property that gives the bailee exclusive possession of the property, and the bailee must knowingly accept the bailed property. If either element is lacking, there is no bailment relationship and no liability on the part of the bailee hotel. The facts clearly indicate that the bailee hotel took exclusive possession and control of Curtis's car, and it knowingly accepted the car when the attendant took the car from Curtis and parked it in the underground guarded garage, retaining the keys. Thus, a bailment was created as to the car, and, because a mutual-benefit bailment was created, the hotel owes Curtis the duty to exercise reasonable care over the property and to return the bailed car at the end of the bailment. Failure to return the car creates a presumption of negligence (lack of reasonable care), and unless the hotel can rebut this presumption, the hotel is liable to Curtis for the loss of the car. As to the fur coat, the hotel neither knew nor expected that the trunk contained an expensive fur coat. Thus, although the hotel knowingly took exclusive possession of the car, the hotel did not do so with the fur coat. (But for a regular coat and other items likely to be in the car, the hotel would be liable.) Because no bailment of the expensive fur coat was created, the hotel has no liability for its loss.

24.2A. HYPOTHETICAL QUESTION WITH SAMPLE ANSWER

Wiley understandably wants a general warranty deed, as this type of deed will give him the most extensive protection against any defects of title claimed against the property transferred. The general warranty would have Gemma warranting the following covenants, or promises:

1. Covenant to convey—a warranty that the seller has good title and power to convey.
2. Covenant against adverse claims of third parties—a guaranty by the seller that, unless stated, there are no outstanding encumbrances (claims) or liens against the property conveyed.
3. Covenant of quiet enjoyment—a warranty that the grantee's possession will not be disturbed by others claiming a prior legal right. Gemma, however, is conveying only ten feet along a property line that may not even be accurately surveyed. Gemma therefore does not wish to make these warranties. Consequently, she is offering a quitclaim deed, which does not convey any warranties but conveys only whatever interest, if any, the grantor owns. Although title is passed by the quitclaim deed, the quality of the title is not warranted. Because Wiley really needs the property, it appears that he has three choices: (1) he can accept the quitclaim deed; (2) he can increase his offer price to obtain the general warranty deed he wants; or (3) he can offer to have a title search made, which should satisfy both parties.

25.2A. HYPOTHETICAL QUESTION WITH SAMPLE ANSWER

Each system has its advantages and its disadvantages. In a common law system, the courts independently develop the rules governing certain areas of law, such as torts and contracts. This judge-made law exists in addition to the laws passed by a legislature. Judges must follow precedential decisions in their jurisdictions, but courts may modify or even overturn precedents when deemed necessary. Also, if there is no case law to guide a court, the court may create a new rule of law. In a civil law system, the only official source of law is a statutory code. Courts are required to interpret the code and apply the rules to individual cases, but courts may not depart from the code and develop their own laws. In theory, the law code will set forth all the principles needed for the legal system. Common law and civil law systems are not wholly distinct. For example, the United States has a common law system, but crimes are defined by statute as in civil law systems. Civil law systems may allow considerable room for judges to develop law: law codes cannot be so precise as to address every contested issue, so the judiciary must interpret the codes. There are also significant differences among common law countries. The judges of different common law nations have produced differing common law principles. The roles of judges and lawyers under the different systems should be taken into account. Among other factors that should be considered in establishing a business law system and in deciding what regulations to impose are the goals that the system and its regulations are intended to achieve and the expectations of those to whom both will apply, including foreign and domestic investors.

Glossary

A

abandoned property ■ Property with which the owner has voluntarily parted, with no intention of recovering it.

acceptance ■ A voluntary act by the offeree that shows assent, or agreement, to the terms of an offer; may consist of words or conduct. In negotiable instruments law, the drawee's signed agreement to pay a draft when it is presented.

acceptor ■ A drawee who is legally obligated to pay an instrument when the instrument is presented for payment.

accession ■ Occurs when an individual adds value to personal property by the use of either labor or materials. In some situations, a person may acquire ownership rights in another's property through accession.

accord and satisfaction ■ A common means of settling a disputed claim, whereby a debtor offers to pay a lesser amount than the creditor purports is owed. The creditor's acceptance of the offer creates an accord (agreement), and when the accord is executed, satisfaction occurs.

accredited investors ■ In the context of securities offerings, "sophisticated" investors, such as banks, insurance companies, investment companies, the issuer's executive officers and directors, and persons whose income or net worth exceeds certain limits.

act of state doctrine ■ A doctrine providing that the judicial branch of one country will not examine the validity of public acts committed by a recognized foreign government within its own territory.

actionable ■ Capable of serving as the basis of a lawsuit. An actionable claim can be pursued in a lawsuit or other court action.

actual malice ■ The deliberate intent to cause harm, which exists when a person makes a statement either knowing that it is false or showing a reckless disregard for whether it is true. In a defamation suit, a statement made about a public figure normally must be made with actual malice for the plaintiff to recover damages.

actus reus ■ A guilty (prohibited) act. The commission of a prohibited act is one of the two essential elements required for criminal liability, the other element being the intent to commit a crime.

adhesion contract ■ A "standard-form" contract, such as that between a large retailer and a consumer, in which the stronger party dictates the terms.

adjudicate ■ To render a judicial decision. In the administrative process, adjudication is the trial-like proceeding in which an administrative law judge hears and decides issues that arise when an administrative agency charges a person or a firm with violating a law or regulation enforced by the agency.

administrative agency ■ A federal or state government agency established to perform a specific function. Administrative agencies are authorized by legislative acts to make and enforce rules in order to administer and enforce the acts.

administrative law judge (ALJ) ■ One who presides over an administrative agency hearing and has the power to administer oaths, take testimony, rule on questions of evidence, and make determinations of fact.

administrative law ■ The body of law created by administrative agencies (in the form of rules, regulations, orders, and decisions) in order to carry out their duties and responsibilities.

administrative process ■ The procedure used by administrative agencies in the administration of law.

adverse possession ■ The acquisition of title to real property by occupying it openly, without the consent of the owner, for a period of time specified by a state statute. The occupation must be actual, open, notorious, exclusive, and in opposition to all others, including the owner.

after-acquired property ■ Property that is acquired by the debtor after the execution of a security agreement.

agreement ■ A meeting of two or more minds in regard to the terms of a contract; usually broken down into two events—an offer by one party to form a contract and an acceptance of the offer by the person to whom the offer is made.

alien corporation ■ A designation in the United States for a corporation formed in another country but doing business in the United States.

alienation ■ The process of transferring land out of one's possession (thus "alienating" the land from oneself).

alternative dispute resolution (ADR) ■ The resolution of disputes in ways other than those involved in the traditional judicial process. Negotiation, mediation, and arbitration are forms of ADR.

answer ■ Procedurally, a defendant's response to the plaintiff's complaint.

anticipatory repudiation ■ An assertion or action by a party indicating that he or she will not perform an obligation that the party is contractually obligated to perform at a future time.

antitrust law ■ Laws protecting commerce from unlawful restraints.